T0192165

Deep Learning Projects Using TensorFlow 2

Neural Network Development with Python and Keras

Vinita Silaparasetty

Apress®

Deep Learning Projects Using TensorFlow 2: Neural Network Development with Python and Keras

Vinita Silaparasetty
Bangalore, India

ISBN-13 (pbk): 978-1-4842-5801-9   ISBN-13 (electronic): ISBN 978-1-4842-5802-6
https://doi.org/10.1007/978-1-4842-5802-6

Managing Director, Apress Media LLC: Welmoed Spahr
Acquisitions Editor: Aaron Black
Development Editor: James Markham
Coordinating Editor: Jessica Vakili

Distributed to the book trade worldwide by Springer Science+Business Media New York, 233 Spring Street, 6th Floor, New York, NY 10013. Phone 1-800-SPRINGER, fax (201) 348-4505, e-mail orders-ny@springer-sbm.com, or visit www.springeronline.com. Apress Media, LLC is a California LLC and the sole member (owner) is Springer Science + Business Media Finance Inc (SSBM Finance Inc). SSBM Finance Inc is a **Delaware** corporation.

For information on translations, please e-mail rights@apress.com, or visit http://www.apress.com/rights-permissions.

Apress titles may be purchased in bulk for academic, corporate, or promotional use. eBook versions and licenses are also available for most titles. For more information, reference our Print and eBook Bulk Sales web page at http://www.apress.com/bulk-sales.

Any source code or other supplementary material referenced by the author in this book is available to readers on GitHub via the book's product page, located at www.apress.com/978-1-4842-5801-9. For more detailed information, please visit http://www.apress.com/source-code.

Printed on acid-free paper

Table of Contents

About the Author

Vinita Silaparasetty is a data science trainer who is passionate about AI, machine learning, and deep learning. She is experienced in programming with Python, R, TensorFlow, and Keras.

She is currently pursuing her master's degree in Data Science at NewCastle University, U.K.

She has written two award-winning research papers on machine learning. The first is titled " Python vs. R" and is a comparative study of Python and R. The second is titled "Machine Learning for Fraud Detection: Employing Artificial Intelligence in the Banking Sector" and it proposes a new system for real-time fraud detection in the banking sector. She is also a reviewer for the Oxford Publication entitled *The Computer Journal.*

She is the co-organizer of the "Bangalore Artificial Intelligence Meetup" group as well as the "AI for Women" meetup group, where she conducts training sessions on Python, R, machine learning, and deep learning.

You can find her on Facebook at `https://www.facebook.com/VinitaSilaparasetty/`

About the Technical Reviewer

 **Mezgani Ali** is a Ph.D. student in artificial intelligence (Mohamed V. University in Rabat) and a researcher at Native LABS, Inc. He likes technology, reading, and his little daughter Ghita. His first program was a Horoscope in Basic in 1993. He has done a lot of work on the infrastructure side in system engineering, software engineering, managed networks, and security.

Mezgani worked for NIC France, Capgemini, and HP, and he was part of the (SRE) Site Reliability Engineer team responsible for keeping data center servers and customers' applications up and running. He is fanatical about Kubernetes, REST API, MySQL, and Scala, and he is the creator of the functional and imperative programming language, PASP.

Acknowledgments

I would like to thank my father, Mr. S. Mohan Kumar, for his guidance and valuable input that made this book a great resource for beginners and seasoned professionals alike.

I would like to thank my mother, Mrs. Agnes Shanthi Mohan, for her constant support, encouragement, and love.

I would like to thank my younger sister, Ms. Nikita Silaparasetty, for her valuable feedback and support.

Special thanks to Aaron Black, the senior editor, for accepting my book proposal and giving me the opportunity to write this book.

Thanks to Jessica Vakili, the coordinating editor, for ensuring that the process of writing this book was smooth and for clarifying even the smallest doubts I had as a first-time author.

Thanks to James Markham, the editor, for his guidance on formatting each chapter as well as his keen eye for detail, which make this book easy to understand.

Thanks to Mezgani Ali, the technical reviewer, for ensuring that the source code is well formatted.

Finally, I would like to thank the awesome team at Apress, for their effort in making this book possible.

Preface

TensorFlow 2.0 was officially released on September 30th, 2019. However, the new version is very different than what most users are familiar with. While programming with TensorFlow 2.0 is much simpler, most users still prefer to use older versions. This book aims to help long-time users of TensorFlow adjust to TensorFlow 2.0 and to help absolute beginners learn TensorFlow 2.0.

Why use TensorFlow?

Here are some advantages to using TensorFlow for your deep learning projects.

- It is open source.

- It is reliable (has minimal major bugs).

- It is ideal for perceptual and language understanding tasks.

- It is capable of running on CPUs and GPUs.

- It is easier to debug.

- It uses graphs for numeric computations.

- It has better scalability, as libraries can be deployed on a gamut of hardware machines, starting from cellular devices to computers with complex setups.

- It has convenient pipelining, as it is highly parallel and designed to use various backend software (GPU, ASIC, etc.).

- It uses the high-level Keras API.

- It has better compatibility.

- It uses TensorFlow Extended (TFX) for a full production ML pipeline.

- It also supports an ecosystem of powerful add-on libraries and models to experiment with, including Ragged Tensors, TensorFlow Probability, Tensor2Tensor, and BERT.

TensorFlow 1.x	TensorFlow 2.0
Global variables	decorator tf.function so that the following function block is run as a single graph.
Sessions	Functions
Layers	Keras Layers
Placeholders	Eager Execution
tf.app,tf.flags,tf.logging	absl-py
-	The tf.function() will create a separate graph for every unique set of input shapes and datatypes.

Figure I-1. *Comparison of TensorFlow 1.x and TensorFlow 2.0*

About the Book Projects

The projects in this book mainly cover image and sound data. They are designed to be as simple as possible to help you understand how each neural network works. Consider them to be a skeletal structure for your own projects. You are encouraged to build on the models in this book and experiment with them using different datasets. The projects in this book were designed keeping in mind the latest developments in deep learning and will be the perfect addition for an impressive data science portfolio.

System Specifications

The projects in this book require powerful computing resources or a good cloud platform. You are strongly advised to use a system with the following minimum requirements:

> **GPU:** Model: 16-bit Memory: 8GB and CUDA Toolkit support
>
> **RAM:** Memory: 10GB
>
> **CPU:** PCIe lanes: 8 Core: 4 threads per GPU
>
> **SSD:** Form Factor: 2.5-inch and SATA interface
>
> **PSU:** 16.8 watts
>
> **Motherboard:** PCIe lanes: 8

If you are unable to acquire a system with these requirements, try using a cloud computing platform, such as one of the following:

- BigML

- Amazon Web Services

- Microsoft Azure

- Google Cloud

- Alibaba Cloud

- Kubernetes

Tips to Get the Most Out of This Book

To get the most value out of the projects in this book, follow these guidelines:

- **Create separate environments.** To prevent problems, it's best to create separate environments for each project. This way you will have only the libraries necessary for that particular project and there will not be any clashes.

- **Save your projects in separate folders.** To keep your work organized and handy for future reference, create separate folders for each project. You can store the script, datasets, and results that you have obtained in that folder. Each project in this book provides the code to set your file path to work directly in the project folder that you created.

- **Use data wisely.** Ensure that you have enough data to divide into training and test sets. I suggest that you use 80% of the data for training and 20% for testing.

- **Be organized.** By creating a folder for your project, you know that all the data, output files, etc. are available in one place.

- **Make backups.** Make copies of each notebook before experimenting. This way you have one working copy as a template for future projects. Then make copies of it and modify it as required.

- **Plan.** Understand the problem statement and create a rough flowchart of your approach to solving the problem.

- **Consider your presentation.** As a data scientist, your inferences will be discussed by members of a company who have technical knowledge as well as those who do not. So be sure that you can convey your findings in a manner that anyone can understand.

- **Network.** Join online communities where you can ask questions and help others with solutions to their questions. This is the best way to learn. I recommend the following:

  - StackOverflow

  - Quora

  - Reddit

  - StackExchange

  - CodeProject

  - Google Groups

  - CodeRanch

  - Programmers Heaven

- **Practice:** Need inspiration for more projects? Join online communities that have hackathons, competitions, etc., to help you practice and learn. I recommend the following:

  - Hackerearth

  - Kaggle

  - Challengerocket

  - Angel Hack

CHAPTER 1

Getting Started: Installation and Troubleshooting

In order to make the best use of this book, you'll need to satisfy the following prerequisites:

- Install Python 3, the latest version of Python

- Install Jupyter Notebooks

- Install TensorFlow 2.0

- Install Keras

- Install NumPy

- Install SciPy

- Install Matplotlib

- Install Pandas

- Install Scikit-Learn

This chapter will help you install all the necessary packages. It also provides troubleshooting tips for some common errors that may occur during installation.

© Vinita Silaparasetty 2020
V. Silaparasetty, *Deep Learning Projects Using TensorFlow 2*,
https://doi.org/10.1007/978-1-4842-5802-6_1

Note   It is good practice to create a separate virtual environment for these projects. Before installing the packages mentioned here, create a virtual environment and activate it.

Installing Python 3

Python is a general-purpose interpreted, imperative, object-oriented, high-level programming language. It is one of the oldest programming languages around. However, with the onset of machine learning, Python has been given a new lease on life. It has become a popular tool for both machine learning and deep learning. Currently, Python is available as two distinct versions—Python 2 and Python 3.

All the projects in this book use Python 3, so it is best to ensure that it is installed.

Method 1: Direct Installation from the Official Python Website

This method works well with Windows, Linux, and macOS X systems. It is the standard method of installation, whereby you download Python directly from the official website and then install it on your system.

1. Go to `https://www.python.org/` and select the Downloads tab. A drop-down menu will appear (see Figure 1-1).

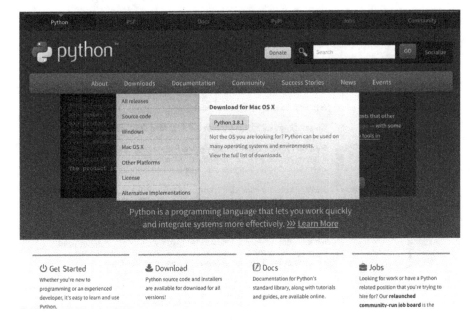

Figure 1-1. *Official Python website*

2. To the right of the drop-down menu, you will see the latest versions of Python that are available for your specific system. The first button provides the latest version of Python 3. Once you click it, the download will begin.

3. Once the download is complete, double-click the package in the Download bar. This will start the installation process.

4. In the dialog box that pops up, select Continue (see Figure 1-2).

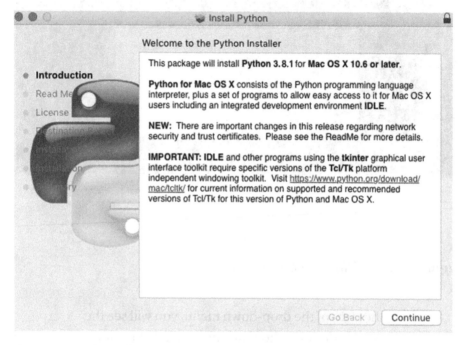

Figure 1-2. *Introduction window of the Python installation*

5. In the new dialog box, you will be presented with important information regarding the changes made to Python (see Figure 1-3). Once again, select Continue.

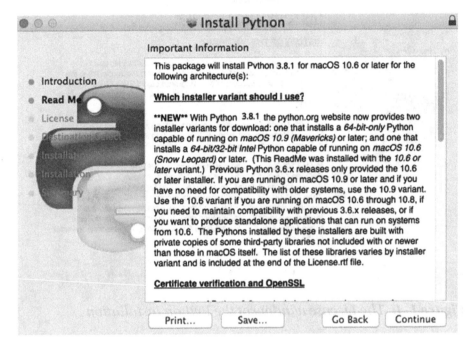

Figure 1-3. *The Read Me window of the Python installation*

6. Now you will be shown the license agreement for using Python. Select Continue (see Figure 1-4).

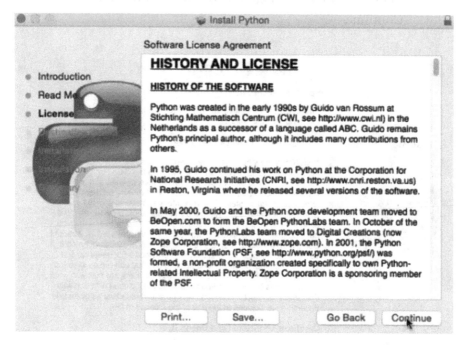

Figure 1-4. *The License window of the Python installation*

7. A mini dialog box will appear requesting you to agree to the terms and conditions listed. Select Agree.

8. Select the file path for the new Python installation.

9. Select the type of installation. See Figure 1-5.

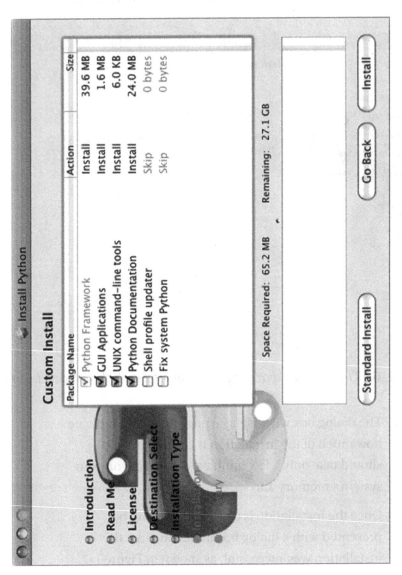

Figure 1-5. *The Installation type window of the Python installation*

10. Finally, you will be told how much memory will be used on your system. Select Install (see Figure 1-6).

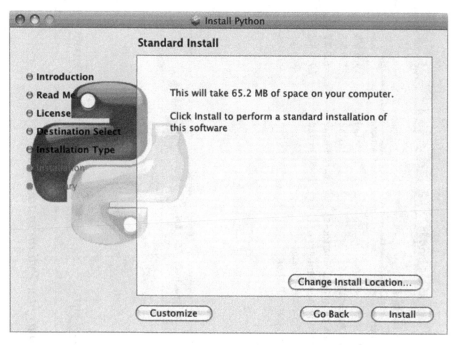

Figure 1-6. *The Storage warning window of the Python installation*

11. The dialog box will display a progress bar to indicate how much of the installation is complete. This should take only a few minutes, depending on your system's memory and speed.

12. Once the installation is complete, you will be presented with a dialog box indicating that the installation was successful, as shown in Figure 1-7.

Figure 1-7. *The Summary window of the Python installation*

13. To test the installation, open the terminal (see
     Figure 1-8), type python 3, and press Enter.

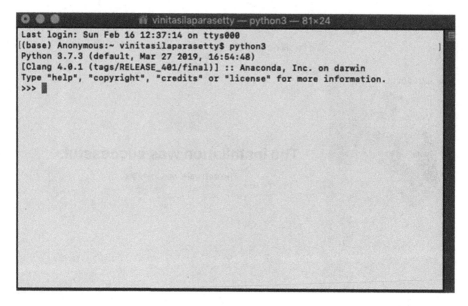

Figure 1-8. Running Python in the terminal

14. Now type the command print ("Hello World!") and press Enter.

15. This will print the words 'Hello World!' in the terminal, as shown in Figure 1-9.

```
Last login: Sun Feb 16 12:40:22 on ttys000
(base) Anonymous:~ vinitasilaparasetty$ python3
Python 3.7.3 (default, Mar 27 2019, 16:54:48)
[Clang 4.0.1 (tags/RELEASE_401/final)] :: Anaconda, Inc. on darwin
Type "help", "copyright", "credits" or "license" for more information.
>>> "Hello World!"
'Hello World!'
>>> 
```

Figure 1-9. *Testing the Python installation*

Troubleshooting Tips

On a Linux system, you may get an error message saying that `pip` requires `ssl`, as shown in Figure 1-10.

Figure 1-10. *The PIP requires SSL warning*

To install `ssl`, use following the command:

```
sudo apt-get install libssl-dev openssl
```

Once this is completed, use the following command:

```
sudo make install
```

Python should now be successfully installed on your system. On a Windows system, follow these steps:

1. Test the installation by opening the terminal.

2. Type `python -version` and press Enter.

3. The version of the Python installation should show up.

Method 2: Using Anaconda

This method is suitable for Windows and Linux systems. Anaconda is a desktop graphical user interface (GUI) that allows you to launch applications and easily manage conda packages, environments, and channels without using the command-line.

1. Download and install Anaconda from `https://www.anaconda.com/distribution/`. See Figure 1-11.

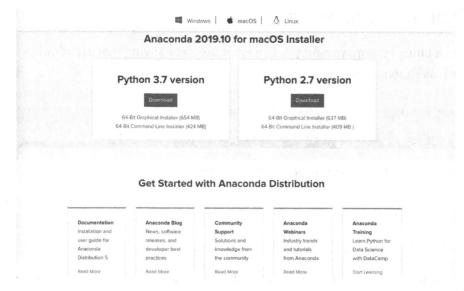

Figure 1-11. *Anaconda's official website*

2. Select the graphical installer for Python 3 as it is the easiest one to use.

3. In the pop-up window, select Continue. See Figure 1-12.

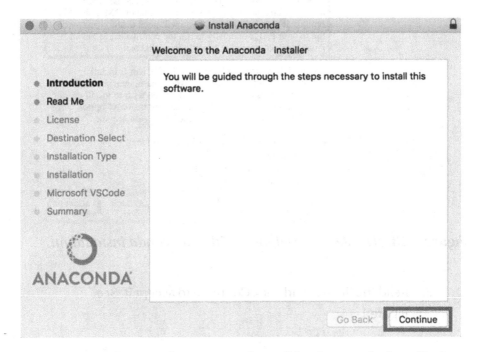

Figure 1-12. *The Introduction window of the Anaconda installation*

4. Read the important information and click Continue. See Figure 1-13.

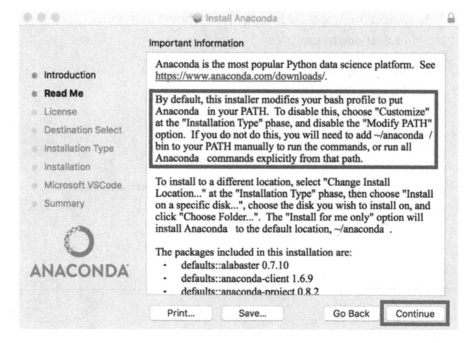

Figure 1-13. *The Read Me window of the Anaconda installation*

5. Read the license and click Continue to accept it. See
    Figure 1-14.

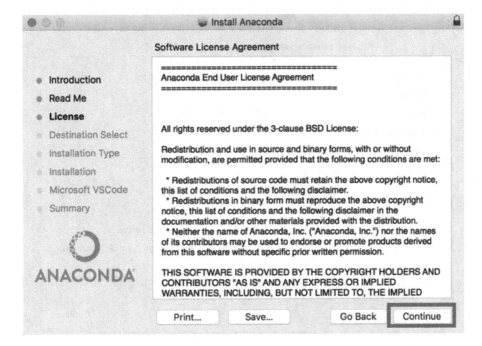

Figure 1-14. *The License window of the Anaconda installation*

6. Select Install for Just Me (unless you are installing for all users) and click Next.

7. Select a destination folder to install Anaconda and click the Next button. See Figure 1-15.

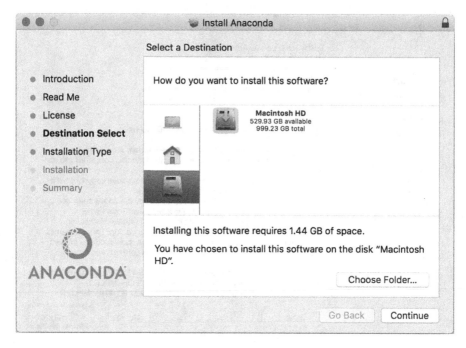

Figure 1-15. *The Select a Destination window of the Anaconda installation*

8. In the dialog box, select Add Anaconda to My PATH Environment Variable, as this will automatically create the path in the bash file. See Figure 1-16.

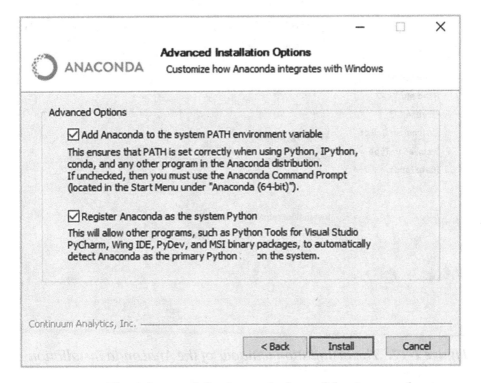

Figure 1-16. *The Advanced Options window of the Anaconda installation*

9. Choose whether to register Anaconda as your default Python version. Unless you plan on installing and running multiple versions of Anaconda, or multiple versions of Python, accept the default and leave this box checked.

10. Click the Install button. The installation will begin, as shown in Figure 1-17.

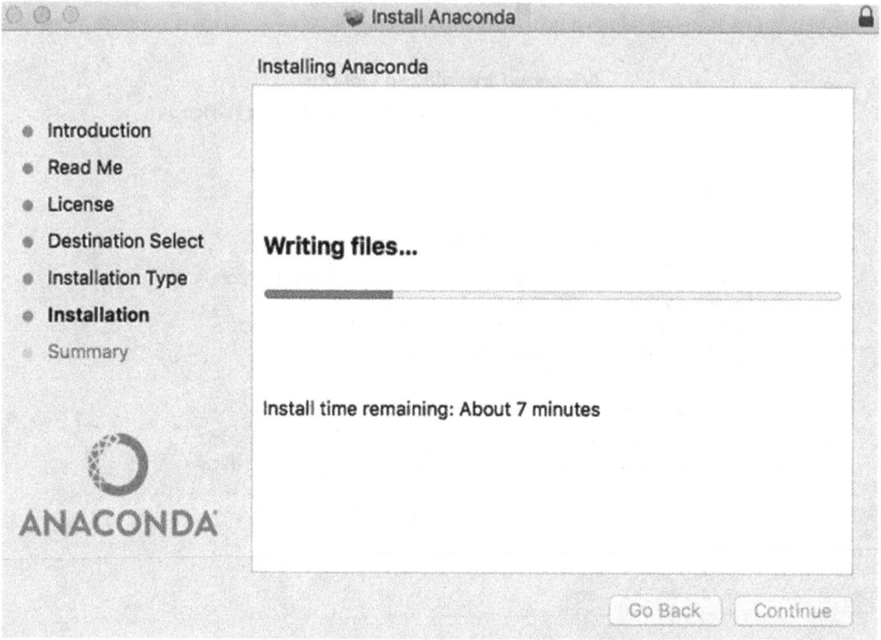

Figure 1-17. *The Installation window of the Anaconda installation*

11. Click the Next button.

12. Once the installation is complete, click the Anaconda icon to run Anaconda.

Figure 1-18. *The Anaconda icon*

13. Create a new environment by clicking
    Environments, as shown in Figure 1-19.

Figure 1-19. *The Environments button*

14. Next, click the Create button, as shown in Figure 1-20.

Figure 1-20. *The Create button*

15. Enter the name of the new environment and select Python 3.7 as the default language. See Figure 1-21.

Figure 1-21. *Select Python 3.7 (the latest version of Python as of the publication of this book)*

16. To test the installation, type `source activate vin` in the terminal, where `vin` is the name of your environment. See Figure 1-22.

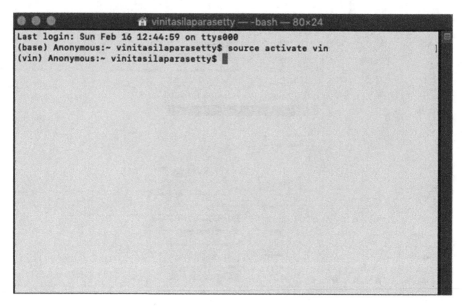

Figure 1-22. *Activating the newly created environment from the terminal*

17. To test the Python installation, type python 3 and press Enter. See Figure 1-23.

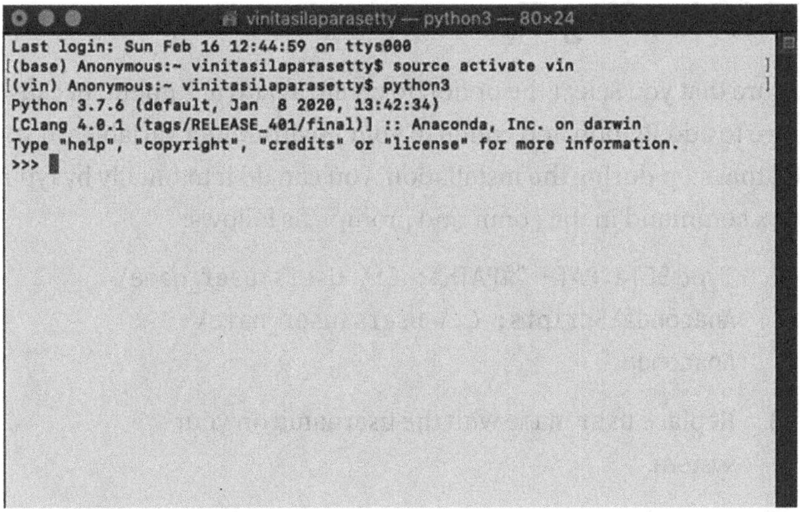

```
● ● ●                    vinitasilaparasetty — python3 — 80×24
Last login: Sun Feb 16 12:44:59 on ttys000
[(base) Anonymous:~ vinitasilaparasetty$ source activate vin
[(vin) Anonymous:~ vinitasilaparasetty$ python3
Python 3.7.6 (default, Jan  8 2020, 13:42:34)
[Clang 4.0.1 (tags/RELEASE_401/final)] :: Anaconda, Inc. on darwin
Type "help", "copyright", "credits" or "license" for more information.
>>> █
```

Figure 1-23. *Running Python*

18. Now type "Hello World!" and press Enter. This will
    print the words 'Hello World!' in the terminal, as
    shown in Figure 1-24.

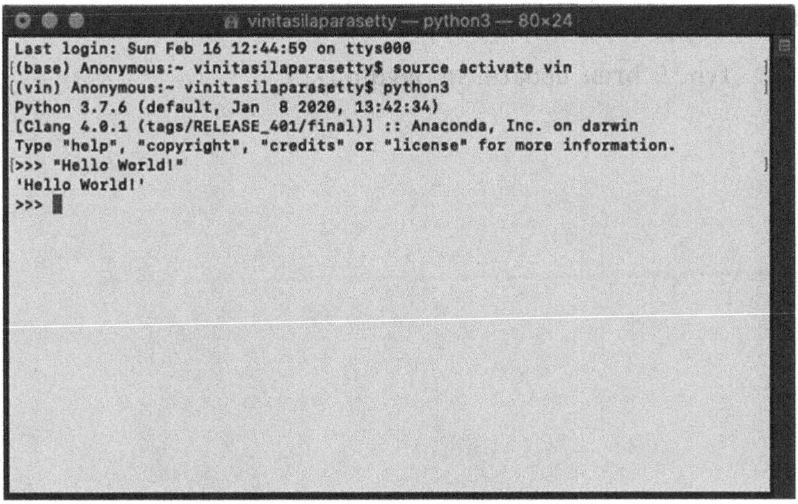

```
● ● ●                    vinitasilaparasetty — python3 — 80×24
Last login: Sun Feb 16 12:44:59 on ttys000
[(base) Anonymous:~ vinitasilaparasetty$ source activate vin
[(vin) Anonymous:~ vinitasilaparasetty$ python3
Python 3.7.6 (default, Jan  8 2020, 13:42:34)
[Clang 4.0.1 (tags/RELEASE_401/final)] :: Anaconda, Inc. on darwin
Type "help", "copyright", "credits" or "license" for more information.
[>>> "Hello World!"
'Hello World!'
>>> █
```

Figure 1-24. *Testing Python in the terminal*

Troubleshooting Tips

Make sure that you select the option to create a path argument, because you have to add Python and conda to your environment variables. If you missed that step during the installation, you can do it manually by typing the `setx` command in the command prompt, as follows:

1. Type `SETX PATH "%PATH%; C:\ Users\user_name\ Anaconda\Scripts; C:\ Users\user_name\ Anaconda`.

2. Replace `user_name` with the username on your system.

3. Close the current command prompt and open a new one.

4. Try typing `python` and `conda` in the command prompt to see if the paths are saved.

Note that the direct installation method works on all systems. If direct installation from the official Python website causes you trouble, use `brew` as an alternative method:

1. Type `$ brew update`. See Figure 1-25.

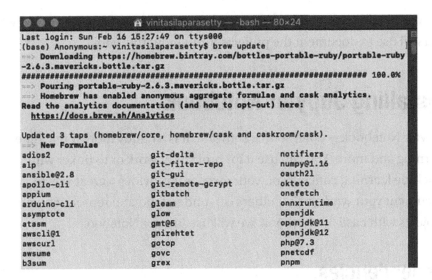

Figure 1-25. *Updating brew in the terminal*

2. Then type $ `brew install python3`. See Figure 1-26.

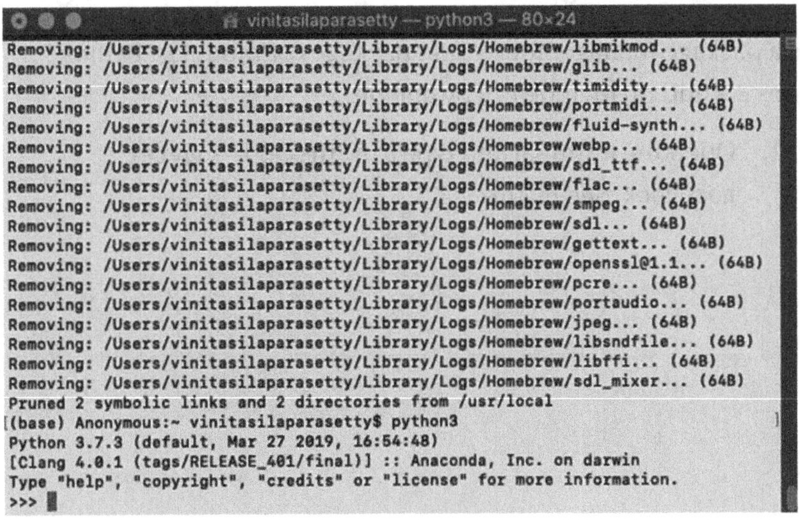

Figure 1-26. *Opening Python in the terminal*

With Python installed, you are ready to install Jupyter Notebook, which you will use to document the projects throughout this book.

Installing Jupyter Notebook

Jupyter Notebook is open source software. It is a handy tool for machine learning and more. You can use it for projects at work or to tinker with machine learning concepts on your own, as it provides a great way to document your work so that others can understand and reproduce your projects with ease. In this book, we will use Jupyter Notebook.

Dependencies

- Python 3

Method 1: Using the PIP Installation Package

PIP is a package manager for Python packages or modules. Python versions 3.4 and up include PIP by default.

1. Open the terminal and type `pip install jupyter notebook`. See Figure 1-27.

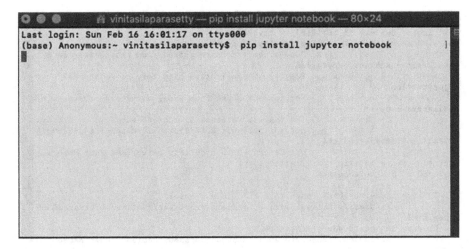

Figure 1-27. *Installing Jupyter Notebook using the terminal*

2. The installation will take a few seconds.

3. To test the installation, type `jupyter notebook` at the command prompt in the terminal. See Figure 1-28.

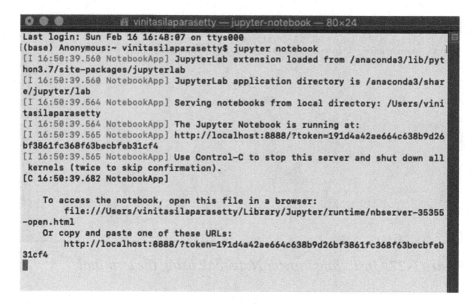

Figure 1-28. *Running Jupyter Notebook via the terminal*

4. Information about the notebook will be shown in
    the terminal. Then the Jupyter Notebook dashboard
    will open in the browser. See Figure 1-29.

Figure 1-29. *The Jupyter Notebook interface*

Troubleshooting Tips

Sometimes you may need to type `jupyter-notebook` in the command prompt to launch it.

Method 2: Using Anaconda

If you installed Anaconda, Jupyter Notebook has already been installed for you. You can open Anaconda to launch Jupyter Notebook using the following steps:

1. Open the Anaconda Navigator dashboard.

2. Click Jupyter Notebook. See Figure 1-30.

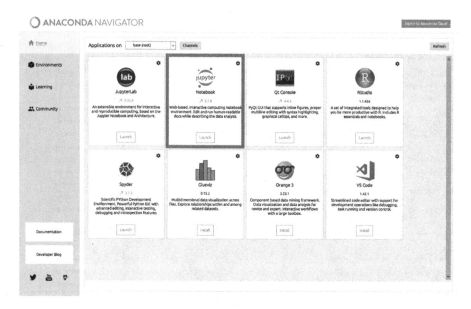

Figure 1-30. *The Jupyter Notebook in Anaconda*

A new web browser will open with the Jupyter dashboard.

Troubleshooting Tips

Be sure the Anaconda directory PATH has been properly added to
Environment Variables section. If this path is not added, you'll need
to locate the Anaconda directory/file path and manually add it to
Environment Variables.

Now that you have installed Jupyter Notebook, you are ready to install
TensorFlow 2.0.

Installing TensorFlow 2.0

TensorFlow is an open source machine learning library for research
and production, developed by Google. It had a steep learning curve, but
with the introduction of version 2.0, which is currently in the beta phase,
TensorFlow has become much more user friendly. We are going to use
TensorFlow 2.0 for all the projects in this book.

Dependencies

- Python 3

Method 1: Using the PIP Installation Package

PIP provides an easy way to install TensorFlow with a single line of code.

1. Open the terminal and type `pip install`
   `tensorflow==2.0.0`. See Figure 1-31.

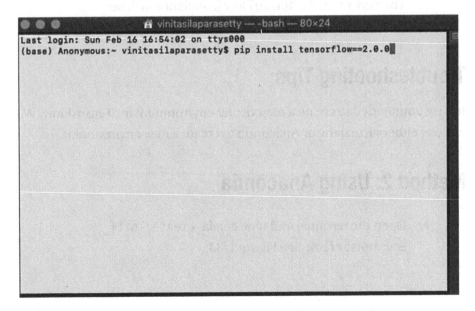

Figure 1-31. *Installing TensorFlow 2.0 via the terminal*

2. The installation will take a few seconds.

3. Open a new notebook in Jupyter.

4. To test the installation, type `import tensorflow` in a new cell, as shown in Figure 1-32.

Figure 1-32. *Testing TensorFlow 2.0 installation via Jupyter Notebook*

5. Now type `tensorflow.__version__`.

6. Run the cell.

7. The version of the TensorFlow installation will be shown under the cell.

Troubleshooting Tips

It is recommended to create a new virtual environment for TensorFlow. We can use either virtualenv or Anaconda to create a new environment.

Method 2: Using Anaconda

1. Open the terminal and type `conda create -n tf_ env tensorflow`. See Figure 1-33.

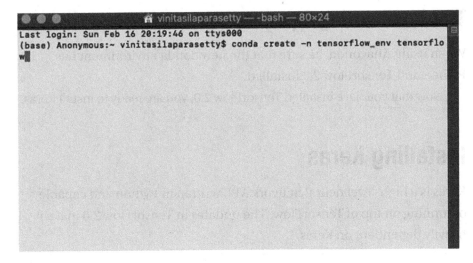

Figure 1-33. *Installing TensorFlow 2.0 using Anaconda*

2. The setup takes a few seconds.

3. Now type `conda activate tf_env`. See Figure 1-34.

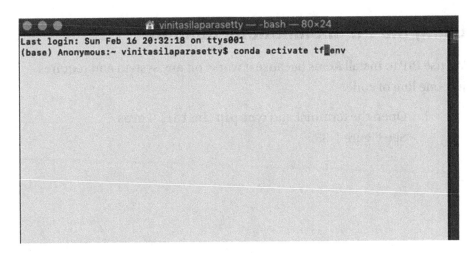

Figure 1-34. *Activating the newly created environment with TensorFlow 2.0*

Troubleshooting Tips

When using Anaconda, be sure that the new conda environment has Python and TensorFlow 2.0 installed.

Now that you have installed TensorFlow 2.0, you are ready to install Keras.

Installing Keras

Keras is a high-level neural network API, written in Python and capable of running on top of TensorFlow. The updates in TensorFlow 2.0 make it heavily dependent on Keras.

Dependencies

- Python 3
- TensorFlow 2.0

Using the PIP Installation Package

We use PIP to install Keras because it works on any system and requires just one line of code.

1. Open the terminal and type `pip install keras`.
   See Figure 1-35.

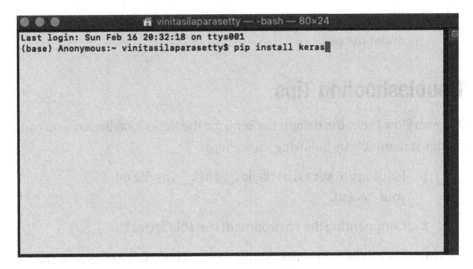

Figure 1-35. *Installing Keras via the terminal*

2. The installation will take a few seconds.

3. Open a new notebook in Jupyter.

4. To test the installation, type import keras in a new cell.

5. Now type pip list | grep Keras and run the cell. See Figure 1-36.

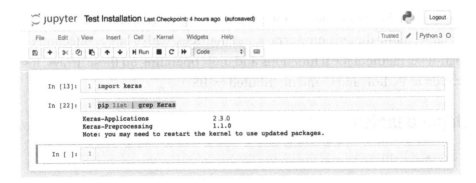

Figure 1-36. *Testing the Keras installation via Jupyter Notebook*

6. The version of the Keras installation will be shown under the cell.

Troubleshooting Tips

If TensorFlow is not the default backend for the Keras installation, you can change it manually by following these steps:

1. Finding the `keras.backend.__init__.py` file on your system.

2. Commenting the environment variable `import`.

Now that you have installed Keras, you are ready to install the basic Python libraries.

Installing Python Libraries

Throughout this book we will be using basic Python libraries for data preprocessing. The best way to install all the Python libraries easily is using PIP.

Installing NumPy

NumPy is a library for the Python programming language. It adds support for large, multi-dimensional arrays and matrices, with a large collection of high-level mathematical functions and tools operating on these arrays. It's written in Python and C and distributed by BSD.

Dependencies

- Python 3

Using the PIP Installation Package

1. Open the terminal and type `pip install numpy`.
    See Figure 1-37.

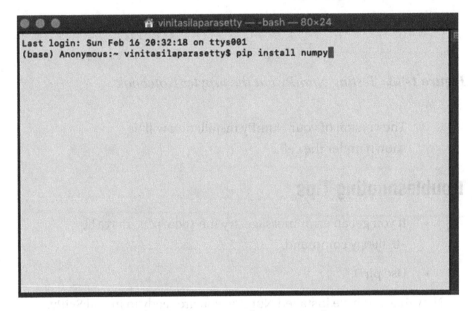

Figure 1-37. *Installing NumPy via the terminal*

2. The installation will take a few seconds.

3. Open a new notebook in Jupyter.

4. To test the installation, type `import numpy` in a
    new cell.

5. Now type `numpy.version.version` and run the cell.
    See Figure 1-38.

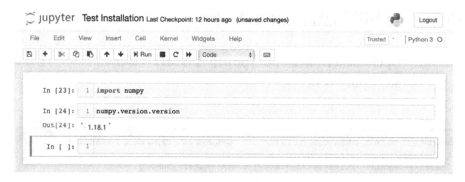

Figure 1-38.   *Testing NumPy via the Jupyter Notebook*

6. The version of your NumPy installation will be
    shown under the cell.

Troubleshooting Tips

- If you get an error message, try the `sudo pip install`
  `-U numpy` command.

- Use pip3.

Now that you have installed NumPy, you are ready to install SciPy.

Installing SciPy

SciPy is a free and open source Python library used for scientific and
technical computing. SciPy contains modules for optimization, linear
algebra, integration, interpolation, special functions, FFT (fast Fourier
transform), signal and image processing, ODE solvers, and other tasks
common in science and engineering. It's written in Python, Fortran, C, and
C++ and distributed under a BSD-new license.

Dependencies

- Python 3
- NumPy

Using the PIP Installation Package

1. Open the terminal and type `pip install scipy`.
   See Figure 1-39.

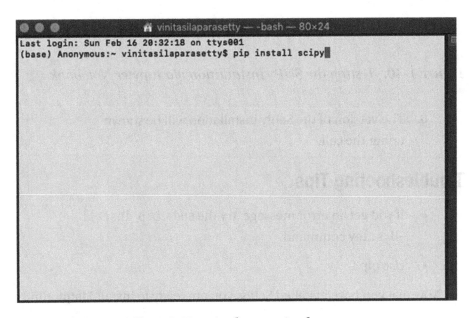

Figure 1-39. *Installing SciPy via the terminal*

2. The installation will take a few seconds.

3. Open a new notebook in Jupyter.

4. To test the installation, type `import scipy` in a new cell.

5. Now type `scipy.version.version` and run the cell.
    See Figure 1-40.

Figure 1-40. *Testing the SciPy installation via Jupyter Notebook*

6. The version of the SciPy installation will be shown
    under the cell.

Troubleshooting Tips

- If you get an error message, try the `sudo pip install`
  `-U scipy` command.

- Use pip3.

Now that you have installed SciPy, you are ready to install Matplotlib.

Installing Matplotlib

Matplotlib is a plotting library for the Python programming language and
the NumPy numerical mathematics extension. Matplotlib provides an
object-oriented API for embedding plots into applications using general-
purpose GUI toolkits.

Dependencies

- Python 3
- NumPy
- SciPy

Using the PIP Installation Package

1. Open the terminal and type `pip install matplotlib`. See Figure 1-41.

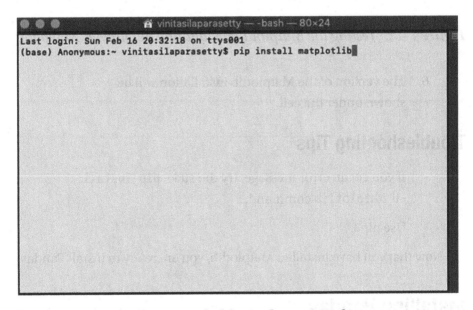

Figure 1-41. *Installing Matplotlib via the terminal*

2. The installation will take a few seconds.

3. Open a new notebook in Jupyter.

4. To test the installation, type `import matplotlib` in a new cell.

41

5. Now type `matplotlib.version.version` and run the cell. See Figure 1-42.

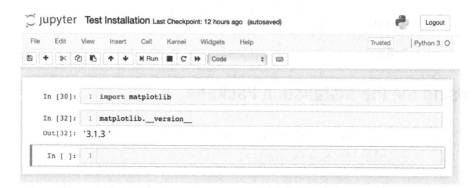

Figure 1-42. *Testing the Matplotlib installation via Jupyter Notebook*

6. The version of the Matplotlib installation will be shown under the cell.

Troubleshooting Tips

- If you get an error message, try the `sudo pip install -U matplotlib` command.

- Use pip3.

Now that you have installed Matplotlib, you are ready to install Pandas.

Installing Pandas

Pandas is a software library written for the Python programming language for data manipulation and analysis. It offers data structures and operations for manipulating numerical tables and time series.

It is free software released under the three-clause BSD license. It's written in Python, and C and the original author is Wes McKinney.

Dependencies

- Python 3

- NumPy

- SciPy

- Matplotlib

Using the PIP Installation Package

1. Open the terminal and type pip install pandas. The installation will take a few seconds. See Figure 1-43.

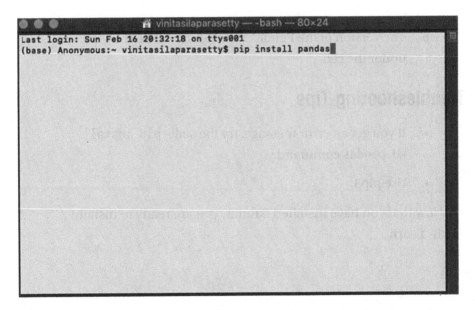

Figure 1-43. *The Pandas installation via the terminal*

2.   Open a new notebook in Jupyter.

3.   To test the installation, type import pandas in a new cell.

4.   Now type pandas.__version__ and run the cell. See Figure 1-44.

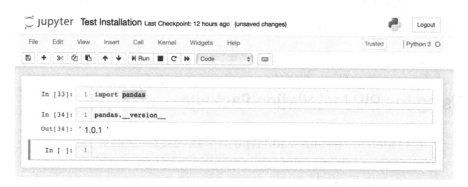

Figure 1-44. *Testing Pandas via Jupyter Notebook*

5.   The version of the Pandas installation will be shown under the cell.

Troubleshooting Tips

- If you get an error message, try the sudo pip install -U pandas command.

- Use pip3.

Now that you have installed Pandas, you are ready to install Scikit- Learn.

Installing Scikit-Learn

Scikit-Learn is a free software machine learning library for the Python programming language. It features various classification, regression, and clustering algorithms, including support vector machines.

It's available for Linux, macOS, and Windows and is distributed under a BSD license.

Dependencies

- Python 3
- NumPy
- SciPy
- Matplotlib
- Pandas

Using the PIP Installation Package

1. Open the terminal and type `pip install sklearn`. See Figure 1-45.

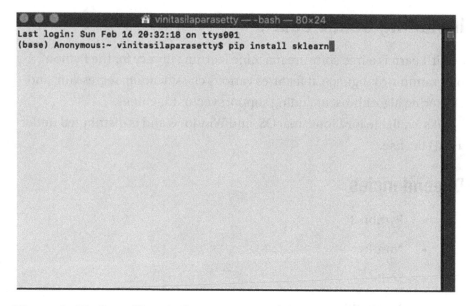

Figure 1-45. *Installing Scikit-Learn via the terminal*

2. The installation will take a few seconds.

3. Open a new notebook in Jupyter.

4. To test the installation, type import sklearn in a new cell.

5. Now type sklearn.__version__ and run the cell. See Figure 1-46.

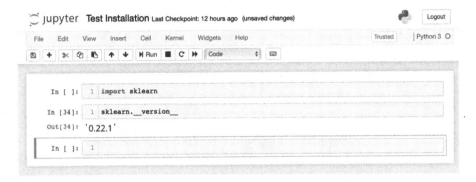

Figure 1-46. *Testing the Scikit-Learn installation via Jupyter Notebook*

6. The version of the sklearn installation will be shown under the cell.

Troubleshooting Tips

- If you get an error message, try the sudo pip install -U sklearn command.

- Use pip3.

With Scikit-Learn installed, you are ready to learn the basics of deep learning using TensorFlow 2.0.

Summary

In this chapter, you learned how to install all the necessary packages to follow along in the remaining chapters.

CHAPTER 2

Perceptrons

Before we get started with deep learning and discuss how we can use neural networks, we need to understand what a neural network is. In particular, we need to understand the most basic unit of the neural network, the perceptron. A *perceptron* is the elementary unit of a neural network and is modeled in a very similar manner to a neuron found in the human brain.

Biological Neurons

The biological neuron is the inspiration for artificial neurons. By emulating the way a biological neuron works, humans have enabled machines to think on their own. Biological neurons are the basic structural and functional unit of the human nervous system (see Figure 2-1). There are about 86 billion neurons in the human brain, which comprise roughly 10% of all brain cells. They interconnect to form a network that is involved in processing and transmitting chemical and electrical signals. The cell nucleus processes the information received from dendrites. The *axon* is a cable that is used by neurons to send information. Every neuron is made of the following:

- Cell body (also called the *soma*)
- Dendrites
- Axon

© Vinita Silaparasetty 2020
V. Silaparasetty, *Deep Learning Projects Using TensorFlow 2,*
https://doi.org/10.1007/978-1-4842-5802-6_2

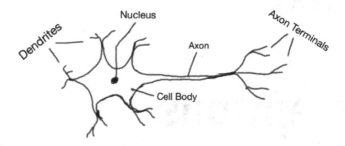

Figure 2-1. *Basic neuron structure*

This gives us a clear understanding of how a biological neuron works. Now, let's compare the workings of a biological neuron with that of an artificial neuron.

Artificial Neurons

An *artificial neuron* is a mathematical function, modeled on the working of a biological neuron. Each neuron takes inputs, weighs them separately, sums them up, and passes this sum through a nonlinear function to produce an output. Every neuron holds an internal state called the *activation signal.* Each neuron is connected to another neuron via a connection link.

Components of an artificial neuron include the following:

- Input signal

- Weights

- Bias

- Net input

- Activation function

- Output signal

The simplest artificial neuron is called a perceptron. Let's look at perceptrons in detail.

Perceptrons

A perceptron is an algorithm for supervised learning of binary classifiers. The perceptron algorithm learns the weights of the input signals in order to draw a linear decision boundary.

It is a classification algorithm that makes all of its predictions based on a linear predictor function that combines a set of weights with the feature vector.

There are two types of perceptrons:

- Single layer perceptrons, which have limited processing power.

- Multilayer perceptrons, or feedforward neural networks, have greater processing power, as they contain two or more layers.

To get a better idea of how perceptrons work, let's discuss the *Perceptron Learning Rule.*

Perceptron Learning Rule

The Perceptron Learning Rule states that an algorithm will automatically learn the optimal weight coefficients. The perceptron receives multiple input signals, and if the sum of the input signals exceeds a certain threshold, it either sends a signal or does not return an output. In the context of supervised learning and classification, this can then be used to predict the class of a sample.

Before we can start creating a perceptron, we need to know how to "activate" it, to help it process the data correctly and obtain useful output. Let's take a look at the basic activation functions.

Types of Activation Functions

To keep things simple, we are covering the three most commonly used activation functions in this chapter:

- Sigmoid function

- ReLU function

- Softmax function

The Sigmoid Activation Function

A Sigmoid function is a mathematical function with a Sigmoid curve, also called an "S" curve (see Figure 2-2). It is a special case of the logistic function and leads to a probability of the value between 0 and 1.

This is useful as an activation function when we want to focus on probability mapping rather than on the precise values of the input parameter.

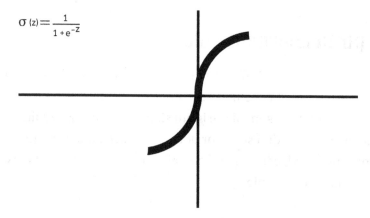

$$\sigma(z) = \frac{1}{1 + e^{-z}}$$

Figure 2-2. *Sigmoid S curve*

Advantages of the Sigmoid function are as follows:

- It is especially used for models in which we have to predict the probability as an output. Since the probability of anything exists only between the range of 0 and 1, Sigmoid is the right choice.

- We can find the slope of the Sigmoid curve at any two points. This means the function is differentiable.

- The function is monotonic but its derivative is not. This means the function varies in such a way that it either never decreases or never increases, but the derivatives of the Sigmoid function are not monotonic.

Limitations of the Sigmoid function are as follows:

- The Sigmoid output is close to zero for highly negative input.

- This can be a problem in neural network training and can lead to slow learning and the model getting trapped in local minima during training.

- The Sigmoid function cannot be used in networks with many layers due to the vanishing gradient problem.

The ReLU Function

A rectifier or ReLU (Rectified Linear Unit) allows us to eliminate negative values in an artificial neural network, as it is a piecewise linear function. It will output the input directly if positive; otherwise, it will give 0 as the output (see Figure 2-3).

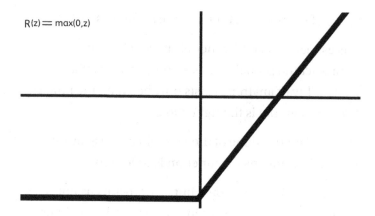

$R(z) = max(0,z)$

Figure 2-3. *ReLU activation function*

Advantages of ReLU functions include the following:

- Allow for faster and effective training of deep neural architectures on large and complex datasets.

- Sparse activation of only about 50% of units in a neural network (as negative values are eliminated).

- Efficient gradient propagation, which means no vanishing or exploding gradient problems.

- Efficient computation with the only comparison, addition, or multiplication.

- Scale well.

Limitations of ReLU functions include:

- Non-differentiable at zero. This means that values close to zero may give inconsistent or intractable results.

- Non-zero centered. This creates asymmetry around data (since only positive values are handled), leading to uneven handling of data.

- The output value has no limit and can lead to computational issues with large values being passed through.

- When the learning rate is too high, ReLU neurons can become inactive and "die."

The Softmax Function

The Softmax, or normalized exponential, function is a generalization of the logistic function that outputs the probability of the result belonging to a certain set of classes. It converts a K-dimensional vector of arbitrary real values to a K-dimensional vector of real values in the range (0, 1) that add up to 1 (see Figure 2-4). It is akin to categorization logic at the end of a neural network.

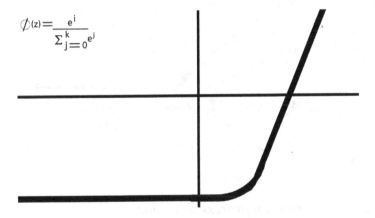

$$\varnothing(z) = \frac{e^i}{\sum_{j=0}^{k} e^j}$$

Figure 2-4. *Softmax activation function*

Advantages of the Softmax function include the following:

- Highlights the largest values.

- Suppresses values that are significantly below the maximum value.

- It is quick to train and predict.

Disadvantages of the Softmax function include the following:

- It does not support null rejection, so we need to train the algorithm with a specific null class if we need one.

Now that you know what a perceptron is and have been introduced to the activation functions required for it, let's see how a perceptron works.

Perceptrons in Action

A perceptron process consists of four stages (see Figure 2-5). The following sections discuss each one.

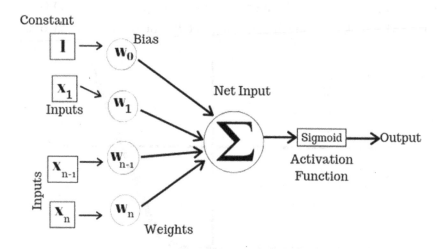

Figure 2-5. *A perceptron processing inputs*

Stage 1: Forward Propagation of Inputs

A perceptron accepts inputs in the form of features and processes them to predict the output. This output is compared to the labels to measure the error. This is known as *forward propagation*.

The inputs of the perceptron in the diagram are denoted by [x1,x2.....x (n)], where x represents the feature value and n represents the total number of features. In Figure 2-5, we take 1 as a constant so that it can be multiplied by the bias without changing its value.

Next, the net input is calculated.

Stage 2: Calculation of the Net Input

Weights

The *weights* are the values that are computed over time when training the model. We represent the weights of a perceptron using [w1,w2,.....w(n)].

The weights of the perceptron algorithm are estimated from the training data using gradient descent.

Bias

In algebraic terms, the *bias* allows a classifier to translate its decision boundary to the left or to the right by a constant distance in a specified direction. The bias helps to train the model faster and with better quality.

In the example shown in Figure 2-5, the bias is denoted by $\mathbf{w_0}$.

Net Input

The net input is the result of two calculations that occur successively:

- First is the multiplication of each weight [w(n)] by its associated feature value [x(n)].

- Then the bias [w_0] is added to the product.

Now that we have the net input, it is time to apply the activation function.

Stage 3: Activation Function

The activation function provides nonlinearity to the perceptron. In the current example, we use the Sigmoid function as the activation function. A Sigmoid function is defined for real input values and has a non-negative derivative at each point. The output lies between 0 and 1.

The Sigmoid function is expressed as `f(x) = 1/1+e^-x`.

At this point, forward propagation is complete, but the beauty of perceptrons and artificial neurons in general lies with the process of backward propagation, where a recalculation occurs.

Stage 4: Backward Propagation

Backward propagation of errors is sometimes called *back-propagation* for short. It is a mechanism used in supervised learning of artificial neural networks using gradient descent.

Gradient descent is an optimization algorithm used to find the values of parameters of a function that minimize a cost function. This method calculates the gradient of the error function with respect to the neural network's weights. Error calculation is done by comparing the output with the labels.

The prediction process takes the input and generates, using the internal state, the most likely output according to its past "training experience." The loss function is calculated during each iteration and is minimized using an optimization function until convergence is achieved. The loss function is a calculation of the error in the models' calculations. Optimization is the method of minimizing the loss.

The calculation of the gradient proceeds backward through the network. This means the gradient of the output of the last layer of the neural network is calculated first and the gradient of the first layer is calculated last.

Partial computations of the gradient from one layer are reused to compute the gradient of the previous layer. This backward flow of information allows for efficient computation of the gradient at each layer.

The way this optimization algorithm works is that each training instance is shown to the model one at a time. The model makes a prediction for a training instance, the error is calculated, and the model is updated in order to reduce the error for the next prediction. This procedure can be used to find the set of weights in a model that result in the smallest error for the model on the training data. The bias is updated in a similar way, except without an input, as it is not associated with a specific input value.

Let's get a better understanding of the working of a perceptron by creating our own perceptron using TensorFlow 2.0.

Project Description

In this tutorial, we are classifying structured data using a perceptron. These are the steps that will occur inside our perceptron:

- The features and weights are taken as matrices and multiplied.

- The product of the matrix multiplication is then added to the bias.

- The error is calculated using the loss function and optimization is done.

Figure 2-6 provides a simple example to help show how an individual perceptron works.

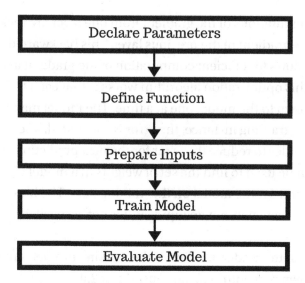

Figure 2-6. *Perceptron flowchart*

Important Terminology

- **Target/label:** The expected output of the function.

- **Loss function:** It computes the error for each iteration. The error is calculated as the difference between the expected output value and the prediction value.

- **Optimizer:** It minimizes the loss function.

- **Iteration:** The number of times training is to be done.

- **Confusion matrix:** It compares the predicted value with the target value and represents the number of correct and incorrect observations in a matrix.

Required Libraries

We will be working with the following libraries:

- TensorFlow 2.0
- Keras
- NumPy
- SciPy
- Pandas
- Matplotlib
- Scikit-Learn

Procedure

In this tutorial, we'll implement the perceptron by classifying structured data using TensorFlow.

Step 1. Import Libraries

Begin by importing the necessary libraries.

```
import numpy as np
import pandas as pd
import tensorflow as tf

from tensorflow import feature_column #reformats structured
data for ease in calculations
from tensorflow.keras import layers #to create the layer in the
neural network.
from sklearn.model_selection import train_test_split #splits
the data for us
```

```
from sklearn.metrics import confusion_matrix #calculates the
confusion matrix
from sklearn.metrics import accuracy_score #calculates the
accuracy score

import matplotlib.pyplot as plt
%matplotlib inline
#so that plots remain within the cell
```

Step 2. Declare Parameters

In this tutorial, we will take two features as the input. Here, units indicates the number of neurons present in the current layer.

```
Number_of_features=2
Number_of_units=1 #indicates number of neurons
```

Step 3. Declare the Weights and Bias

Initialize a variable for the weights using tf.Variable() and name it weights. Set the weights variable to 0 using tf.zeros(). Next, initialize a variable for the bias using tf.Variable() and name it bias. Set the bias variable to 0 using tf.zeros().

```
weight=tf.Variable(tf.zeros([Number_of_features,Number_of_
units])) #initializing to zero
bias=tf.Variable(tf.zeros([Number_of_units]))#Initializing to zero
```

Step 4. Define the Perceptron Function

Define the perceptron function using def perceptron(x). Inside the function, I computes the matrix multiplication of x and weight using tf.matmul(x,weight), then adds the product to bias using tf.add(bias). tf.sigmoid(I) calculates the output using the Sigmoid activation function.

```
def perceptron(x):
    I=tf.add(tf.matmul(x,weight),bias)
    output=tf.sigmoid(I)
    return output
```

Step 5. Define the Loss Function and Optimizer

The individual loss function is calculated as the reduced mean of the Sigmoid cross-entropy of the labels y, where the logits are the outputs of the perceptron(x) function.

The Sigmoid cross-entropy is used to quantify the difference between two probability distributions, in this case, 0 and 1. Initialize optimizer and employ the Adam optimizer using tf.optimizers.Adam(.01):

individual_loss=lambda: abs(tf.reduce_mean(tf.nn.sigmoid_cross_entropy_with_logits(labels=y,logits=perceptron(x))))

optimizer=tf.keras.optimizers.Adam(.01)

Step 6. Read in the Data

Read in the data using pd.read_csv('data.csv'). Then check if the data has been read correctly by viewing the first few lines of the data frame using dataframe.head().

```
dataframe = pd.read_csv('data.csv')
dataframe.head()
```

Step 7. Visualization of Labels

To familiarize yourself with the data, you can do a quick visualization of the labeled data using plt.scatter().

plt.scatter(dataframe.x1,dataframe.x2,c=dataframe.label)

The output is shown in Figure 2-7.

Visualization of Labels

```
[9] plt.scatter(dataframe.x1,dataframe.x2,c=dataframe.label)
```

```
<matplotlib.collections.PathCollection at 0x7f98e4bec048>
```

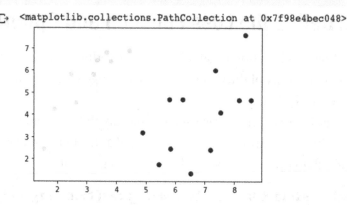

Figure 2-7. *Scatterplot of labels*

Step 8. Prepare Inputs

Format the input data x_input as a matrix using .as_matrix() and format the labels y_label as a matrix using .as_matrix(). This will separate the inputs and labels from the dataset.

```
x_input=dataframe[['x1','x2']].as_matrix()
y_label=dataframe[['label']].as_matrix()

#View the input matrix
x_input
```

Step 9. Initialize Variables

Initialize x as a variable using `tf.Variable()`. and the dataframe object `x_input`.

```
#Initialize the variable x
x=tf.Variable(x_input)
```

Change the datatype of x to `float32` using `x=tf.cast()`.

```
#Change the datatype of x to 'float32'
x=tf.cast(x,tf.float32)
```

Initialize y as a variable using `tf.Variable()` and the dataframe object `y_label`.

```
#Create the variable y
y=tf.Variable(y_label)
```

Change the datatype of y to `float32` using `tf.cast()`.

```
#Change the datatype of y to 'float32'
y=tf.cast(y,tf.float32)
```

Step 10. Train the Model

Train the model using a `for` loop. Set the number of iterations to 1000 using in `range(1000):`. The loss is minimized using `optimizer.minimize(individual_loss,[weight,bias])`.

```
for i in range(1000):
    optimizer.minimize(individual_loss,[weight,bias])
```

Step 11. New Values for Weights and Bias

View the new weights and bias by printing their values using
tf.print(weight,bias).

```
tf.print(weight,bias)
```

Here is the output:

```
[[-2..42329407]
[1.85045445]] [1.74988687]]
```

Step 12. View the Final Loss

View the final loss by calculating it using the following:

```
final_loss=tf.reduce_mean(tf.nn.sigmoid_cross_entropy_with_logi
ts(labels=y,logits=perceptron(x)))
```

Now print the value of the final loss using tf.print(final_loss).

```
final_loss=tf.reduce_mean(tf.nn.sigmoid_cross_entropy_with_logi
ts(labels=y,logits=perceptron(x)))
```

```
tf.print(final_loss)
```

Here is the output:

```
0.534005582
```

Step 13. Predicting Using the Trained Model

Round off the output values to make them either 1 or 0 using
ypred=perceptron(x) and then ypred=tf.round(ypred).

```
ypred=perceptron(x)
ypred=tf.round(ypred) #Round off the output value to 1 or 0, to
make the comparison with the target easier.
```

Step 14. Evaluate the Model

Calculate the accuracy score using accuracy_score(y, ypred). This
indicates the accuracy of the model after comparing the predicted output
to the target.

```
accuracy_score(y, ypred)
```

Here is the output:

```
1.0
```

Generate the confusion matrix using confusion_matrix(y, ypred).
If all the observations fall within the diagonal of the matrix, and the rest of
the values are 0, then the model is 100% accurate.

```
confusion_matrix(y, ypred)
```

Note   When initializing a variable in TensorFlow, always use a
capital V.

Now you know how a perceptron works. In the next chapter, you learn
how a collection of perceptrons work together in the form of an artificial
neural network.

Summary

Here's a recap of what you learned in this chapter:

- An artificial neuron is a mathematical function that is modeled after a biological neuron.

- A perceptron is the elementary unit of a neural network that certain computations use to detect features or business intelligence in the input data. It maps its input, x, which is multiplied by the learned weight coefficient, and generates an output value, $f(x)$.

- The Perceptron Learning Rule states that the algorithm will automatically learn the optimal weight coefficients.

- A multilayer perceptron, or feedforward neural network with two or more layers, has more processing power and can process nonlinear patterns as well.

- A perceptron accepts features as inputs.

- Every perceptron has weights and a bias.

- Forward propagation occurs when the inputs are fed at the input layer and are processed successively until they reach the output layer.

- Backward propagation occurs when the gradient of the last layer is calculated and each partial calculation is fed to the predecessor until the first layer of the neural network is reached.

- Commonly used activation functions are Sigmoid, ReLU, and Softmax.

- Weighted summation is the sum of the values that we get after the multiplication of each weight.

- A Sigmoid function is a mathematical function with a Sigmoid curve.

- A rectifier, or ReLU (Rectified Linear Unit), allows us to eliminate negative values in an artificial neural network.

- The Softmax, or normalized exponential function, is a generalization of the logistic function.

- In the project in this chapter, you learned how to make predictions for a binary classification problem, how to optimize a set of weights, how to calculate the accuracy score, and how to view the confusion matrix.

CHAPTER 3

Neural Networks

Here's some food for thought: if a single neuron is powerful enough to perform a binary classification, as you saw in the previous chapter, how much more powerful is a collection of neurons? That's what we are going to discover in this chapter. Several neurons together make up a neural network. In this tutorial, we will create a multi-layer neuron and then classify the MNIST dataset with it. In Keras, a single iteration is referred to as an *epoch*. Let's study neural networks more in detail.

What Is a Neural Network?

A neural network is also called an Artificial Neural Network (ANN). It contains layers of interconnected nodes called *neurons*. The neural network utilizes a series of algorithms to detect underlying relationships in a dataset. Neural networks adapt to internal and external parameters. The network generates the best possible output without having to modify the output criteria. Neural networks are based on adaptive learning. They use several principles, including gradient-based training, fuzzy logic, and Bayesian methods. Artificial neural networks are used in sequence and pattern recognition systems, data processing, robotics, and many more systems.

© Vinita Silaparasetty 2020
V. Silaparasetty, *Deep Learning Projects Using TensorFlow 2*,
https://doi.org/10.1007/978-1-4842-5802-6_3

Neural Network Components

A neural network consists of the following main components:

- **Input layer:** The inputs that are fed into the neural network.

- **Hidden layer:** Contains any number of neurons, depending on the goal we want to achieve.

- **Output layer:** The final output obtained.

Advantages of Neural Networks

Neural networks offer the following advantages:

- When an element of the neural network fails, it will continue to function. This is due to its parallel nature.

- A neural network does not need to be reprogrammed for unseen data, as it is an adaptive, intelligent system.

- Neural networks are excellent at solving complex problems.

- A neural network is capable of greater fault tolerance than a traditional network. Without the loss of stored data, the network can regenerate a fault in any of its components.

Disadvantages of a Neural Networks

Neural networks have the following setbacks:

- Require lots of processing time for large neural networks.

- The architecture of a neural network is different from the architecture and history of microprocessors, so they have to be emulated.

- Increasing the number of neutrons increases the complexity of the network.

- An optimal amount of data is required to successfully train the network.

- A bit of trial and error is involved to determine the number of layers as well as the number of neurons per layer. This is time consuming.

We know what a neural network is in theory, but what about in practice? Let's take a look at how a neural network functions.

How a Neural Network Works

As you saw in the previous chapter, the process that happens within the neuron is:

1) Forward propagation

   Inputs ➤ Calculation of Net Input ➤ Activation Function Applied ➤ Output

2) Back propagation

   Output ➤ Activation Function Applied ➤ Calculation of Net Input ➤ Inputs

Now let's extend this process to a multitude of neurons within the neural network.

Let's take the example of a shallow neural network with ten neurons. In this type of network, there is just one hidden layer (see Figure 3-1).

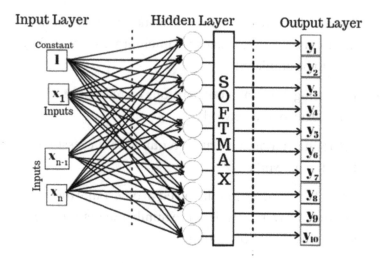

Figure 3-1. *Example of a shallow neural network using MNIST*

Forward Propagation

The inputs are fed to each neuron in the hidden layer. This means that within the hidden layer, each neuron has its own set of weights and a bias. The entire process is in the forward direction, hence it is known as forward propagation. The following is a breakdown of the three layers:

> **Input layer:** According to Figure 3-1, there are four inputs. Here, x1, xn-1, and xn are the variables. We take one as a constant so that it does not affect the bias.

> **Hidden layer:** In Figure 3-1, there are four inputs, so each neuron has four weights and a single bias. The activation function is applied to the net input in each neuron. According to the diagram, we get ten outputs from the hidden layer. That is one from each neuron. In this case, we use the Softmax activation function.

Output layer: We obtain ten categories, one for each digit, y1, y2 ..... y10 .

Note   The hidden layer can have either a Sigmoid function or a Softmax function, depending on the number of expected outputs. If two outputs are expected, Sigmoid is used. If more than two outputs are expected, Softmax is used.

For a neural network with multiple hidden layers, the most popular activation function used between the layers is the ReLU function.

Once the inputs have been fed in and processed in the forward direction, it is time to check them and adjust them to get better results via backward propagation.

Backward Propagation

We saw in the previous chapter that back propagation occurs in each layer of the neural network. The weights and bias of each neuron, within each layer, are adjusted until convergence is achieved. The process moves from the output layer, to the hidden layers, and finally to the input layer.

With this knowledge of neural networks, let's take a look at the most common types of neural networks at our disposal.

Types of Neural Networks

In the previous example, we learned what a shallow neural network is. Now, let's take a quick look at how neural networks are broadly classified.

There are several variations and combinations of each neural network. So, in reality there are several neural networks available. For the projects in this book, we focus on the broad categories of ANNs.

Feedforward Neural Network

In a feedforward neural network, data moves in only one direction from the first tier onward until it reaches the output node (see Figure 3-2). This is also known as a *front propagated wave,* which is usually achieved by using a classifying activation function. There is no back propagation and it may have a single layer or multiple hidden layers.

The uses of a feedforward neural network include:

- Face recognition

- Computer vision

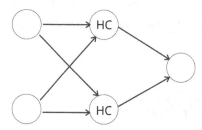

Figure 3-2. *Sample feedforward neural network (HC indicates hidden cell)*

Convolutional Neural Networks

A convolutional neural network (CNN) is a regularized version of multilayer neurons and contains one or more convolutional layers (see Figure 3-3). These layers can either be completely interconnected or pooled. The convolutional layer uses a convolutional operation on the input.

The uses of a CNN include:

- Image and video recognition

- Natural language processing

- Recommender systems

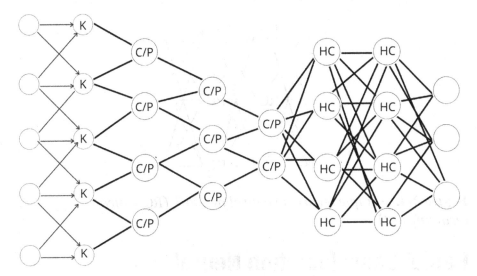

Figure 3-3. *Sample convolutional neural network (K indicates kernel, C/P indicate convolution or pooling, and HC indicates hidden cell)*

Recurrent Neural Network (RNN)

A recurrent neural network (RNN) saves the output of a particular layer and feeds it back as input. The recurrent neural network process begins in the layers after the first layer. Each node acts as a memory cell while computing and carrying out operations, so that during back propagation it can compare the previous values with the new ones (see Figure 3-4). RNNs are discussed more in detail in Chapter 9.

Uses of an RNN include text-to-speech conversion technology.

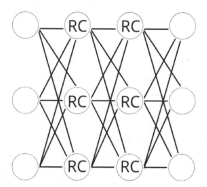

Figure 3-4. *Sample recurring neural network (RC indicates recurring cell)*

Radial Basis Function Neural Network (RBNN)

An RBNN considers the distance of any point relative to the center. It applies the radial basis function as its activation function (see Figure 3-5). There are two layers. In the inner layer, the features are combined with the radial basis function. Then the output of these features is taken into account when calculating the same output in the next time-step. In this way, it achieves linear separability.

The uses of an RBNN include power restoration systems.

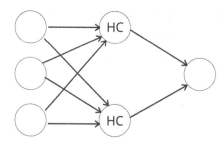

Figure 3-5. *Sample radial basis function neural network (HC indicates hidden cell)*

Now you are aware of the basic categories of neural networks. As we work on the projects in this book, we will use neural networks that fall under the subcategories discussed here.

Project Description

In this project, we use a single layer neural network to classify a set of handwritten digits. We first flatten the data from a two-dimensional matrix to a one-dimensional array. Then we feed it into the neural network with a Softmax activation function. The output is a digit from 0-9. Figure 3-6 shows a flowchart of this process.

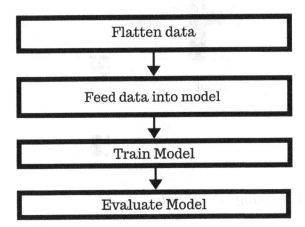

Figure 3-6. *Flowchart using a simple neural network on MNIST data*

Flattening Data

The data in MNIST consists entirely of two-dimensional images of handwritten digits. That means the data is in the form of a two-dimensional matrix. This is not easy for the neural network to process. So we "flatten" it by converting it to one-dimensional data. The two-dimensional matrix is converted into a one-dimensional array. This way the neural network can process the data better and give better results. See Figure 3-7.

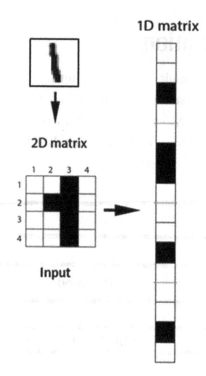

Figure 3-7. *Flattening MNIST data*

About the Dataset

Name: MNIST database

Contents: The MNIST database of handwritten digits has a training set of 60,000 examples and a test set of 10,000 examples. It is a subset of the larger set available from MNIST. The digits have been size-normalized and centered in a fixed-size image.

Source: http://yann.lecun.com/exdb/mnist/

Required Libraries

Our project requires the following libraries:

- Keras
- TensorFlow 2.0

Neural Network Architecture

We will use a simple neural network architecture composed of the following:

- **Input layer:** The data is fed into the input layer as features. The neuron calculates the net input function.

- **Output layer:** This layer contains ten neurons , for each of the possible categories of the data.

- **Activation function:** Softmax

- **Loss function:** Sparse Categorical Cross Entropy

- **Optimizer:** Adam

- **Metric:** Accuracy

Procedure

Follow these steps to create a multi-layer neuron:

1. Import the libraries. Use the `import` command to import both TensorFlow 2.0 and Keras.

   ```
   #import libraries.
   import keras
   import tensorflow as tf
   ```

2. Read in the data. Keras comes loaded with a collection of datasets. MNIST is one of them. So you can load it directly from Keras. Then split the data into two sets for testing and training, respectively.

```
mnist=tf.keras.datasets.mnist
```

```
#split data
(x_train, y_train), (x_test, y_test) = mnist.load_
data()
```

Our output should look like this.

```
Downloading data from https://storage.googleapis.com/
tensorflow/tf-keras-datasets/mnist.npz
11493376/11490434 [==============================] - 0s 0us/
step
```

3. Data processing. The MNIST dataset consists of two-dimensional images. Flatten them into one-dimensional images for convenience.

```
x_train, x_test = x_train / 255.0, x_test / 255.0
```

4. Create the neural network. Create a single hidden layer, using the Sequential module. This hidden layer has ten neurons. The activation function that we will use is Softmax. Next, you can define the optimizer. We will use the Adam optimizer, as we are just doing a basic categorization of data. We will define the loss function as Sparse Categorical Cross Entropy, because the output can be only one of ten possible categories. To test the capability of this model, use the accuracy metric.

```
digit = tf.keras.models.Sequential([
    tf.keras.layers.Flatten(input_shape=(28, 28)),
    tf.keras.layers.Dense(10, activation=tf.nn.softmax)
])

#compile model
digit.compile(optimizer='adam',
              loss='sparse_categorical_crossentropy',
              metrics=['accuracy'])
```

5. Train the model. Using the fit module, train the newly created model. Set the iterations for the model. To begin, set it to three epochs and check the accuracy score.

```
digit.fit(x_train, y_train, epochs=3)
```

Our output should look similar to this:

```
Train on 60000 samples
Epoch 1/3
60000/60000 [==============================] - 3s 47us/
sample - loss: 0.4670 - acc: 0.8788
Epoch 2/3
60000/60000 [==============================] - 3s 44us/
sample - loss: 0.3036 - acc: 0.9151
Epoch 3/3
60000/60000 [==============================] - 3s 45us/
sample - loss: 0.2834 - acc: 0.9204
<tensorflow.python.keras.callbacks.History at 0x7f8709047358>
```

6. Evaluate the model. Using the `evaluate` module, test the model. Once the test is complete, check the accuracy score. With just three iterations, you get an accuracy score of 92%.

```
digit.evaluate(x_test, y_test)
```

The output should look similar to this:

```
10000/10000 [==============================] - 0s 26us/sample -
loss: 0.2765 - acc: 0.9229
[0.2764906617820263, 0.9229]
```

7. Further experimentation. Try changing the number of epochs to see how it affects the accuracy.

Summary

Here's a recap of all that you learned in this chapter:

- A neural network is also called an artificial neural network (ANN).

- Neural networks are based on adaptive learning.

- Neural networks use several principles, including gradient-based training, fuzzy logic, and Bayesian methods.

- Neural networks have a parallel nature.

- Without the loss of stored data, the network is able to regenerate a fault in any of its components.

- Large neural networks require a lot of processing time.

- Increasing the number of neutrons increases the complexity of the network.

- An optimal amount of data is required to train the network successfully.

- A bit of trial and error is involved to determine the number of layers as well as the number of neurons per layer. This is time consuming.

- The hidden layer can have either a Sigmoid function or a Softmax function, depending on the number of expected outputs. If there are two expected outputs, Sigmoid is used. If there are more than two expected outputs, Softmax is used.

- A feedforward neural network is an ANN wherein connections between the nodes do not form a cycle.

- A recurrent neural network applies backward propagation.

- RBNN is a single layer neural network whose activation function is the radial basis function. It achieves linear separability.

- Flattening data involves converting it from one format to another. For example, in this project, we flattened the MNIST data by converting it from a two-dimensional matrix to a one-dimensional array.

- Through this first project, you learned how to work with a large dataset, how to split a dataset into testing and training datasets, and how to prepare data for a model.

- You should now have a good idea of how to structure a simple neural network, how to train it with training data, and how to test it with testing data.

References

Here are the resources used in this chapter:

- Advantages and disadvantages: `www.linkedin.com/pulse/artificial-neural-networks-advantages-disadvantages-maad-m-mijwel/`

- Types of neural networks: `www.digitalvidya.com/blog/types-of-neural-networks/`

CHAPTER 4

Sentiment Analysis

In the previous chapter, we learned about the different types of neural networks. In this chapter, we learn about long short-term memory (LSTM) neural networks. The project in this chapter is meant to be simple, to help us adjust to TensorFlow 2.0. We will first learn what an LSTM is and why we need it. Then we will take a look at how an LSTM works. After that, we will learn what sentiment analysis is and its various types. We will also learn how to save a trained model and reload it, so that we can save models and reuse them in future projects. Keep in mind that we cover the process of saving and reloading a trained model only in this project; however, any project that you work on, within this book or your own, can be saved and reloaded.

LSTM Review

Let's begin by learning what an LSTM is in theory. An LSTM is capable of learning long-term dependencies. It maintains a relatively constant error that allows recurrent nets to continue to learn over multiple steps to link causes and effects remotely. This error is back-propagated through time and layers. Figure 4-1 shows a basic LSTM where the M indicates the memory cells. The first column of neurons is the input layer and the last column of neurons is the output layer.

© Vinita Silaparasetty 2020
V. Silaparasetty, *Deep Learning Projects Using TensorFlow 2*,
https://doi.org/10.1007/978-1-4842-5802-6_4

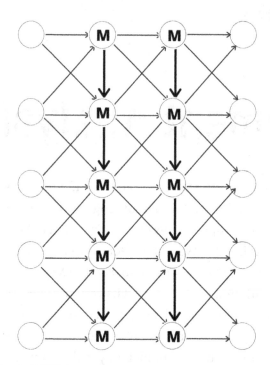

Figure 4-1. *Basic LSTM structure*

The LSTM contains information outside the normal flow of the recurrent network in a gated cell. It essentially acts as a memory cell in which information can be stored, written to, or read from.

The cell makes decisions about what to store and when to allow read and write privileges via analog gates. These gates are implemented with element-wise multiplication by Sigmoids, which are all in the range of 0-1. Analog has the advantage of being differentiable, which makes it suitable for back propagation.

The cells learn when to allow data to enter, leave, or be deleted through the iterative process of making guesses, back propagating error, and adjusting weights via a gradient descent.

It is the perfect solution to the "vanishing gradient" problem. The vanishing gradient problem occurs when we try to train a neural network model using gradient-based optimization techniques.

During backward propagation, the gradient diminishes as it moves backward through the neural network. This means that the neurons in the initial layers learn very slowly as compared to the neurons in the later layers. The initial layers in the network are the slowest to train. The training process takes a very long time and the prediction accuracy of the model decreases.

LSTM solves the problem by creating a connection between the forget gate activations and the gradients' computation. This connection creates a path for information flow through the forget gate, thus ensuring that information is not forgotten.

The applications of LSTM include:

- Handwriting recognition

- Speech recognition

- Disease prediction

- Music composition

Now that you know what an LSTM is, as well as its applications in real-life scenarios, let's look at the process within an LSTM.

How an LSTM Works

The best way to understand an LSTM is to picture it as a chain-like structure with two nonrepeating modules and one repeating module. (see Figure 4-2). Within this structure, the repeating module has three gates. They are the *input gate,* the *output gate,* and the *forget gate.* The cell state connects the entire chain, with minimal linear interactions.

LSTMs use a structure called a gate to regulate the flow of data in to and out of a cell. They work in a similar manner as conditional gates (and, or, xor, etc.). Based on a set of conditions, they decide which information to allow through the gate. The conditions are decided by the LSTM and do not need to be explicitly programmed.

- **Forget gate:** The output of the forget gate tells the cell state which information to forget by multiplying a position in the matrix by zero. If the output of the forget gate is 1, the information is kept in the cell state.

- **Input gate:** This gate determines which information should enter the cell state. The important component here is the activation function. The input gate has a Sigmoid function that has a range of [0,1]. The equation of the cell state is a summation between the previous cell states, so the Sigmoid function alone will only add memory and not be able to remove memory. If you can only add a float number between [0,1], that number will never be zero. This makes it incapable of forgetting. This is why the input modulation gate has an tanh activation function. tanh has a range of [-1, 1] and allows the cell state to forget memory.

- **Output gate:** This gate takes into account all the possible values and utilizes a Sigmoid activation function to decide which information should go to the next hidden state.

The input for an LSTM is in the form of a three-dimensional array. Where the first dimension represents the batch size, the second dimension represents the number of time-steps we are feeding a sequence and the third dimension represents the number of units in one input sequence.

- $S_{(t-1)}$ is the cell state
- $f_{(gt)}$ is the forget gate
- $i_{(gt)}$ is the input gate
- $o_{(gt)}$ is the output gate

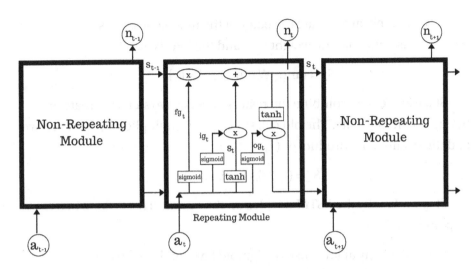

Figure 4-2. *An inside look at the workings of an LSTM*

Stage 1: The LSTM decides what information to discard from the cell state. This decision is made by the forget gate layer, which uses a Sigmoid activation function. This means a value between 0 and 1 will be assigned. The value 1 represents "store" and 0 represents "discard."

Let's assume that the weight is W_{fg} and the bias is b_{fg}. Now according to the diagram, we have two inputs—$n_{(t-1)}$ and a. Both values will be multiplied by the weight (W_{fg}) and then the resulting product will be added to the bias (b_{fg}). Finally, the Sigmoid activation function will be applied to the result.

It can be derived mathematically as follows:

$$f_{gt} = \text{Sigmoid}(\ W_{fg}\,.[n_{(t-1)}\,,\,a] + b_{fg})$$

Stage 2: From the remaining information, the LSTM decides what new information to store in the cell state. This is done in a two-step process:

1.   The input gate layer uses a Sigmoid function to decide which values will be updated. Let's assume that the weight is W_{ig} and the bias is b_{ig}.

$$i_{gt} = \text{Sigmoid}(\ W_{ig}\,.[n_{(t-1)}\,,\,a] + b_{ig})$$

2. A tanh layer creates a vector of the new values. Let's assume that the weight is W_c and the bias is b_c.

$$S_{t1} = \tanh(\ W_c \cdot [n_{(t-1)}, a] + b_c)$$

Stage 3: We now combine the results of these two steps to create an update to the cell state. The old cell state $S_{(t-1)}$ is multiplied by f_{gt}. Then we add the result to the product of $(i_{gt} * S_{t1})$.

$$S_{t2} = (f_{gt} * S_{t-1}) + (i_{gt} * S_{t1})$$

Stage 4: Finally the LSTM decides on the output. This is done in a two-step process:

1. The output layer uses a Sigmoid layer to decide what parts of the cell state will be the output. Let's assume that the weight is W_c and the bias is b_c:

$$o_{gt} = \text{Sigmoid}(\ W_{og} \cdot [n_{(t-1)}, a] + b_{og})$$

2. The result is passed through a tanh activation function, to get values between -1 and 1. Then the result is multiplied by the output of the Sigmoid gate.

$$n_t = o_{gt} * S_t$$

Layers in an LSTM

In order to design an effective LSTM, it is not enough to know how an LSTM works. We also need to understand which layers can be used to design an LSTM. It can have the following types of layers:

> **Embedding layer:** Used to create word vectors for incoming words. It lies between the input and the LSTM layer. The output of the embedding layer is the input to the LSTM layer.

LSTM layer: A recurrent neural net layer that takes a sequence as an input and can return either a sequence or a matrix.

Dropout layer: A regularization technique that consists of setting a fraction of input units to 0 at each update during the training to prevent overfitting.

Dense layer: A fully connected layer where each input node is connected to each output node.

Activation layer: Determines which activation function the LSTM uses to calculate the output of a node.

Now that you understand how an LSTM works, you are ready to put it into action in the project.

Project Description

In this project we are going to use an LSTM on Amazon reviews to identify emotions in a sentence and determine their polarity. Essentially, we will find out how positive or negative a review is. Deep learning models require numerical data as their input. Since we're working on text classification, we need to translate our text data into numerical vectors. To do this, we're going to use a method called *word embeddings*. This method encodes every word into an n-dimensional dense vector, in which similar words will have similar encoding. For this purpose, we're going to use a Keras embedding layer.

We first take only 20% of the total reviews and create the main dataframe that we will work with. This is to avoid overloading our system and potentially causing it to crash. Then we clean the data by removing punctuation and numbers, converting all uppercase letters to lowercase, and removing single characters. To prepare the data for the model, we split it into 70% for the training set and 30% for the test set. After this, we convert the newly cleaned data into arrays and use a tokenizer to help the model understand each word. To avoid incompatibility issues with the array size, we use padding. We proceed to create the model and train it. Finally, we evaluate the performance of the model by checking its accuracy. The process is shown in Figure 4-3.

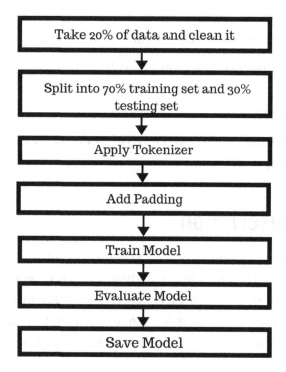

Figure 4-3. *LSTM sentiment analysis project workflow*

About the Dataset

Name: Amazon_Review_Polarity

Contents: 656MB (688,340,758 bytes) compressed archive of negative, positive, and neutral reviews on Amazon

Source: https://drive.google.com/open?id=0Bz8a_
Dbh9QhbaW12WVVZS2drcnM
Created by: Xiang Zhang

Note   It is advisable to create a rough flowchart for all your projects, even ones that you are doing on your own, to help you structure your projects better.

Understanding Sentiment Analysis

Sentiment analysis (see Figure 4-4) is the contextual mining of text that identifies and extracts subjective information in the source material. However, analysis of social media streams is usually restricted to just basic sentiment analysis and count-based metrics.

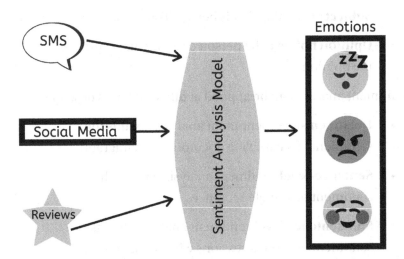

Figure 4-4. *Sentiment analysis is conducted on various online sources*

Sentiment analysis is an automated process of analyzing text data and classifying opinions as negative, positive, or neutral. Sentiment analysis is the most common text classification tool; its applications include:

- Social media monitoring

- Brand monitoring

- Voice of customer (VoC)

- Customer service

- Market research

- Automatically analyze survey responses, product reviews, and social media comments

We can extract other attributes of expression, such as:

- **Polarity:** When the speaker express a positive or negative opinion

- **Subject:** The thing that is being talked about

- **Opinion holder:** The person or entity that expresses the opinion

Sentiment analysis can be applied at different levels of scope:

- **Document-level** sentiment analysis obtains the sentiment of a complete document or paragraph.

- **Sentence-level** sentiment analysis obtains the sentiment of a single sentence.

- **Sub-sentence level** sentiment analysis obtains the sentiment of sub-expressions within a sentence.

Before we can start our project, there are a few concepts we need to understand, such as the different types of sentiment analysis and how they are applied in real life. Then we need to understand one-hot encoding, as we will apply it to our dataset. Once we have designed our model, we also need to test it to ensure that it performs well.

Types of Sentiment Analysis

There are many types of sentiment analysis and SA tools that range from systems that focus on polarity (positive, negative, neutral) to systems that detect feelings and emotions (angry, happy, sad, etc.) or identify intentions.

Fine-Grained Sentiment Analysis

We can be more precise about the level of polarity of the opinion, by extending the basic categories of emotions—positive, neutral, or negative opinions—to the following categories:

- Very positive

- Positive

- Neutral

- Negative

- Very negative

This is usually referred to as fine-grained sentiment analysis.

Emotion Detection

Emotion detection aims at detecting emotions such as happiness, frustration, anger, sadness, etc. Many emotion detection systems resort to lexicons (i.e., lists of words and the emotions they convey) or complex machine learning algorithms. One of the downsides of resorting to lexicons is that the way people express their emotions varies a lot. Some words that would typically express anger might also express happiness.

Aspect-Based Sentiment Analysis

Usually, when analyzing the sentiment in subjects, we might be interested in not only whether people are talking with a positive, neutral, or negative polarity about the product, but also which particular aspects or features of the product people talk about.

Intent Analysis

Intent analysis basically detects what people want to do with text rather than what people say with that text (see Figure 4-5). Sometimes, the intended action can be inferred from the text, but other times, inferring the intention requires contextual knowledge.

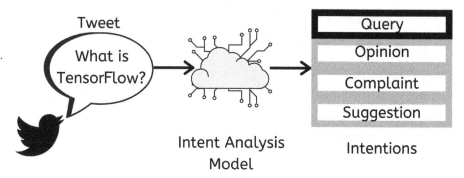

Figure 4-5. *A simple example of intent analysis conducted on a tweet*

Multilingual Sentiment Analysis

Multilingual sentiment analysis is a difficult task. It involves heavy preprocessing of the data. Most of these resources are available online (e.g., sentiment lexicons), but many others have to be created (e.g., translated corpora or noise detection algorithms). The use of the resources available requires a lot of coding experience and can take a long time to implement.

An alternative to that would be detecting language automatically, then training a custom model for the language of our choice (if the text is not written in English), and finally, performing the analysis.

Sentiment Analysis Algorithms

There are many methods and algorithms to implement sentiment analysis systems, and they can be classified as follows:

- **Rule-based** systems perform sentiment analysis based on a set of manually crafted rules. Usually, rule-based approaches define a set of rules that identify subjectivity, polarity, or the subject of an opinion. The rules may use a variety of inputs, such as the following:

  - Classic NLP techniques like stemming, tokenization, part of speech tagging, and parsing.

  - Other resources, such as lexicons (i.e., lists of words and expressions). This system is very naïve since it doesn't take into account how words are combined in a sequence.

- **Automatic** systems rely on machine learning techniques to learn from data.

- **Hybrid** systems combine rule-based and automatic approaches.

Sentiment Analysis Metrics for Evaluation

Once we have designed our model, we need to test it to see how well it works for sentiment analysis. We can do this by using certain metrics as described in the following sections.

Cross-Validation

This involves splitting the training data into a certain number of training folds (with 75% of the training data) and the same number of testing folds (with 25% of the training data). We then use the training folds to train the classifier and test it against the testing folds to obtain performance metrics. The process is repeated multiple times and an average for each of the metrics is calculated.

If our testing set is always the same, we might be overfitting to that testing set, which means we might be adjusting our analysis to a given set of data so much that we fail to properly analyze a different set.

Precision

This measures how well the text was predicted as belonging to a given category out of all of the text that *was predicted (correctly and incorrectly)* as belonging to the category.

Recall

This measures how the text was predicted correctly as belonging to a given category out of all the text that *should have been predicted as* belonging to the category. The more data we feed into our classifiers, the better recall will be.

Accuracy

This measures how much of the text was predicted correctly (both as belonging to a category and not belonging to the category) from the text in the corpus.

Most frequently, precision and recall are used to measure performance, since accuracy alone does not say much about how good or bad a classifier is.

Hybrid Approaches

When we combine various sentiment analysis methods and techniques together, we get hybrid ones.

Parameters Affecting Model Performance

The factors that affect the performance of our model are parameters, the most common ones are discussed next.

Subjectivity and Tone

The detection of subjective and objective text is just as important as analyzing its tone. In fact, so-called *objective* text does not contain explicit sentiments. All *predicates* (adjectives, verbs, and some nouns) should not be treated the same with respect to how they create sentiment.

Context and Polarity

All utterances are made in context. Analyzing sentiment without context gets pretty difficult. However, machines cannot learn about context if it is not mentioned explicitly. A good deal of preprocessing or post-processing will be needed if we are to take into account at least part of the context in which the text was produced.

Irony and Sarcasm

Differences between literal and intended meaning (i.e., irony) and the more insulting or ridiculous version of irony (i.e., sarcasm) usually change positive sentiment into negative, whereas negative or neutral sentiment might be changed to positive. However, detecting irony and sarcasm takes a good deal of analysis of the context in which the text was produced and, therefore, is really difficult to do automatically.

Comparisons

Sentiment analysis is still not advanced enough to understand comparisons. It tends to make errors with these kinds of statements.

Defining Neutral Emotions

Defining our categories—and, in this case, the *neutral* tag—is one of the most important parts of the problem. Since tagging data requires that tagging criteria be consistent, a good definition of the problem is a must.

Neutral tags may contain:

- Objective text

- Irrelevant information

- Text containing wishes

Tokenizer

The tokenizer is used to vectorize a text corpus (the text data that we are working with), by turning the text into either a sequence of integers (each integer being the index of a token in a dictionary) or into a vector where the coefficient for each token could be binary or based on word count.

Note   0 is a reserved index that won't be assigned to any word.

By setting verbose to 0, 1, or 2, you determine how you want the training progress for each epoch to be displayed.

verbose=0 will show you nothing (silent).

verbose=1 will show you an animated progress bar like this:

```
[===============================]
```

verbose=2 will mention the number of epoch like this:

Epoch 1/10

H5 File

In order to save our model, we need to store the weight in an H5 file. It is a data file saved in the Hierarchical Data Format (HDF). It contains multidimensional arrays of scientific data.

JSON File

When saving our model, the JSON file stores information about the layers and the number of each layer used, so that it can be reloaded easily. A JSON file stores simple data structures and objects in JavaScript Object Notation (JSON) format, which is a standard data interchange format. It is primarily used for transmitting data between a web application and a server. JSON files are lightweight, text-based, human-readable, and can be edited using a text editor.

You should now have a clear understanding of what this project is about and have learned some new terms. We can begin.

Required Libraries

For this project, you will use the basic libraries that you installed in the first chapter of this book. In addition, there are some other libraries that we require. The following is a list of all the libraries required for this project:

- NumPy (See Chapter 1 for installation instructions)

- TensorFlow (See Chapter 1 for installation instructions)

- Pandas (See Chapter 1 for installation instructions)

- Keras (See Chapter 1 for installation instructions)

- Scikit-Learn (See Chapter 1 for installation instructions)

- re (built-in Python library)

Looks like we have all the required libraries specific to this project. Let's focus on the types of layers and the number of each type of layer we want to use in our project.

LSTM Architecture

The model that we will use for this project is a simple LSTM. We want to focus on identifying the basic emotions, both positive (happy, excited, etc.) and negative (sad, worried, etc.). We will not get into complex emotions such as being passive aggressive or similar. Figure 4-6 is a visual representation of the structure of this LSTM.

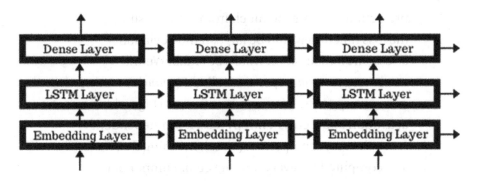

Figure 4-6. *LSTM architecture for sentiment analysis*

In order to get a good understanding of how our model works, let's take a look at the "blueprints" for the LSTM. We are working with only 20% of the dataset, so our model does not need to be too complex. Our model is going to consist of the following:

- Embedding layers - 1

- LSTM layers - 1

- Dense layers - 1

We're going to use a Keras embedding layer to train our own custom word embedding model. The layer is initialized with random weights and is defined as the first hidden layer of a network. The LSTM layer learns what a positive and negative emotion is, respectively. It then stores this information so that it can identify and categorize data as positive or negative emotions. Finally, the dense layer is a fully connected layer that ensures that the model learns well and improves its accuracy.

> **Activation function:** We will use the Softmax function, as it can identify emotions and categorize them.

> **Loss function:** The model learns by means of a loss function. It's a method of evaluating how well specific algorithms work on the given data. If

predictions deviate too much from actual results, the loss function would be large. If the deviation is less, the loss function would be small. We will use *binary cross-entropy,* also called *Sigmoid cross-entropy* loss. It is a combination of a Sigmoid activation and a cross-entropy loss. It is independent for each vector component (class), meaning that the loss computed for every output vector component is not affected by other component values. This makes it ideal for multi-label classification, where an element belonging to a certain class should not influence the decision of another class. It's called binary cross-entropy loss because it sets up a binary classification problem for every class.

Optimizer: The Adam optimizer is ideal for most projects. The project in this chapter is fairly simple, so the Adam optimizer is just fine.

Metric: In order to check how our model works, we will measure just the accuracy for now.

We have our architecture planned out. All that is left is to implement the model.

Procedure

Let's review the code that we will use for this project.

Step 1. Import Libraries

Begin by importing the necessary libraries for this project.

```
import tensorflow as tf
import numpy as np
import pandas as pd
import re
import keras
from keras import Model
from tensorflow.keras.layers import Flatten,LSTM, Dense,
Flatten, Embedding
from tensorflow.keras.preprocessing.sequence import pad_
sequences
from tensorflow.keras.utils import to_categorical
from tensorflow.keras.models import Sequential
from keras_preprocessing.text import Tokenizer
from keras.initializers import glorot_uniform
from sklearn import model_selection
```

Step 2. Load the Data

Load the data, which is in .csv format. Then use file.readlines() to read each line in the reviews.

```
#Read in data
with open('train.csv', 'r') as file:
    text = file.readlines()
```

Now you create an empty dataframe named x_train using Pandas. This will be used to store only the data needed for the analysis.

```
#create empty dataframe
x_train = pd.DataFrame()
```

You need to initialize two lists. The word list stores all the words from the reviews as strings. Using a for loop, you then indicate that words are separated by a space. The loop then detects words in the reviews and stores them as strings. Finally, these lists are converted into series, which are ready to be stored in the dataframe. The first series is named consumer_review and the second series is named polarity_label. At this point, the data has been loaded onto the system. Now it is time to prepare the data for the model.

```
# fill in dataframe
word=[]
label=[]
for n in text:
    n=n.split()
    label.append(1) if n[0] =="__label__2" else label.append(0)
    word.append(" ".join(n[1:]))
x_train['consumer_review'] = word
x_train['polarity_label'] = label
#view dataframe
x_train
```

Step 3. Prepare the Data

As mentioned in the project description, we will use only 20% of the total data for now. So you use the model_selection.train_test_split function in sklearn to indicate that, out of the entire dataset, you want only 20% of it to be used.

```
#use only 20% of data to avoid overloading your system. You can
reduce or increase this number according to your convenience.
_, x_set,_, y_set = \
    model_selection.train_test_split(x_train['consumer_review'],
                                     x_train['polarity_label'],
                                     test_size=0.02)
```

Step 4. Clean the Data

Computers cannot read text the way humans do. So you need to reformat the reviews in the dataset to make them easier for the system to understand. This means you need to remove capitalization, punctuation, and articles (a, an, and the). To do this, you'll define a custom function.

```
#data cleaning function
def data_prep(in_tex):
    # Remove punctuations and numbers
    out_tex = re.sub('[^a-zA-Z]', ' ', in_tex)
    # Convert upper case to lower case
    out_tex="".join(list(map(lambda x:x.lower(),out_tex)))
    # Remove single character
    out_tex= re.sub(r"\s+[a-zA-Z]\s+", ' ', out_tex)
    return out_tex
```

Store this newly cleaned dataset in a new list named text_set:

```
#create new list with clean data
text_set=[]
for reviews in list(x_set):
    text_set.append(data_prep(reviews))
```

Now you create a new dataframe to store the clean data. If you use the same dataframe as previously, the original data will be overwritten with the clean data.

```
x_train= pd.DataFrame()
x_train['consumer_review'] = text_set
x_train['polarity_label'] = list(y_set)
```

This data is clean, but still needs more preprocessing. First split it into 70% for the training dataset and 30% for the testing dataset. You use the same split function from sklearn as before.

```
#split data into 70% train and 30% test
x_train, x_test, y_train, y_test = \
    model_selection.train_test_split(x_train['consumer_review'],
                                     x_train['polarity_label'],
                                     test_size=0.30)
```

In order to apply a tokenizer, you need to convert the lists into arrays. This makes it easier to process.

```
#convert to array
x_train=np.array(x_train.values.tolist())
x_test=np.array(x_test.values.tolist())
y_train=np.array(y_train.values.tolist())
y_test=np.array(y_test.values.tolist())
```

Apply the tokenizer.

```
#tokenizer
tokenizer = Tokenizer()
tokenizer.fit_on_texts(x_train)
word_index=tokenizer.word_index
total_size = len(word_index)+1

print(total_size)
```

Output:

```
22259
```

Convert the text input to sequences. This is the form that is the easiest for the model to process.

```
#text to sequence
x_train = tokenizer.texts_to_sequences(x_train)
x_test = tokenizer.texts_to_sequences(x_test)
```

To avoid incompatibility due to array size, you have to add padding to the data.

```
#add padding to ensure the same length
max_length = 100
x_train = pad_sequences(x_train, padding='post', maxlen=max_length)
x_test = pad_sequences(x_test, padding='post', maxlen=max_length)
```

Step 5. Structure the Model

Structure the model using a Keras embedding layer, an LSTM layer, and a dense layer.

```
#Create Model
model = Sequential()
model.add(Embedding(total_size, 20, input_length=max_length))
model.add(LSTM(32,dropout=0.2, recurrent_dropout=0.2))
model.add(Dense(1, activation='sigmoid'))
```

Step 6. Compile the Model

Next, you specify that the optimizer to be used is Adam, the loss function is binary cross-entropy, and the metric you want to focus on is accuracy.

```
#compile
model.compile(optimizer='adam', loss='binary_crossentropy',
metrics=['acc'])
print(model.summary())
```

Step 7. Train the Model

Now train the model by setting the batch size to 128, the epochs to 5, and the verbose to 1. These settings can be fine-tuned to get even better results.

```
model.fit(x_train, y_train, batch_size=128, epochs=5,
verbose=1, validation_data=(x_test, y_test))
```

Step 8. Save the Model (Optional)

You can save the model in its current state for future use if you want.

```
model.save("model.h5")
```

Step 9. Import the Pretrained Model (Optional)

This code is used to reload the model that you trained, so that you can use it on the same or different dataset.

```
model = keras.models.load_model("model.h5")
```

You have successfully completed the sentiment analysis. The accuracy is pretty good, but the model definitely needs more training if you want to put it to use.

Further Tests

The sentiment analysis you did in this project is really simple. It has a lot of room for experimentation. Here are some ideas to modify and learn more through this project:

- Add more LSTM layers

- Add more dense layers

- Try a different optimization function

Troubleshooting

Here are some common errors that may pop up but can be easily fixed:

- "Warning: No read.me file". This indicates that the package.json file is missing. The package.json file keeps track of the dependencies of the project. Use npm init first, before installing the modules, because it will create the package.json file for you.

- "Error: Missing DLL". This error message could mean one of the following:

  - Your version of Windows is not updated. You must ensure that you are using the latest version of Windows.

  - The project doesn't have full access to the C:\ Users\\AppData\Local\Microsoft\Windows\ or C:\Users\\AppData\Local\Temp folder. It is best to use the admin account, which has full access to all files, or request access from the admin.

    "Cannot execute binary file". There are two methods to resolve this error:

  - Create a symlink by passing the -s option to the ln command followed by the target file and the name of the link.

  - Don't install with apt-get, as it is not the same thing.

- "npm WARN package.json chat@4.5.0 No repository field".

```
npm WARN package.json chat@4.5.0 No README data
npm ERR! Windows_NT 6.1.7600
node_modules\\npm\\bin\\npm-cli.js" "install"
npm ERR! node v4.5.0
npm ERR! npm v2.15.9
npm ERR! code ENOENT
npm ERR! errno ENOENT
npm ERR! syscall getaddrinfo
npm ERR! enoent getaddrinfo ENOENT registry.npmjs.
org:443
npm ERR! enoent This is most likely not a problem with
npm itself
npm ERR! enoent and is related to npm not being able to
find a file.
npm ERR! enoent
npm ERR! Please include the following file with any
support request:
npm ERR! C:\xampp\htdocs\chat\npm-debug.log. "
```

These errors indicate that you already have NodeJS installed. If Keras Tokenizer causes trouble, use the following as an alternative:

```
from keras.preprocessing import text
tokenizer = text.Tokenizer(...)
```

Note keras/preprocessing/__init__.py doesn't import nor expose the text submodule. So sometimes it may cause an error. However, this error can be handled using the fix discussed in this section.

Summary

Here's a quick recap of all that you learned in this chapter:

- An LSTM is capable of learning long-term dependencies. The applications of LSTM include handwriting recognition, speech recognition, disease prediction, and music composition.

- Analog has the advantage of being differentiable, which makes it suitable for back propagation.

- LSTMs are the perfect solution to the "vanishing gradient" problem, which occurs when we try to train a neural network model using gradient-based optimization techniques.

- The gates in an LSTM are the forget gate, the input gate, and the output gate.

- The LSTM decides what information is discarded from the cell state. This decision is made by the "forget gate layer," which uses a Sigmoid activation function.

- The accuracy is a measure of how good our machine learning model is at predicting a correct class for a given observation. Don't use accuracy on imbalanced problems.

- The model learns by means of a loss function. It's a method of evaluating how well specific algorithms work on the given data. If predictions deviate too much from actual results, the loss function is large. If the deviation is small, the loss function is also small.

- Sentiment analysis is the contextual mining of text that identifies and extracts subjective information from the source material. However, analysis of social media streams is usually restricted to basic sentiment analysis and count-based metrics. Sentiment analysis is an automated process of analyzing text data and classifying opinions as negative, positive, or neutral. It is the most common text classification tool.

- With fine-grained sentiment analysis, we can be more precise about the level of polarity of the opinion, by extending the basic categories of positive, neutral, and negative opinions to the following categories: very positive, positive, neutral, negative, and very negative.

- There are many methods and algorithms to implement sentiment analysis systems, and they are classified as rule-based, automatic, and hybrid.

- Cross-validation involves splitting the training data into a certain number of training folds (with 75% of the training data) and the same number of testing folds (with 25% of the training data). You then use the training folds to train the classifier and test it against the testing folds to obtain performance metrics. The process is repeated multiple times and an average for each of the metrics is calculated. If the testing set is always the same, you run the risk of overfitting to that testing set, which means you might be adjusting your analysis to a given set of data so much that you will fail to analyze a different set.

- Precision measures how well the text is predicted correctly as belonging to a given category out of all of the text that *was predicted (correctly and incorrectly)* as belonging to the category.

- Recall measures how well the text was predicted correctly as belonging to a given category out of all the text that *should have been predicted* as belonging to the category. The more data we feed into our classifiers, the better recall will be.

References

Here are the resources used in this chapter:

- Sentiment Analysis: `https://monkeylearn.com/sentiment-analysis/`

- Keras Tokenizer: `https://keras.io/preprocessing/text/`

Further Reading

Are you interested in learning more about some of the topics covered in this chapter? Here are some great links to check out:

- About LSTM: `https://colah.github.io/posts/2015-08-Understanding-LSTMs/`

- Word embedding with Keras: `https://machinelearningmastery.com/use-word-embedding-layers-deep-learning-keras/`

- Difference between polarity and topic-based sentiment analysis: `https://blog.bitext.com/polarity-topic-sentiment-analysis`

- Polarity and intensity of text: `www.aclweb.org/anthology/W18-3306/`

- Polarity for sentiment analysis: `www.kdnuggets.com/2018/08/emotion-sentiment-analysis-practitioners-guide-nlp-5.html`

- Saving and loading pretrained models: `www.tensorflow.org/tutorials/keras/save_and_load`

CHAPTER 5

Music Generation

Everyone loves music. No matter what our mood or preference, there is a song out there for all of us. With that in mind, in this chapter, we'll generate a song using a neural network called Gated Recurrent Unit (GRU). Don't worry, you don't need to be an expert musician to generate music using deep learning.

GRU Overview

GRUs aim to solve vanishing gradient problems that come with a standard recurrent neural network (RNN). The vanishing gradient problem occurs in deep neural networks when the gradient becomes increasingly small, which prevents the weight from changing its value.

To solve the vanishing gradient problem, GRUs use an update gate and a reset gate. These gates are two vectors that decide what information should be passed to the output. They can be trained to store information from long ago, without erasing it through time. They can also remove information that's irrelevant to the prediction.

Instead of having a simple neural network with four nodes, as the RNN had previously, a GRU has a cell containing multiple operations. The GRU carries information forward over several time periods in order to influence a future time period. In other words, the value is stored in memory for a certain amount of time. At a critical point, it is pulled out and used with the current state to be updated at a future date. GRU networks involve

© Vinita Silaparasetty 2020
V. Silaparasetty, *Deep Learning Projects Using TensorFlow 2*,
https://doi.org/10.1007/978-1-4842-5802-6_5

fewer parameters, which make them faster to train. The network learns how to use gates to protect its memory so that it's able to make long-term predictions for a longer duration. Similar to vanilla RNNs, a GRU network generates an output at each time-step and this output is used to train the network using gradient descent.

Applications of a GRU network include:

- Polyphonic music modeling

- Speech signal modeling

- Handwriting recognition

- Speech recognition

- Research on the human genome

- Stock market analysis

How a GRU Works

A GRU is a gated version of the recurrent neural network. The hidden state is used to transfer information. A GRU is intuitive, as it is able to determine how much of the past information to pass to the future, without explicit programming. Unlike an LSTM, a GRU has only two gates:

- **Update gate**: The update gate helps the model determine how much of the past information (from previous time-steps) needs to be passed to the future. That is really powerful because the model can decide to copy all the information from the past and eliminate the risk of the vanishing gradient problem.

- **Reset gate**: Essentially, this gate is used from the model to decide how much of the past information to forget.

Figure 5-1 shows the internal workings of a GRU. Here, Rg(t) is the reset gate and Ug(t) is the update gate.

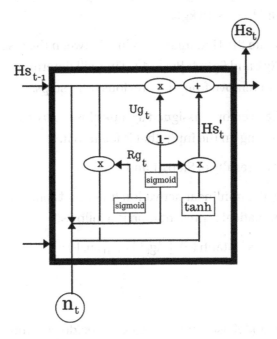

Figure 5-1. *Inside a GRU*

GRU Stages

Let's take a look at the process at each stage of a GRU. Remember, the input for a GRU is in the form of a three-dimensional array.

Stage 1

The current memory functions very much like a gate, but is incorporated into the reset gate and is used to introduce some nonlinearity into the input and make the input zero-mean. Additionally, it reduces the effect that previous information has on the current information, which is passed into the future. Follow these steps:

121

1. Introduce new memory content that will use the reset gate to store the relevant information from the past. The input nt gets multiplied by the weight W and Hs(t-1) with Rgt.

2. Calculate the Hadamard product between the reset gate Rgt and Rgt * Hs(t-1). This will determine what to remove from the previous time-steps.

3. The Rgt vector is assigned a value close to 0 or 1, depending on the input that is fed into it.

4. Sum the results of Steps 1 and 2.

5. Apply the nonlinear activation function tanh. The mathematical representation is a follows:

$$Hs_t' = \tanh (W [Rg_t * Hs_{(t-1)} , n_t])$$

Stage 2

Essentially, the model uses the reset gate to decide how much of the past information to forget. It is analogous to the combination of the input gate and the forget gate in an LSTM recurrent unit. The total error is given by the summation of errors at all time-steps. Similarly, the value can be calculated as the summation of the gradients at each time-step. Follow these steps:

1. Multiply the input nt by the weight Wrg and Hst-1 with Wrg.

2. Calculate the sum of the products from Step 1.

3. Apply Sigmoid to the result.

The model can learn to set the vector Rg_t close to 0 or 1. If the vector Rgt is close to 0, a big portion of the current content will be ignored since it is irrelevant for our prediction. At the same time, since Rgt will be close to 0 at this time-step, 1-Rgt will be close to 1, allowing the majority of the past information to be kept.

The mathematical representation is as follows:

$$Rg_t = \text{Sigmoid} (W_{rg} [Hs_{t-1}, n_t])$$

Stage 3

The update gate is where the model can decide to copy all the information from the past and eliminate the risk of the vanishing gradient problem. Follow these steps:

1. Multiply the input nt by the weight Wug and Hst-1 with Wug.

2. Calculate the sum of the products from Step 1.

3. Step 3: Apply Sigmoid to the result.

The model can learn to set the vector Ug_t close to 0 or 1. If the vector Ugt is close to 0, a big portion of the current content will be ignored since it is irrelevant for our prediction. At the same time, since Ugt will be close to 0 at this time-step, (1-Ugt) will be close to 1, allowing the majority of the past information to be kept.

The mathematical representation is as follows:

$$Ug_t = \text{Sigmoid} (W_{ug} [Hs_{t-1}, n_t])$$

Stage 4

The memory at the current time-step is the final stage of the GRU. The network calculates Hst, the vector that holds information for the current unit, and passes it down to the network.

In order to do that, the update gate determines what to collect from the current memory content, Hst, and what to collect from the previous steps, Hs(t-1). That is done as follows:

1. Apply element-wise multiplication to the update gate Ugt and Hs(t-1).

2. Apply element-wise multiplication to (1-Rgt) and Hst'.

3. Sum the results from Steps 1 and 2.

$$Hs_t = (1 - Rg_t) * (Hs_{t-1}) + Ug_t * Hs_t'$$

GRU Layers

In order to design an effective GRU, we can utilize the following types of layers:

- **Embedding layer:** Used to create word vectors for incoming words. It lies between the input and the GRU layer. The output of the embedding layer is the input to the GRU layer.

- **GRU layer:** A recurrent neural net layer that takes a sequence as an input and can return either a sequence or a matrix.

- **Dropout layer:** A regularization technique that consists of setting a fraction of input units to 0 at each update during the training to prevent overfitting.

- **Dense layer:** A fully connected layer in which each input node is connected to each output node.

- **Activation layer:** Determines which activation function the GRU uses to calculate the output of a node.

Note   `keras.layers.CuDNNGRU` offers a fast GRU implementation backed by cuDNN. The NVIDIA CUDA Deep Neural Network library (cuDNN) is a GPU-accelerated library of primitives for deep neural networks. cuDNN provides highly tuned implementations for standard routines such as forward and backward convolution, pooling, normalization, and activation layers.

Comparing GRU and LSTM

At first glance, LSTMs and GRUs appear to be very similar. However, there are subtle differences between the two that need to be noted:

- A GRU has only two gates whereas an LSTM has three.

- LSTMs control the exposure of memory content (the cell state), while GRUs expose the entire cell state to other units in the network. The LSTM unit has separate input and forget gates, while the GRU performs both of these operations together via its reset gate.

- LSTM gives us the most control and, thus, better results. It does come with more complexity and greater operating cost.

GRU uses fewer training parameters and therefore uses less memory, executes faster, and trains faster than LSTM, whereas LSTM is more accurate on a dataset using longer sequences.

You now know what a GRU is and how it differs from an LSTM. It's time to see how you can turn a GRU into a music DJ.

Project Description

In this project, we are going to create a GRU that will generate music based on a given sequence of notes. Once the model is trained, it should be able to predict the sequence of notes that comes next, when a random set of notes is provided as the input. The dataset consists of MIDI files from which we extract musical components to feed as features to our model. The GRU model requires the following two objects to generate music:

- **Note objects:** Contain information about the pitch, octave, and offset.

- **Chord objects:** Containers for a set of notes.

The note and chord objects are then converted to integer vectors using the process of *one-hot encoding*. This enables the model to learn the patterns in various pieces of musical compositions. This prediction is then reconverted from integer vectors to musical notes and saved as a MIDI file. The objective is to obtain a MIDI file that sounds as similar as possible to the original song.

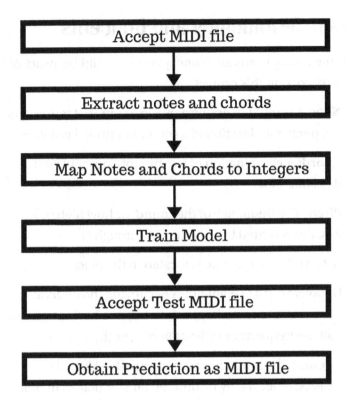

Figure 5-2. GRU music project workflow

About the Dataset

Name: 130,000 MIDI file collection

Genres included: Pop, classical (Piano/Violin/Guitar), EDM, VideoGame, and movie/TV themes

Source: www.reddit.com/r/datasets/comments/3akhxy/the_ largest_midi_collection_on_the_internet/

Created by: Midi Man

Before you can begin generating music, there are a few terms and concepts you need to understand.

Important Terminology and Concepts

Here are some handy terms and concepts you should be aware of before you can get to work on this project.

- **Note:** A symbol denoting a musical sound. It represents the pitch and duration of a sound in musical notation.

- **Chord:** A combination of two or more notes played at the same time.

- **Pitch:** The frequency of the sound, or how high or low it is. Represented by the letters A through G.

- **Offset:** Where the note is located in the piece.

- **Octave:** Series of eight notes occupying the interval between (and including) two notes, one having twice or half the frequency of vibration of the other.

- **Stream:** The fundamental container for Music21 objects; objects may be ordered and/or placed in time based on offsets from the start of this container in Music21.

- **MIDI file:** (pronounced "mid-ee"): The abbreviation for Musical Instrument Digital Interface file. It has two extensions—.MID or .MIDI. It does not contain actual audio, just the information such as pitch, chord, notes, etc.

- **Categorical cross-entropy:** A loss function that is used for single label categorization. This is when only one category is applicable to each data point.

- **RMSprop optimizer:** Similar to the gradient descent algorithm, but with momentum. It restricts oscillations to the vertical direction.

- **One-hot encoding:** A process by which categorical variables are converted into integers or a vector of zeros and ones. For example, in Figure 5-3 we have a dataset with the elements A, B, C, and A. Currently they are characters. However, our model can only accept numeric values. Therefore, we use one-hot encoding to convert the characters into vectors, each with one row and three columns to represent each category. For the purpose of this example, the mapping is that the last column represents category A, the middle column represents category B, and the first column represents category C. Hence, the one is used to indicate which category a variable belongs to.

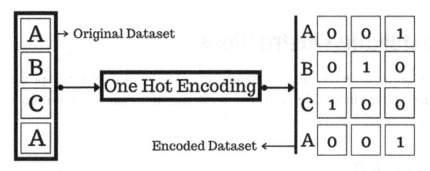

Figure 5-3. *One-hot encoding workflow*

Finally, you are ready to start on the project. Let's start by preparing the packages for this project.

Required Libraries

Let's take a look at the list of required libraries for this project.

- Os (built-in Python)
- Os.path (built-in Python)

- Random (built-in Python 2 and up)

- Shutil (built-in Python library)

- NumPy (see Chapter 1 for installation instructions)

- Pandas (see Chapter 1 for installation instructions)

- Matplotlib (see Chapter 1 for installation instructions)

- TensorFlow (see Chapter 1 for installation instructions)

- Keras (see Chapter 1 for installation instructions)

- Music21(installation instructions in this chapter)

It looks like all we need to do is install Music21 and Random2. Let's do that now.

Installation Instructions

In Chapter 1, we installed the standard libraries required for each project. These are the installation instructions for the additional libraries used in this particular project.

Using PIP

To ensure that we can install these libraries regardless of our system, we will use the Python package, PIP.

1. Use the following command in the terminal to install Music21.

   ```
   Pip3 install Music21
   ```

2. Use the following command in the terminal to check the installation of Music21.

   ```
   Pip3 show Music21
   ```

3. Use the following command in the terminal to install Random2.

```
Pip3 install random2
```

4. Use the following command in the terminal to check the installation of Random2.

```
Pip3 show random2
```

5. Install MuseScore. Since we are working with MIDI files, we need the software to open and view these files. Go to the official website at `https://musescore.org/en` (see Figure 5-4). MuseScore is open source and free. The website automatically detects which system you are using and suggests the appropriate version of MuseScore. Just click the Free Download button.

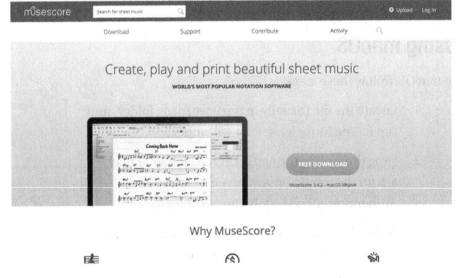

Figure 5-4. *Official MuseScore website*

After this, the instructions vary a bit depending on the operation system you're using.

Using Windows

In Windows, follow these steps:

1. Find the location where the file is downloaded and double-click the installer to begin the installation.

2. Click the Next button on each screen until the Install button appears. Click this button, and MuseScore will be installed.

3. Once the Finish button pops up, it means that MuseScore has been successfully installed. Exit the installer.

4. Start MuseScore by going to the Start menu and choosing All Programs ➤ MuseScore.

Using macOS

In macOS, follow these steps:

1. Locate the file (usually in the Downloads folder) and run it. The MuseScore icon will appear.

2. Drag the icon to the Applications folder. It may ask for the admin password; enter it and click Authenticate. The installation will begin.

3. To run MuseScore, navigate to the Applications folder and click the MuseScore icon.

Using Linux

In Linux, follow these steps:

1. In the terminal type:

   sudo apt-get install musescore

2. Then press Return.

3. When prompted, press Y and then Return again. MuseScore will be installed.

4. MuseScore can be opened via the application menu or by typing musescore into the terminal and pressing Return.

Installation Troubleshooting

Here are some very common errors that may pop up but can be easily fixed:

- Ensure that all installations are up to date.

Note   random2 provides a Python 3 ported version of Python 2.7's random module. It has also been back-ported to work in Python 2.6.

- Try not to install anything manually. Instead use the pip installer.

- If you get a "not in the sudoers file" error it can be fixed by editing the file. You will need to su to the root in a terminal, then run visudo and search for a line that looks like root ALL=(ALL) ALL. Duplicate that line, replacing root with the username. Then save the file. Alternatively, you can just set the user to be an administrator in the Users preference panel. Then you will have admin permissions.

- In Windows, you have to add the Python path to the environment variables before using pip.

These are the most common problems that you may come across. For more help, there is a Google group where users post queries regarding Music21. The link to the group can be found in the "Resources" section at the end of this chapter.

GRU Architecture

To generate music with a GRU, you need a model with the right number of layers and in the correct order. Figure 5-5 shows the model we will use for this project.

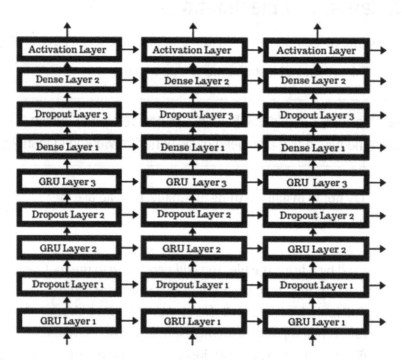

Figure 5-5. *Architecture of the GRU for this project*

Let's take a look at the "blueprints" for the GRU. This model is going to consist of four layers:

- GRU layers - 3

- Dropout layers - 3

- Dense layers - 2

- Activation layer - 1

The GRU layers learn the patterns in a musical composition. They utilize the reset gate and update gate to extract the pattern and "memorize" it. The dropout layer does exactly as it implies. By "dropping" sections of the pattern that the model learns, we avoid overfitting the model. Finally, the dense layer is a fully connected layer that improves the accuracy of the model.

- **Activation function:** We will use the Softmax function, as it ideal for the identification and categorization of the components in a musical composition.

- **Loss function:** Since we are treating this project as a classification problem, the categorical cross-entropy loss function will give us the best results. It is specifically designed for classification.

- **Optimizers:** We use the RMSprop optimizer as it has pseudo-curvature information. Additionally, it can deal with stochastic objectives. These two features are important for mini-batch learning, which is the process our model uses.

Note   The embedding layer is normally used for text analysis. So we will not be using it in our model.

Procedure

You are finally ready to implement the GRU. Let's open a new Jupyter Notebook and get to work.

Step 1. Import Libraries

Import the necessary libraries for this project.

```
import tensorflow as tf
from music21 import converter, instrument, note, chord,stream
import numpy as np
import matplotlib.pyplot as plt
import pandas as pd
import os
import random
from keras.layers.core import Dense, Activation, Flatten
from keras.layers import GRU,Convolution1D,Convolution2D,
Flatten, Dropout, Dense
from keras import utils as np_utils
from tensorflow.keras import layers
```

Set the file path so that the Jupyter Notebook can access this dataset. Use the os.chdir command and enter the file path.

```
os.chdir("//Users//vinitasilaparasetty//Downloads//Project 1-
GRU//Input//music_files")#enter the file path from your system.
```

Declare the variables that will be used for feature extraction:

```
musical_note = []
offset = []
instrumentlist=[]
```

Step 2. Load the Data

Create the `filenames` variable, which selects and loads MIDI files at random using the random module. We can set the number of files to be chosen randomly; in this case we picked 5. Create the `musiclist` variable, which loads all the MIDI files present in the dataset.

```
filenames = random.sample(os.listdir('D:\\Proj\\vinita\\Project
1- GRU\Input\\music_files\\'), 5) #Only 5 files are taken at
random
musiclist = os.listdir('D:\\Proj\\vinita\\Project 1- GRU\
Input\\music_files\\')
```

Step 3. Feature Extraction

Append the pitch of every note object using its string notation since the most significant parts of the note can be recreated using the string notation of the pitch. Follow these steps:

1. Parse the notes using `string_midi = converter. parse(r1)` and initialize the `parsednotes = None` variable.

2. Detect the type of instrument using `parts = instrument.partitionByInstrument(string_ midi)` and update the instrument counter using `instrumentlist.append(parts.parts[0]. getInstrument().instrumentName)`.

3. Extract sharp notes using `if parts: parsednotes = parts.parts[0].recurse()`.

4. Extract flat notes using `else: parsednotes = string_midi.flat.notes`.

5. Extract offsets using `for element in parsednotes:` `offset.append(element.offset)`.

6. Begin adding the notes to the `musical_note[ ]` array using `if isinstance(element, note.Note):` and `musical_note.append(str(element.pitch))`.

7. Use a `.` to separate each note: `elif isinstance(element, chord.Chord):` and `musical_note.append('.'.join(str(n) for n in element.normalOrder))`.

```
for file in filenames:
    matching = [s for s in musiclist if file.split('_')
    [0] in s]
    print(matching)
    r1 = matching[random.randint(1, len(matching))]
    string_midi = converter.parse(r1)
    parsednotes = None
    parts = instrument.partitionByInstrument(string_midi)
    instrumentlist.append(parts.parts[0].
    getInstrument().instrumentName)
    if parts: # file has instrument parts
        parsednotes = parts.parts[0].recurse()
    else: # file has flat notes
        parsednotes = string_midi.flat.notes
    for element in parsednotes: #detect offsets
        offset.append(element.offset)
        if isinstance(element, note.Note):
            musical_note.append(str(element.pitch))
        elif isinstance(element, chord.Chord):
            musical_note.append('.'.join(str(n) for n in
            element.normalOrder))
```

Step 4. Exploratory Data Analysis (EDA)

Count the number of unique instruments in the MIDI file using the following:

```
pd.Series(instrumentlist).value_counts()
pd.Series(instrumentlist).value_counts()
```

Count the number of notes and chords using the following:

```
pd.Series(musical_note).value_counts()
pd.Series(musical_note).value_counts()
```

Visualize the offsets in the MIDI file using the following:

```
offset = [float(item) for item in offset]
offset = [float(item) for item in offset]
plt.plot(offset)
plt.show() # this shows that offset is normally started from 0
for each musical file
```

The output should look similar to Figure 5-6.

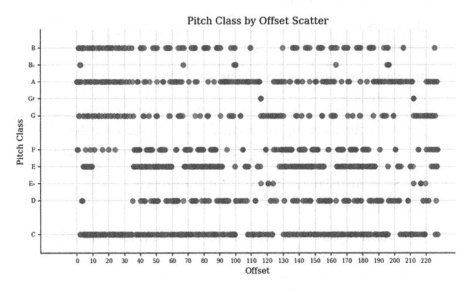

Figure 5-6. *Generate a scatterplot of the offsets*

Step 5. Data Preparation (Input)

Take a sequence of the first 100 notes as the input using the variable sequence_length = 100 variable.

Now let's arrange the notes:

1. In the musical_note[ ] array, in ascending order, use pitchcategory = sorted(set(item for item in musical_note)).

2. Then use one hot-encoding by mapping the notes in the MIDI file to integers.

3. Create a dictionary to hold the mapped notes using the following:

   note_encoding = dict((note, number) for number, note in enumerate(pitchcategory))

4. Create the input for the model by declaring the model_input_original = [] variable.

5. Collect the output from the model using model_output = [].

6. Separate the notes that will be fed as the input sequence:

   for i in range(0, len(musical_note) - sequence_length, 1):
   sequence_in = musical_note[i:i + sequence_length]

7. Separate the notes that will be in the expected output:

   sequence_out = musical_note[i + sequence_length]

8. Add the input sequence to the dictionary:

```
model_input_original.append([note_encoding[char] for
char in sequence_in])
```

9. Add the output sequence of notes:

```
model_output.append(note_encoding[sequence_out])
```

The pattern of the composition of the MIDI file is stored in the n_patterns = len(model_input_original) variable. Now that we have the input, it is time to reshape it so that it can be used on the model. Use the following line to reshape the data.

```
model_input = np.reshape(model_input_original, (n_patterns,
sequence_length, 1))
```

After reshaping the data, it is time to standardize it to get accurate results and avoid problems during training.

```
sequence_length = 100

# Arranging notes and chords in ascending order
pitchcategory = sorted(set(item for item in musical_note))

# One hot encoding
note_encoding = dict((note, number) for number, note in
enumerate(pitchcategory))
model_input_original = []
model_output = []

# Prepare input and output data for model
for i in range(0, len(musical_note) - sequence_length, 1):
    sequence_in = musical_note[i:i + sequence_length]
    sequence_out = musical_note[i + sequence_length]
```

```
model_input_original.append([note_encoding[char] for char in
sequence_in])
model_output.append(note_encoding[sequence_out])

n_patterns = len(model_input_original)

# converting data for compatibility with GRU
model_input = np.reshape(model_input_original, (n_patterns,
sequence_length, 1))

# standardizing model input data
model_output = np_utils.to_categorical(model_output)
Len_Notes = model_output.shape[1]
model_input = model_input / float(Len_Notes)
```

Step 6. Structure the Model

You are now ready to create the GRU model. Follow these steps:

1. Initialize the model using model_GRU = tf.keras. models.Sequential().

2. Add the first GRU layer using model_GRU. add(layers.GRU(16,input_shape=(model_input. shape[1], model_input.shape[2]),return_ sequences=True)). This layer returns values after the data has been processed.

3. Add the dropout layer using model_GRU. add(layers.Dropout(0.3)).

4. This is followed by a second GRU layer using model_GRU.add(layers.GRU(64, return_ sequences=True)).

5. Add the second dropout layer using `model_GRU. add(layers.Dropout(0.3))`.

6. Add the final GRU layer using `model_GRU. add(layers.GRU(64))`.

7. Add the first dense layer using `model_GRU. add(layers.Dense(16))`.

8. Add the final dropout layer using `model_GRU. add(layers.Dropout(0.3))`.

9. You're ready for the final dense layer using `model_ GRU.add(layers.Dense(Len_Notes))`.

10. Now you just need to add the last layer, which is the activation layer. Use `model_GRU.add(layers. Activation('softmax'))` to set Softmax as the activation function.

11. To complete the setup of the model, add the compilation features using `model_GRU. compile(loss='categorical_crossentropy', optimizer='rmsprop')`. This is where you set the loss function to categorical cross-entropy and the optimizer to `rmsprop`.

12. Now set the epochs and batch size for the model using `model_GRU.fit(model_input, model_ output, epochs=30, batch_size=64)`. For the first run, you will start with 30 epochs and a batch size of 6. This can be changed later to improve the model.

13. To ensure that the architecture of the model is correct, you can use `model_GRU.summary()` to get an overview of the structure of the model.

```
model_GRU = tf.keras.models.Sequential()
model_GRU.add(layers.GRU(16,input_shape=(model_input.
shape[1], model_input.shape[2]),return_sequences=True))
model_GRU.add(layers.Dropout(0.3))
model_GRU.add(layers.GRU(64, return_sequences=True))
model_GRU.add(layers.Dropout(0.3))
model_GRU.add(layers.GRU(64))
model_GRU.add(layers.Dense(16))
model_GRU.add(layers.Dropout(0.3))
model_GRU.add(layers.Dense(Len_Notes))
model_GRU.add(layers.Activation('softmax'))
model_GRU.compile(loss='categorical_crossentropy',
optimizer='rmsprop')
model_GRU.summary() #Displays model architecture
```

Step 7. Train the Model

Follow these steps to train the model:

1. Initialize a new dictionary for the notes using `int_to_note = dict((number, note) for number, note in enumerate(pitchcategory))`.

2. Initialize a new array to detect the pattern in the MIDI file using `pattern = model_input_original[0]`.

3. Initialize a new array to store the predicted notes using `prediction_output = [ ]`.

```
# initializing data for model prediction
int_to_note = dict((number, note) for number, note in
enumerate(pitchcategory))
pattern = model_input_original[0]
```

```
prediction_output = []
model_GRU.fit(model_input, model_output, epochs=30,
batch_size=64)
```

Step 8. Prediction

You can predict the next 500 notes by using for note_index in range(500) and following these steps:

1. The prediction input must be reshaped for compatibility with the GRU using prediction_input = np.reshape(pattern, (1, len(pattern), 1)).

2. The input needs to be standardized using prediction_input = prediction_input / float(Len_Notes).

3. Next, obtain the predicted notes using prediction_ GRU = model_GRU.predict(prediction_input, verbose=0).

4. Find the note with the maximum frequency using index_GRU = np.argmax(prediction_GRU).

5. Reconvert the integer to its corresponding note using:

```
index = index_GRU
  result = int_to_note[index]
```

6. Add the note to the array using:

```
      prediction_output.append(result)
      pattern = np.append(pattern,index)
      pattern = pattern[1:len(pattern)]
```

```
# generate 500 notes
```

```
for note_index in range(500):
    prediction_input = np.reshape(pattern, (1,
    len(pattern), 1))
    prediction_input = prediction_input / float(Len_Notes)
    prediction_GRU = model_GRU.predict(prediction_input,
    verbose=0)
    index_GRU = np.argmax(prediction_GRU)
    index = index_GRU
    result = int_to_note[index]
    prediction_output.append(result)
    pattern = np.append(pattern,index)
    pattern = pattern[1:len(pattern)]
```

Step 9. Data Preparation (Offset)

Follow these steps to prepare the offset:

1. Use offlen = len(offset) to find the length of the offset.

2. Now find the differential of the offset using
    DifferentialOffset = (max(offset)-
    min(offset))/len(offset).

3. Create a copy of the offsets that you collected using
    offset2 = offset.copy().

4. Initialize the array for output notes using output_
    notes = [ ] and set the counter to zero using i = 0.

5. Now initialize the array for offsets using offset = [ ]
    and set the counter to zero using initial = 0.

6. Begin counting the offsets using the following:

```
for i in range(len(offset2)):
    offset.append(initial)
    initial  = initial+DifferentialOffset
```

7. Now it is time to detect the notes and chords. Ensure the counter is at zero by resetting it using i=0.

8. Search for the full stops to detect when each note begins using the following:

```
for pattern in prediction_output:
    if ('.' in pattern) or pattern.isdigit():
```

9. Separate the chords from the string and add them to the array for notes using the following:

```
notes_in_chord = pattern.split('.')
    notes = [ ]
```

10. Detect notes and separate them using the following:

```
for check_note in notes_in_chord:
    gen_note = note.Note(int(check_note))
    gen_note.storedInstrument = instrument.Guitar()
    notes.append(gen_note)
    gen_chord = chord.Chord(notes)
```

11. Detect the offsets using the following:

```
gen_chord.offset = offset[i]
    output_notes.append(gen_chord)
```

12. To prevent exceptions, use the following code:

```
else:
        gen_note = note.Note(pattern)
        gen_note.offset = offset[i]
        gen_note.storedInstrument = instrument.Guitar()
        output_notes.append(gen_note)
    i=i+1
```

```python
# prepare notes , chords and offset separately
offlen = len(offset)
DifferentialOffset = (max(offset)-min(offset))/
len(offset)
offset2 = offset.copy()
output_notes = []
i = 0
offset = []
initial = 0
for i in range(len(offset2)):
    offset.append(initial)
    initial  = initial+DifferentialOffset
# Differentiate notes and chords
i=0
for pattern in prediction_output:
    if ('.' in pattern) or pattern.isdigit():
        notes_in_chord = pattern.split('.')
        notes = []
        for check_note in notes_in_chord:
            gen_note = note.Note(int(check_note))
            gen_note.storedInstrument = instrument.
            Guitar()
            notes.append(gen_note)
        gen_chord = chord.Chord(notes)
        gen_chord.offset = offset[i]
        output_notes.append(gen_chord)
    else:
        gen_note = note.Note(pattern)
        gen_note.offset = offset[i]
        gen_note.storedInstrument = instrument.Guitar()
        output_notes.append(gen_note)
    i=i+1
```

Step 10. Store the Output as a MIDI File

Follow these steps to store the output as a MIDI file:

1. Specify file path to store the MIDI file using `os.chdir('D:\\Proj\\vinita\\Project 1- GRU\Output\\')`.

2. Create a stream with the output using `midi_stream = stream.Stream(output_notes) #create stream`.

3. Create a MIDI file with the stream using the following code:

```
midi_stream.write('midi', fp='GRU_output.mid') #create
MIDI file using stream

os.chdir('D:\\Proj\\vinita\\Project 1- GRU\Output\\')
#Specify file path to store the MIDI file.
midi_stream = stream.Stream(output_notes) #create
stream
midi_stream.write('midi', fp='GRU_output.mid') #create
MIDI file using stream
```

We can now view the MIDI file using MuseScore (see Figure 5-7). Compare the original musical composition with the generated output to see how well the GRU performs.

Figure 5-7. *View the generated output using MuseScore*

Further Tests

Here are some ideas to experiment with and learn more from this project:

- Try increasing and decreasing the number of layers in the GRU.

- Try increasing the dropout layers.

- Try increasing and decreasing the number of epochs to see how that affects the results of the model.

Troubleshooting

Here are some common errors you may get that can be easily fixed:

- You may get this error when you start training the model:

  ```
  WARNING: Logging before flag parsing goes to stderr.
  ```

Do not worry about this. It will not affect your program.

- If you make a layer stateful, remember to specify the size.

- Ensure that all your path files are correct.

- The data is quite large, which may exhaust the RAM. To avoid this problem, reduce the number of files in the training set.

- When testing other datasets, if there is a problem recognizing instruments, ensure that the dataset consists of musical pieces played on a single instrument.

- Play the MIDI file directly in a Jupyter Notebook by using `.show('midi')`.

Summary

Here's a recap of all that you learned in this chapter.

- A GRU is capable of learning long-term dependencies as opposed to a vanilla RNN.

- During backward propagation, the gradient diminishes as it moves backward through the neural network. This is known as the vanishing gradient problem.

- GRUs have a simpler architecture than LSTMs and are quicker to train.

- The applications of GRUs include polyphonic music modeling, speech signal modeling, handwriting recognition, speech recognition, research on the human genome, and stock market analysis.

- A GRU has two gates: the reset gate and the update gate.

- The different layers in a GRU are the embedding layer, the GRU layer, the dropout layer, and the dense layer.

- We can set RNN layers to be stateful, which means that the states computed for the samples in one batch will be reused as initial states for the samples in the next batch.

- The input for a GRU is in the form of a three-dimensional array. The first dimension represents the batch size, the second dimension represents the number of time-steps we are feeding into a sequence, and the third dimension represents the number of units in one input sequence.

- The current memory functions very much like a gate, but is incorporated into the reset gate and is used to introduce some nonlinearity into the input and to make the input zero-mean. Additionally, it reduces the effect that previous information has on the current information that's passed into the future.

- The reset gate is used by the model to decide how much of the past information to forget. It is analogous to the combination of the input gate and the forget gate in an LSTM recurrent unit.

- The update gate is where the model can decide to copy all the information from the past and eliminate the risk of the vanishing gradient problem.

- The memory at the current time-step is the final stage of the GRU. The network calculates Hs_t, the vector, which holds information for the current unit and passes it down to the network.

- Categorical cross-entropy is a loss function that is used for single label categorization. This is when only one category is applicable for each data point.

- RMSprop optimizer is similar to the gradient descent algorithm, but with momentum. It restricts oscillations in the vertical direction.

- One-hot encoding is a process by which categorical variables are converted into a form that can be provided to ML algorithms to do a better job in prediction.

References

Here are the references used in this chapter:

- https://towardsdatascience.com/illustrated-guide-to-lstms-and-gru-s-a-step-by-step-explanation-44e9eb85bf21

- www.lifewire.com/midi-file-2621979

- https://towardsdatascience.com/a-look-at-gradient-descent-and-rmsprop-optimizers-f77d483ef08b

- https://peltarion.com/knowledge-center/documentation/modeling-view/build-an-ai-model/loss-functions/categorical-crossentropy

- www.lexico.com/en/definition/octave

Resources

Here are links to additional materials that will aid you in this project.

- Datasets:

  ```
  https://medium.com/@vinitasilaparasetty/list-
  of-midi-file-datasets-for-music-analysis-a49633
  60096e?sk=467d814e336abc52c655e3858eb52ae9
  ```

- Troubleshooting help for Music21:

  ```
  https://groups.google.com/forum/#!forum/
  music21list
  ```

- Troubleshooting help for MuseScore:

  ```
  https://musescore.org/en/forum
  ```

Further Reading

Interested in learning more about some of the topics covered in this chapter? Here are some great links to check out:

- How a GRU solves the vanishing gradient problem:

  ```
  www.geeksforgeeks.org/gated-recurrent-unit-
  networks/
  ```

- More on MIDI files:

  ```
  www.somascape.org/midi/tech/mfile.html
  ```

- More on music theory:

  ```
  https://iconcollective.com/basic-music-theory/
  ```

- Official documentation on Music21:

  ```
  https://web.mit.edu/music21/doc/about/
  index.html
  ```

- Official documentation on cuDNN GRU:

  https://developer.nvidia.com/cudnn

- Stateful in various types of RNNs:

  http://keras.io/layers/recurrent/

- More on one-hot encoding:

  https://medium.com/@vinitasilaparasetty/
  what-is-one-hot-encoding-ffd381f9a8a2

  https://hackernoon.com/what-is-one-hot-
  encoding-why-and-when-do-you-have-to-use-it-
  e3c6186d008f

- More on MuseScore:

  https://musescore.org/en/handbook

CHAPTER 6

Image Colorization

Image colorization is the process of adding color to an originally black and white image. This means the artist needs to plan the color scheme and then spend time painstakingly filling in the colors manually. The current tool of choice is Photoshop or an equivalent. A single picture can take up to one month to colorize. In this chapter, we will implement a simple convolutional neural network (CNN) model to understand how image colorization works.

The CNN model is inspired by human vision. The human eye scans an object and the brain quickly picks up distinct features of the object in order to "recognize" it. The CNN imitates this action of scanning an image and identifying distinct features of the image to recognize it. This makes it ideal for image datasets. Let's first take a look at how human vision works. Then we will compare it to the way a CNN model works.

Human Vision Review

Figure 6-1 shows the entire process of human vision, which requires the brain and eyes to work together simultaneously.

While vision starts in the eyes, the interpretation of what we see happens in the brain, in the *primary visual cortex*. When we see an object, the light receptors in our eyes send signals via the optic nerve to the primary visual cortex, where the input is processed.

© Vinita Silaparasetty 2020
V. Silaparasetty, *Deep Learning Projects Using TensorFlow 2*,
https://doi.org/10.1007/978-1-4842-5802-6_6

We are able to recognize all the objects and people we see in our lives. The deeply complex hierarchical structure of neurons and connections in the brain plays a major role in this process of remembering and labeling objects .

Just as a child learns to recognize objects, we need to introduce an algorithm to millions of labeled pictures before it is able to generalize the input and make predictions about images it has never seen before. Computers visualize objects in the form of numbers. Every image can be represented as a two-dimensional array of numbers, known as pixels.

In vision, a *receptive field* of a single sensory neuron is the specific region of the retina in which something will activate the neuron. Every sensory neuron cell has similar receptive fields, and their fields are overlying.

The concept of *hierarchy* plays a significant role in the brain. Information is stored in sequences of patterns, in sequential order. The *neocortex*, which is the outermost layer of the brain, stores information hierarchically. It is stored in cortical columns, or uniformly organized groupings of neurons in the neocortex.

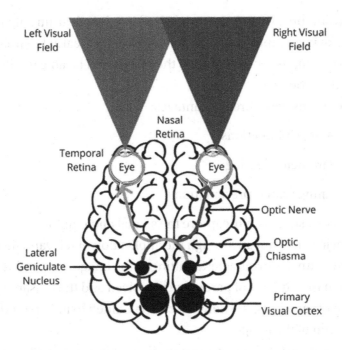

Figure 6-1. *Human vision*

You should now have a rudimentary understanding of how human vision works. Let's see how we can enable machines to "recognize" objects by simulating human vision using a CNN.

Computer Vision Review

Computer vision is an interdisciplinary scientific field that aims to enable machines to view the world as humans do and perceive it in a similar manner. It seeks to automate tasks that the human visual system can do, primarily using CNNs.

The architecture of a CNN is analogous to that of the connectivity pattern of neurons in the human brain and was inspired by the organization of the visual cortex. Individual neurons respond to stimuli only in a restricted region of the visual field, known as the receptive field. A collection of such fields overlaps to cover the entire visual area.

A convolutional neural network (CNN) is a deep learning algorithm that can take in an input image, assign importance (learnable weights and biases) to various aspects/objects in the image, and be able to differentiate one from the other.

Convolutions have three advantages:

- Sparse interactions

- Parameter sharing

- Equivariant representations

A CNN can successfully capture the spatial and temporal dependencies in an image through the application of relevant filters. The architecture performs a better fitting to the image dataset due to the reduction in the number of parameters involved and the reusability of weights. In other words, the network can be trained to understand the sophistication of the image.

The role of the CNN is to reduce the images into a form that's easier to process, without losing features that are critical for making a good prediction. This is important when we want to design an architecture that is not only good at learning features but is also scalable to massive datasets.

Applications of a CNN include:

- Image and video recognition

- Image analysis and classification

- Media recreation

- Recommendation systems

- Natural language processing

Now that you know what a CNN is, as well as its applications in real-life scenarios, let's look at the process within a CNN.

How a CNN Works

The hidden layers of a CNN typically consist of the input layer, convolutional layers, pooling layers, and fully connected layers (see Figure 6-2). Every layer transforms one volume to another through differentiable functions.

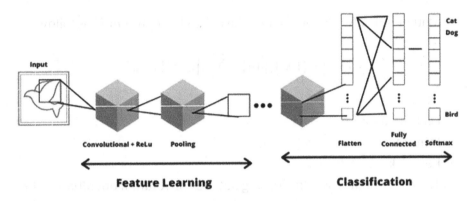

Figure 6-2. *Standard architecture of a CNN*

Input Layer

When a computer sees an image (takes an image as input), it will see an array of pixel values. Depending on the resolution and size of the image, it will see a tensor of R x C x 3, where R indicates the rows, C indicates the columns, and 3 refers to the RGB values. Each of these numbers is given a value from 0 to 255, which describes the pixel intensity at that point. These numbers are the only inputs available to the computer.

Convolution Layer: The Kernel

The convolution layer operates on two signals:

- One-dimensional

- Two-dimensional (it takes two images as input and produces a third as output)

Mathematically, the convolution layer can be represented as follows:

$$f\left[n\right] = \left(i \times k\right)\left[n\right] = \sum_{a=-\infty}^{a=\infty} i\left[a\right]k\left[a+n\right]$$

Feature map: f

Input: i

Kernel: k

The element involved in carrying out the convolution operation in the first part of a convolutional layer is called the *kernel/filter*. The objective of the convolution operation is to extract the low-level features, such as edges, color, gradient orientation, etc., from the input image.

Imagine we are in a dark room and we can view our surroundings using only a flashlight. The flashlight allows us to see only a small section of the room at a time.

A CNN works in a similar manner. The flashlight is called the *filter* and the illuminated area that's covered by the flashlight and is called the *receptive field.*

The filter moves to the right with a certain stride value until it parses the complete width. It then slides or convolves down to the beginning (left) of the image with the same stride value and repeats the process until the entire image is traversed.

In the case of images with multiple channels (e.g., RGB), the kernel has the same depth as that of the input image. All the results are summed with the bias to produce a squashed one-depth channel convoluted feature output.

There are two types of results to the operation:

Valid padding: In which the convolved feature is reduced in dimensionality as compared to the input.

Same padding: The dimensionality is either increased or remains the same.

From the second convolutional layer onward, the input is the activation maps that result from the first layer. So each layer of the input is basically describing the locations in the original image where certain low-level features appear. Now when we apply a set of filters on top of that (pass it through the second convolutional layer), the output will be activations that represent higher-level features. As we go through the network and go through more convolutional layers, we get activation maps that represent more and more complex features. As we go deeper into the network, the filters begin to have a larger and larger receptive field, which means that they are able to consider information from a larger area of the original input volume. (Another way of putting it is that they are more responsive to a larger region of pixel space.)

Note   The depth of the filter must be the same as the depth of the image.

Upsampling Layer

The *upsampling layer* is a simple layer with no weights that will double the dimensions of input. It can be used in a generative model when followed by a traditional convolutional layer.

DepthwiseConv2D

Depthwise separable convolutions perform just the first step in a depthwise spatial convolution (which acts on each input channel separately).

Pooling Layer

Pooling is a sample-based discretization process. The objective is to down-sample an input representation (image, hidden-layer output matrix, etc.), thus reducing its dimensionality and allowing for assumptions to be made about features contained in the sub-regions binned.

Similar to the convolutional layer, the pooling layer is responsible for reducing the spatial size of the convolved feature. It is also referred to as a downsampling layer. This is to decrease the computational power required to process the data. Through dimensionality reduction, the amount of parameters or weights is reduced by 75%, thus lessening the computation cost. Furthermore, it is useful for extracting dominant features that are rotational and positional invariant, thus maintaining the process of effectively training the model.

Pooling works by placing a smaller matrix on the feature map and picking the largest value in that box. The matrix is moved from left to right through the entire feature map, picking a certain value in each pass. These values then form a new matrix called a *pooled feature map.*

There are three types of pooling:

> **Max pooling:** Returns the maximum value from the portion of the image covered by the kernel.
>
> Max pooling also acts as a noise suppressant. It discards the noisy activations altogether and also performs denoising along with dimensionality

reduction. Max pooling performs a lot better than average pooling. Max pooling works to preserve the main features, by selecting the largest values while reducing the size of the image. This helps reduce overfitting.

Min pooling: The minimum pixel value of the batch is selected.

Average pooling: Returns the average of all the values from the portion of the image covered by the kernel. Average pooling simply performs dimensionality reduction as a noise suppressing mechanism.

Fully Connected Layer

Adding a fully connected layer is a (typically) cheap way of learning nonlinear combinations of the high-level features as represented by the output of the convolutional layer. This step is made up of the input layer, the fully connected layer, and the output layer. The fully connected layer is similar to the hidden layer in ANNs, but in this case it's fully connected. The output layer is where we get the predicted classes. The information is passed through the network and the error of prediction is calculated. The error is then back-propagated through the system to improve the prediction. It computes the class scores and outputs the one-dimensional array equal in size to the number of classes.

Now that you understand how a CNN works, you are ready to put it into action in the project.

Project Description

In this project, we take a dataset of colored images. This is our benchmark, so that we know what results we want our model to achieve. We then convert these colored images to grayscale. We split the grayscale images into a training set and test set. We then feed the training set images along with their corresponding color images to our model (a combination of VGG-16 and CNN) to "learn" how an image is colored. Then, to test the model, we feed it a grayscale image as input. It adds color to these images on its own. The objective is to get the model to add colors in such a way that it looks convincingly done and as close to the original image as possible. See Figure 6-3 for a flowchart of the process.

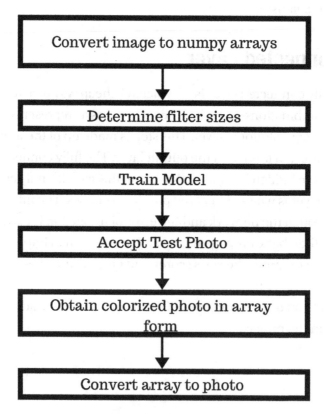

Figure 6-3. *Flowchart for image colorization*

About the Dataset

Name: Colornet
   Source: www.floydhub.com/emilwallner/datasets/colornet
   Created by: Emil Wallner

Important Terminology

Color Space

The first important thing we need to know is that *Lab* color space is used. The reason is simple: in color spaces such as RGB, we need to learn three different channels, whereas in Lab, we only need to learn two. The channel L refers to the lightness, having values between 0 (dark) and 100 (light). The channels a and b are the position in the axis between the red-green and blue-yellow ranges, respectively.

A Lab-encoded image has one layer for grayscale. It then packs three color layers into two. This means that we can use the original grayscale image in our final prediction. Then, we only have two channels to predict.

One good reason to use the Lab color space is that it keeps the light intensity values separate. Black and white pictures can be considered the L channel, and the model won't have to learn how to keep light intensities right when it makes predictions (it will have to do that if RGB is used). The model will only learn how to color images, allowing it to focus on what matters.

The model outputs the AB values, which can then be applied to the black and white image to get the colored version.

The true color values go from -128 to 128, and this is the default interval in the Lab color space. By dividing them by 128, they too fall within the -1 to 1 interval. This enables us to compare the error from our prediction.

After calculating the final error, the network updates the filters to reduce the total error. The network stays in this loop until the error is as low as possible. 1.0/255 indicates that we are using a 24-bit RGB color space. It means that we are using 0-255 numbers for each color channel. This is the standard size of colors and results in 16.7 million color combinations.

Image Colorization

Black and white images can be represented in grids of pixels. Each pixel has a value that corresponds to its brightness. The values span from 0-255, Where 0 indicates black and 255 indicates white. The value 0 in a single channel means that it has no color in this layer. If the value is 0 for all color channels, then the image pixel is black.

Color images consist of three layers:

- Red layer

- Green layer

- Blue layer

The layers not only determine color, but also brightness. For example, to achieve the color white, we need an equal distribution of each color. Thus, a color image encodes the color and the contrast using these three layers.

For the colorization task, the network needs to find the traits that link grayscale images with colored ones. We are searching for the features that link a grid of grayscale values to the three color grids.

We have a grayscale layer for input, and we want to predict two color layers, the *ab* in Lab. To create the final color image, we'll include the L/grayscale image we used for the input, thus creating a Lab image.

To turn one layer into two, we use convolutional filters. Each filter determines what we see in a picture. They can highlight or remove something to extract information from the picture. The network can either create a new image from a filter or combine several filters into one image.

For a convolutional neural network, each filter is automatically adjusted to help with the intended outcome. We'll start by stacking hundreds of filters and then narrow them down into two layers, the a and b layers.

- The input is a grid representing a black and white image.

- It outputs two grids with color values.

- Between the input and output values, we create filters to link them together, a convolutional neural network.

When we train the network, we use colored images. We convert RGB colors to the Lab color space. The black and white layer is our input and the two colored layers are the output.

We have the black and white input, or filters, and the prediction from our neural network.

We map the predicted values to the real values within the same interval. This way, we can compare the values. The interval goes from -1 to 1. To map the predicted values, we use a tanh activation function. For any value we give the tanh function, it will return -1 to 1.

Our neural network finds characteristics that link grayscale images with their colored versions.

The process goes like this:

1. First, we look for simple patterns: a diagonal line, all black pixels, and so on.

2. We look for the same pattern in each square and remove the pixels that don't match.

3. If we scan the images again, we'd see the same small patterns we've already detected. To gain a higher level understanding of the image, we decrease the image size by half.

4. We still only have a three-by-three filter to scan each image. But by combining the new nine pixels with the lower-level filters, we can detect more complex patterns.

5. One pixel combination might form a half circle, a small dot, or a line. Again, we repeatedly extract the same pattern from the image. This time, we generate 128 new filtered images.

As mentioned, we start with low-level features, such as an edge. Layers closer to the output are combined into patterns, then into details, and eventually transformed into a face.

The neural network operates in a trial-and-error manner. It first makes a random prediction for each pixel. Based on the error for each pixel, it works backward through the network to improve the feature extraction.

It starts adjusting for the situations that generate the largest errors. In this case, it's whether to color or not and to locate different objects. Then it colors all the objects brown. It's the color that is most similar to all other colors, thus producing the smallest error.

The main difference from other visual networks is the importance of pixel location. When coloring networks, the image size or ratio stays the same throughout the network. In other networks, the image gets distorted the closer it gets to the final layer.

The max-pooling layers in classification networks increase the information density, but also distort the image. It only values the information, but not the layout of an image. When coloring networks we instead use a stride of 2, to decrease the width and height by half. This also increases information density but does not distort the image.

Two further differences are upsampling layers and maintaining the image ratio. Classification networks only care about the final classification. Therefore, they keep decreasing the image size and quality as it moves through the network. Coloring networks keep the image ratio. This is done by adding white padding. Otherwise, each convolutional layer cuts the images. It's done with the *padding='same'* parameter. To double the size of the image, the coloring network uses an upsampling layer.

Padding essentially makes the feature maps produced by the filter kernels the same size as the original image. This is very useful for deep CNNs, as we don't want the output to be reduced so that we only have a 2x2 region left at the end of the network upon which to predict our result.

Note   Humans can only perceive 2-10 million colors, so it does not make much sense to use a larger color space.

VGG-16

VGG-16 is a convolution neural net (CNN) architecture that's considered to be an excellent vision model architecture (see Figure 6-4). The model has convolution layers with a 3x3 filter and a stride of 1. It always uses the same padding and a max-pool layer of a 2x2 filter and a of stride 2. It follows this arrangement of convolution and max-pool layers consistently throughout the whole architecture. In the end, it has two FCs (fully connected layers) followed by a Softmax optimization function. This network is a pretty large network and it has about 138 million parameters.

The model achieves 92.7% top-five test accuracy in ImageNet, which is a dataset of over 14 million images belonging to 1,000 classes. It is superior to AlexNet, as it replaces large kernel-sized filters (11 and 5 in the first and second convolutional layer, respectively) with multiple 3×3 kernel-sized filters, one after another. It was trained on more than a million images from the ImageNet database. The network is 16 layers deep and can classify images into 1,000 object categories, such as keyboards, mice, pencils, and many animals.

Figure 6-4. *VGG-16 architecture*

MAPE Loss Functions

The mean absolute percentage error (MAPE), also known as mean absolute percentage deviation (MAPD), is a measure of the prediction accuracy of a forecasting method in statistics.

You should now have a clear understanding of what this project is about and have learned some new terms, so let's move on.

Required Libraries

For this project, we will use the basic libraries that you installed in the first chapter of this book. However, there are some additional libraries that we require. The following libraries are required for this project:

- Os (built-in Python2 and up)

- NumPy (see Chapter 1 for installation instructions)

- Pandas (see Chapter 1 for installation instructions)

- Matplotlib (see Chapter 1 for installation instructions)

- TensorFlow (see Chapter 1 for installation instructions)

- Keras (see Chapter 1 for installation instructions)

- PIL (installation instructions are in this chapter)

- math (built-in Python2 and up)

- random (built-in Python2 and up)

- cv2 (installation instructions are in this chapter)

- Scikit-Image (installation instructions are in this chapter)

Installation Instructions

In Chapter 1, we installed the standard libraries required for each project. These are the installation instructions for the additional libraries used in this particular project. To ensure that we can install these libraries regardless of our system, we will use the Python package called PIP.

Installing PIL

PIL is the Python Imaging Library originally developed by Fredrik Lundh and contributors. This library can be used to manipulate images. PIL hasn't seen any development since 2009. Therefore, it is recommended that you use Pillow instead.

Pillow is a fork of PIL, started and maintained by Alex Clark and contributors. It is based on the PIL code, and then evolved to a better version of PIL. It adds support for opening, manipulating, and saving many different image file formats. A lot of its functionality works the same way as the original PIL.

Note   As of the publication of this book, here is the status of the PIL library according to the official website: "The current free version is PIL 1.1.7. This release supports Python 1.5.2 and newer, including 2.5 and 2.6. A version for 3.X will be released later." Python3 users can install a forked version named Pillow.

Use the following command in the terminal to install Pillow.

```
Pip3 install Pillow
```

Then use the following command in the terminal to check the installation.

```
Pip3 show pillow
```

Troubleshooting PIL

- Alternatively, you can install PIL manually by downloading it from the official website at `http://www.pythonware.com/products/pil/`.

- Uninstall any outdated versions of PIL.

- Pillow versions 1.0 and later don't support the `import image` command. Use `from PIL import image` instead.

- Pillow versions 2.1.0 and later don't support `import _imaging`. Use `from PIL.Image import core as _imaging` instead.

Installing CV2

Use the following command in the terminal to install CV2:

```
Pip3 install opencv
```

Then use the following command in the terminal to check the installation of CV2:

```
Pip3 show cv2
```

Troubleshooting CV2

- There are four different packages for opencv and you should select only one of them. Do not install multiple different packages in the same environment.

Installing Scikit-Image

Use the following command in the terminal to install scikit-image.

```
Pip3 install scikit-image
```

Then use the following command in the terminal to check the installation of scikit-image.

```
Pip3 show scikit-image
```

Troubleshooting Scikit-Image

- Ensure that PIP is upgraded.

- Ensure that you have a working and up-to-date C compiler.

- If you get an error while installing directly on your system, try using a virtual environment instead.

- Sometimes skimage gives a false error. To disable errors and warnings from skimage, export the environment variable SKIMAGE_TEST_STRICT_WARNINGS with a value of 0 or False and run the tests as follows:

  ```
  export SKIMAGE_TEST_STRICT_WARNINGS=False
  pytest --pyargs skimage
  ```

175

Now you should have all the required libraries specific to this project. Let's focus on the types of layers and the number of each type of layer we want to use in this project.

CNN+VGG-16 Architecture

To colorize grayscale images using a CNN+VGG-16, we need to first load the VGG-16 model, which is a part of the TensorFlow 2.0 environment. This saves us the trouble of building it from scratch. We then start to build the CNN and insert the VGG-16 as the second layer of the CNN. The first layer of the CNN reshapes the images that are fed as the input, so that they can be easily fed into the VGG-16. From there, the input continues to make its way through the CNN. Figure 6-5 shows the model we will use for this project.

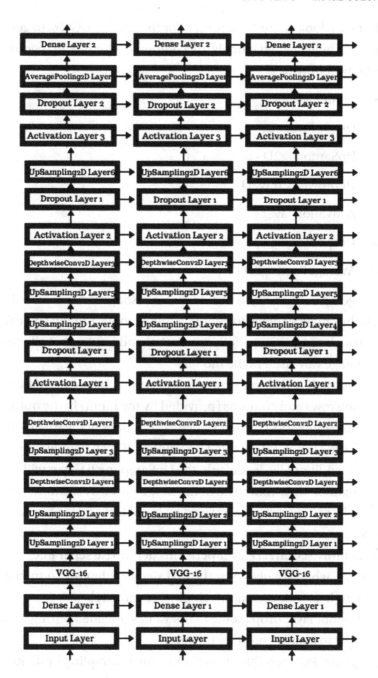

Figure 6-5. *Architecture of the CNN+VGG-16 for this project*

Let's take a look at the "blueprints" for the CNN+VGG-16, to get a better idea of how the two models are combined. Our model is going to consist of the following:

- Input layer - 1

- Dense layer - 2

- UpSampling2D - 6

- DepthwiseConv2D - 3

- Activation layer - 3

- Dropout layer - 3

- AveragePooling2D - 1

We're going to use a Keras input layer to reshape the data into three channels: luminance (black to white), a (green to red), and b (blue to yellow). The dense layers are fully connected and ensure that all the values from the images are used in the model.

The Upsampling2D layer simply doubles the dimensions of the input. It repeats the rows and columns (provided by the input) in the output. The layer has no parameters or model weights, as it does not learn anything; it just doubles the input. By default, UpSampling2D will double each input dimension. Additionally, by default, the UpSampling2D layer will use the nearest neighbor algorithm to fill in the new rows and columns. It is ideal for our model so that valuable image data is not lost as it is processed by the model.

The DepthwiseConv2D layer performs depthwise separable convolutions, which involves just the first step in a depthwise spatial convolution (it acts on each input channel separately).

The dropout layer drops some of the values obtained during training and is crucial to avoid overfitting the model.

The AveragePooling2D layer performs down-sampling by dividing the input into rectangular pooling regions and computing the average values of each region.

For the activation function, we will use ReLU due to the non-saturation of its gradient, which greatly accelerates the convergence of stochastic gradient descent.

For the loss function, we will use MAPE, as explained in the "Important Terminology" section. Due to its advantages of scale-independency and interpretability, it can help us determine how well our model works.

The Adam optimizer is the standard optimizer used for most projects, including this one.

We have our architecture planned out. All that is left is to implement the model.

Procedure

Follow these steps to build this project.

Step 1. Import the Libraries

We begin the project by importing the necessary libraries.

```
# Importing Libraries
import os
import numpy as np
import pandas as pd
import matplotlib.pyplot as plt
import tensorflow as tf
from tensorflow.keras.layers import Dense, Dropout, Input,
InputLayer, Conv2D,UpSampling2D,DepthwiseConv2D
from tensorflow.keras.layers import Flatten,MaxPooling2D,Conv2D
Transpose, AveragePooling2D
from tensorflow.keras.applications.vgg16  import VGG16
from tensorflow.keras.models import Model,Sequential
from tensorflow.keras.optimizers import Adam
```

```
from tensorflow.keras import layers
from tensorflow.keras.preprocessing.image import img_to_
array,load_img
from PIL import Image
from tensorflow.keras.utils import plot_model
from math import ceil
import random
import cv2
from skimage import io, color
```

Set the file path so that the Jupyter Notebook can access the dataset. Use the os.path command and enter the file path.

```
os.path=("Macintosh HD/Users/vinitasilaparasetty□/Downloads/")
```

Step 2. Convert the Images to Grayscale

We'll then convert all the images to grayscale, so that we have a set of color images and their corresponding grayscale versions.

- random.sample() is a built-in function of the random module in Python that returns a list of items of a particular length chosen from a sequence. It is used for random sampling without replacement.

- cv2.cvtColor(rgb, cv2.COLOR_BGR2LAB) is a function in CV2 that is used to convert the color space from RGB to LAB.

- cv2.split(lab_image) splits the image into three channels.

Note   cv2.split() uses more computation time. NumPy indexing is a good alternative but the results may not be as accurate.

```
rootdir = os.getcwd()
filenames = random.sample(os.listdir('D:\\Proj\\vinita\\
colornet\\'), 500)
lspace=[]
abspace=[]
for file in filenames:
    rgb = io.imread(file)
    lab_image = cv2.cvtColor(rgb, cv2.COLOR_BGR2LAB) #convert
    colors space from RGB to LAB
    l_channel,a_channel,b_channel = cv2.split(lab_image)
    lspace.append(l_channel)
    replot_lab=np.zeros((256, 256, 2))
    replot_lab[:,:,0] = a_channel
    replot_lab[:,:,1] = b_channel
    abspace.append(replot_lab)
    transfer = cv2.merge([l_channel, a_channel, b_channel])
    transfer = cv2.cvtColor(transfer.astype("uint8"), cv2.COLOR_
    LAB2BGR)

lspace=np.asarray(lspace) #convert to array
abspace=np.asarray(abspace) #convert to array
```

Step 3. Load the Data

Load lspace as X and abspace as Y. lspace indicates the lightness of the image and abspace is the combined value of the a and b channels, which are the position in the axis between the red-green and blue-yellow ranges.

```
X = np.load("lspace100.npy")
Y = np.load("abspace100.npy")
```

Step 4. Structure the Model

We are ready to create the CNN+VGG-16. Use the following code.

```
model6 = VGG16(weights='imagenet',include_top=False,input_
shape=(256, 256, 3))
model = Sequential()
model.add(InputLayer(input_shape=(X.shape[1], X.shape[2], 1)))
model.add(layers.Dense(units=3))
model.add(Model(inputs=model6.inputs, outputs=model6.
layers[-10].output))
model.add(UpSampling2D((2, 2)))
model.add(UpSampling2D((2, 2)))
model.add(DepthwiseConv2D(32, (2, 2), activation='tanh',
padding='same'))
model.add(UpSampling2D((2, 2)))
model.add(DepthwiseConv2D(32, (2, 2), activation='tanh',
padding='same'))
model.add(layers.ReLU(0.3))
model.add(layers.Dropout(0.4))
model.add(UpSampling2D((2, 2)))
model.add(UpSampling2D((2, 2)))
model.add(DepthwiseConv2D(2, (2, 2), activation='tanh',
padding='same'))
model.add(layers.ReLU(0.3))
model.add(layers.Dropout(0.2))
model.add(UpSampling2D((2, 2)))
model.add(layers.ReLU(0.3))
model.add(layers.Dropout(0.2))
model.add(AveragePooling2D(pool_size = (2, 2)))
model.add(layers.Dense(units=2))
print(model.summary())
```

Step 5. Set the Model Parameters

To complete the architecture of the CNN, we set the optimizer and loss function by creating a function, as shown here:

```
def adam_optimizer():
    return Adam(lr=0.001, beta_1=0.99, beta_2=0.999)
model.compile(loss='mape', optimizer=adam_optimizer())
```

Step 6. Data Preparation

Before feeding the data into the model, we need to reshape it so that the values are fed into the proper channels using this code:

```
X=((X.reshape(X.shape[0],X.shape[1],X.shape[2],1)))
X=(X-255)/255
Y=(Y-255)/255

trainsize= ceil(0.8 * X.shape[0])
testsize= ceil(0.2 * X.shape[0])+1

train_inp=X[:trainsize,]
test_inp=X[testsize:,]

train_out=Y[:trainsize,]
test_out=Y[testsize:,]
```

Step 7. Train the Model

We can now train the model:

```
model.fit(x=train_inp, y=train_out, batch_size=10, epochs=5)
```

Step 8. Obtain Predictions

Now that our model has been trained, it has learned how to add color to an image to make it look as natural as possible. Let's check the results by feeding new grayscale images into the model using this code:

```
train_pred = model.predict(train_inp)
test_pred = model.predict(test_inp)

train_random=random.randint(1,trainsize)
test_random=random.randint(1,testsize)

check=np.interp(train_pred, (train_pred.min(), train_pred.
max()), (0,255))
check1=np.interp(test_pred, (test_pred.min(), test_pred.max()),
(0,255))

l_channel=test_inp[20]*255
a_channel=check1[20,:,:,0]
b_channel=check1[20,:,:,1]

transfer = cv2.merge([l_channel, a_channel, b_channel])
transfer = cv2.cvtColor(transfer.astype("uint8"),
cv2.COLOR_LAB2BGR)
```

Step 9. View the Results

Let's view the results of our image colorization model.

```
plt.imshow(transfer)
```

Some points to consider:

- The dataset we used with this project has only colored images. We need to convert the images to grayscale in order to have one set of color images and one set of grayscale images.

- Most datasets online consist of colored images only, so we have to manually convert the images to grayscale before we can use them to train the model.

- Because most of the training data is quite similar, the network struggles to differentiate between different objects. It will adjust different tones of brown, but fail to generate more nuanced colors.

Troubleshooting

Here are some common errors that you might get that can be easily fixed:

- If the PIL installation is causing you trouble, try uninstalling it and then upgrading it using:

```
pip uninstall PIL
pip install PIL —upgrade
```

- VGG models are rather big and require a decent amount of RAM, so use a system with plenty of RAM or use the cloud.

- If this warning is displayed, you can ignore it, as it will not affect the program:

```
WARNING:tensorflow:From /usr/local/lib/python3.6
/dist-packages/tensorflow/python/framework
/op_def_library.py:263: colocate_with
(from tensorflow.python.framework.ops) is
deprecated and will be removed in a future version.
Instructions for updating: Collocations handled
automatically by placer.
```

Further Tests

Here are some ideas to experiment with and learn more from this project:

- Try using VGG-16 alone and see how the results differ.

- Try training the model with only colorful images and see how the model performs.

- Try other color spaces to see how the results vary.

- Try minimum/maximum pooling instead of average pooling.

- Remove the upsampling layers and see how it affects the results.

- Remove the dropout layers to see how the results differ.

Summary

Here's a quick recap of all that you learned in this chapter.

- Computers visualize objects in the form of numbers. Every image can be represented as a two-dimensional array of numbers, known as pixels.

- A CNN can successfully capture the spatial and temporal dependencies in an image through the application of relevant filters.

- The depth of the filter must be the same as the depth of the image.

- There are three types of pooling: minimum pooling, maximum pooling, and average pooling.

- With RGB, we need to learn three different channels, whereas in Lab, we only need to learn two.

- The Lab color space keeps the light intensity values separate. The true color values go from -128 to 128, which is the default interval in the Lab color space. By dividing them by 128, they too fall within the -1 to 1 interval.

- The channel L refers to the lightness, having values between 0 (dark) and 100 (light).

- Pixel values span from 0 - 255, where 0 indicates black and 255 indicates white.

- The mean absolute percentage error (MAPE), also known as mean absolute percentage deviation (MAPD), is a measure of the prediction accuracy of a forecasting method in statistics.

References

Here are the references used in this chapter:

- www.ncbi.nlm.nih.gov/pmc/articles/PMC1359523/pdf/jphysiol01247-0121.pdf

- https://docs.w3cub.com/tensorflow~python/tf/keras/layers/depthwiseconv2d/

- www.statisticshowto.datasciencecentral.com/mean-absolute-percentage-error-mape/

Further Reading

Interested in learning more about some of the topics covered in this chapter? Here are some great links to check out:

- Color spaces:

  `https://programmingdesignsystems.com/color/`
  `color-models-and-color-spaces/index.html`

- Human vision:

  `www.stat.auckland.ac.nz/~ihaka/120/Notes/`
  `ch04.pdf`

- Computer vision:

  `www.sas.com/en_in/insights/analytics/`
  `computer-vision.html`

CHAPTER 7

Image Deblurring

In the previous chapter we talked about image colorization, which is done using tools like Photoshop. Now let's talk about another task that Photoshop is normally used for, but which we can automate using neural networks. In this chapter we will talk about image deblurring. We are going to use a generative adversarial network (GAN) combined with a VGG-16 for this project. First we will take a look at what a GAN is and how it works. Then we will take a closer look at what image deblurring is.

What Is a GAN?

Generative Adversarial Networks (GANs) are a powerful class of neural networks that are used with unsupervised learning . GANs are made up of two neural network models that compete with each other and are able to analyze, capture, and copy variations within a dataset.

GANs consist of a combination of two components. One is called the *generator*, and it generates new data instances, while the other, called the *discriminator*, evaluates the instances for authenticity. In other words, the discriminator decides whether or not each instance of data that it reviews belongs to the actual training dataset.

Mainstream neural nets often misclassify things when even a small amount of noise is introduced into the original data. This is because most models learn from a limited amount of data, which makes them prone to overfitting. Additionally, the mapping between the input and the output

© Vinita Silaparasetty 2020
V. Silaparasetty, *Deep Learning Projects Using TensorFlow 2*,
https://doi.org/10.1007/978-1-4842-5802-6_7

is almost linear. It may seem that the boundaries of separation between various classes are linear, but in reality, they are composed of linearities and even a small change in a point in the feature space might lead to data misclassification.

Types of GANs

Some of the commonly used ones are as follows:

- **Vanilla GAN:** This is the simplest type of GAN. Here, the generator and the discriminator are simple multi-layer perceptrons. The algorithm is really simple; it tries to optimize the mathematical equation using stochastic gradient descent.

- **Conditional GAN (CGAN):** A CGAN can be described as a deep learning method in which some conditional parameters are put into place. An additional parameter, y, is added to the generator to generate the corresponding data. Labels are also used as input to the discriminator in order to help distinguish the real data from fake generated data.

- **Deep Convolutional GAN (DCGAN):** A DCGAN is one of the most successful implementations of GAN. It is composed of ConvNets in place of multi-layer perceptrons. The ConvNets are implemented without max-pooling. They are replaced with convolutional stride. Additionally, the layers are not fully connected.

- **Laplacian Pyramid GAN (LAPGAN):** The Laplacian Pyramid is a linear invertible image representation consisting of a set of band-pass images, spaced an octave apart, plus a low-frequency residual. This approach uses multiple numbers of generator and discriminator networks and different levels of the Laplacian Pyramid. This approach is mainly used because it produces very high-quality images. The image is down-sampled at each layer of the pyramid and then it is upscaled at each layer in a backward pass, where the image acquires some noise from the conditional GAN until it reaches its original size.

- **Super Resolution GAN (SRGAN):** An SRGAN is a way of designing a GAN in which a deep neural network is used along with an adversarial network in order to produce higher resolution images. It is useful in optimally upscaling native low-resolution images to enhance their details, minimizing errors while doing so.

Applications of GANs include:

- Generating examples for image datasets

- Generating photographs of human faces

- Generating realistic photographs

- Generating cartoon characters

- Image-to-image translation

- Text-to-image translation

- Semantic-image-to-photo translation

- Face frontal view generation

You should now understand what a GAN is, as well as understand its applications in real-life scenarios. Let's look at the process within a GAN.

How a GAN Works

GANs can be broken into two major components, the generator (the first component) and the discriminator (the second component) (see Figure 7-1).

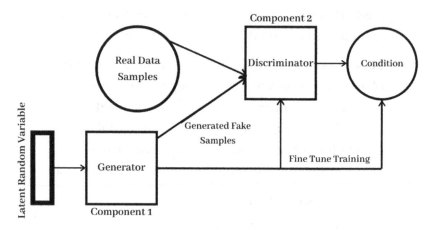

Figure 7-1. *The components of a GAN*

The Generative Model

The generative model describes how data is generated in terms of a probabilistic model. It captures the distribution of data and is trained in such a manner that it tries to maximize the probability of the discriminator making a mistake.

The generator model takes a fixed-length random vector as input and generates a sample in the domain. The vector is drawn randomly from a Gaussian distribution, and the vector is used to seed the generative process. After training, points in this multidimensional vector space will correspond to points in the problem domain, forming a compressed representation of the data distribution.

This vector space is referred to as a latent space, or a vector space composed of latent variables. Latent variables, or hidden variables, are those variables that are important for a domain but are not directly observable.

In the case of GANs, the generator model applies meaning to points in a chosen latent space, such that new points drawn from the latent space can be provided to the generator model as input and used to generate new and different output examples. After training, the generator model is kept and used to generate new samples. See Figure 7-2.

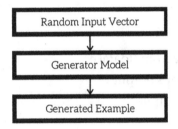

Figure 7-2. *Flowchart of the process of a generator*

Process Within the Generator

The generator is trained while the discriminator is idle. G(z) gives the same shape of the real input. For example, if an image of 10*10 is the real input then G(z) produces the same shape, but we want our generator to maximize the fake data and use a discriminator that maximizes the real data while minimizing the fake data.

$$\textbf{Max V (Di) = En~Rdata(n)[logD(n)]+Ey~Gy(y)[log(1-D(G(z)))]}$$

$$\textbf{Di}$$

$$G_{loss} = \log(1-Di(G(y)))$$

193

Where:

G_{loss} = Generator loss

Di = Discriminator

G(y) = Generator's output

y = Noise vector

Step 1: The generator Ge calculates the loss from its noise as Ge loss.

Step 2: Back propagation

$$V(Di, Ge) = E_{n \sim Rdata(n)}[logD(n)] + E_{y \sim G(y)}[log(1-Di(G(y)))]$$

Where:

Ge = Generator

Di = Discriminator

n = Training sample from Rdata(n)

D(n) = Discriminator's output

G(y) = Generator's output

y = Noise vector

Once we get these two losses, we calculate the gradients with respect to their parameters and back-propagate through their networks independently to learn from the loss (adjusting the parameters with respect to the loss.)

This method is repeated for a few epochs and then manually checked for accuracy. If it seems acceptable, then the training is stopped; otherwise, it's allowed to continue for a few more epochs.

The Discriminator Model

The discriminator is a normal classification model. The goal of the discriminator is to estimate the probability that the sample received is from the training data and not from the generator. The discriminator model takes an example from the domain as input (real or generated) and predicts a binary class label of real or fake (generated sample). See Figure 7-3.

The real example comes from the training dataset. The generated examples are output by the generator model. After the training process, the discriminator model is discarded as we are interested in the generator.

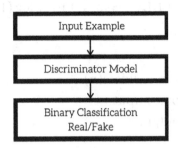

Figure 7-3. *Flowchart of the discriminator process*

Note   Both the generator and the discriminator go through their own individual feedback loops.

The discriminator tries to minimize its reward, V(Di, Ge), and the generator tries to maximize its loss.

Process Within the Discriminator

The discriminator trains while the generator is idle. In this phase, the network is only forward propagated and no back propagation is done. In this phase, the discriminator is trained on the fake generated data as well as the real data to see if it can correctly predict them.

After the discriminator is trained by the generated fake data of the generator, we can get its predictions and use the results for training the generator. This leads to a better result than the previous state, so we can try to fool the discriminator. It returns probabilities in the form of a number between 0 (representing real) and 1 (representing fake). As we can see in the following formula, the D(x) and D(G(z)) give a score between 0 and 1:

$$\textbf{Min V Ge } \mathbf{E_{y\sim py(y)}[log(1\text{-}Di(Ge(y)))]}$$

$$\textbf{Ge}$$

$$DL_{real} = \log\,(Di(n))\ DL_{fake} = \log\,(\,1\text{-}D(G(n)))$$

$$DL = DL_{real} + DL_{fake} => \log\,(D(n)) + \log\,(1\text{-}D(G(y)))$$

Where:

Di = Discriminator

n = Training sample from Rdata(n)

D(n) = Discriminator's output

G(y) = Generator's output

y = Noise vector

DL_{real} = Loss with real samples

DL_{fake} = Loss with fake/generated data

Step 1: We take some noise from the random distribution and feed it to the Ge generator to produce the fake n (label y=0) → (n,y) input-label pair.

Step 2: We take this fake pair and the real pair n (label y =1) and feed them to the Di discriminator alternatively.

Step 3: The Di discriminator is a binary classification neural network, so it runs *twice*. It calculates the loss for both the fake n and the real n and combines them as the final loss, Di loss.

Tips for training a GAN:

- When training the discriminator, hold the generator values constant. When training the generator, hold the discriminator constant. Each should train against a static adversary. This gives the generator a better read on the gradient it must learn by.

- Each side of the GAN can overpower the other. If the discriminator is too good, it will return values so close to 0 or 1 and the generator will struggle to read the gradient. If the generator is too good, it will persistently exploit weaknesses in the discriminator that lead to false negatives. This may be mitigated by the nets' respective learning rates.

Project Description

In this project, we will train a GAN to accept blurry photos as input, remove the blurriness, and return clear, debarred images as the output. GANs take a long time to train. So, for this project we will combine our custom GAN with a pretrained VGG-16 model. This will save computation resources and time and give us better results. The process is shown in Figure 7-4.

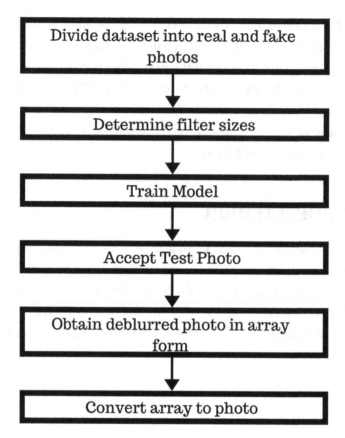

Figure 7-4. *Image deblur flowchart*

About the Dataset

Name: CERTH Image Blur Dataset

Contents:

Training set:

- 630 undistorted images (originals)

- 220 naturally-blurred images (blurred at the instance of taking the photo)

- 150 artificially-blurred images (blurred using software)

Evaluation set consisting of the "natural blur" set and the "artificial blur" set.

Natural blur set:

- 589 undistorted images

- 411 naturally-blurred images

Artificial blur set:

- 30 undistorted images

- 450 artificially-blurred images

Source: https://mklab.iti.gr/results/certh-image-blur-dataset/
Created by: E. Mavridaki and V. Mezaris

Important Terminology and Concepts

Image Deblurring

Image deblurring is the process of removing blurriness from images. Blurriness is generally caused by defocus aberration, motion blur, and Gaussian blur, among others.

Image blurring occurs when a pixel's value is affected by the adjacent pixels.

Defocusing

Defocusing is a kind of blur because the main element is not found only on the pixels that are active, but also on neighboring pixels. It can originate from wrongly adjusted focus distance or from the lack of focusing elements.

Motion Smudging

Motion smudging is also a type of blur because the same signal lands on different receiver cells as the object or if the object is moving.

The objective is to recover a sharp image from a blurred one.

Convolution

Mathematically, this process is represented as follows:

$$BI = SI*BK$$

Where BI is the blurred input image. We need to find the sharp image (SI) and the blur kernel (BK). When we multiply them together, it's called *convolution*. We say that SI is convolved with BK to generate the blurred image (BI), where BK is the blur.

The blur (BK) is typically modeled as a point spread function and is convolved with a hypothetical sharp image (SI) to get the blurred image (BI), where both the sharp image (SI) and the point spread function (BK) are unknown.

This is an example of an inverse problem. In almost all cases, there is insufficient information in the blurred image to uniquely determine a plausible original image, making it an ill-posed problem. In addition, the blurred image contains additional noise, which complicates the task of determining the original image. This is generally solved by using a regularization term to attempt to eliminate implausible solutions.

Deconvolution

The image deblurring problem can be split into two distinct problems:

- **Blind deconvolution:** This involves recovering the Point Spread Function (PSF). In multi-image PSF estimation methods, objects are either followed through the image sequence, or the problem is mathematically constrained to become less and less ill-posed by using multiple blurred images or a blurred noisy image pair. In single image PSF estimation, the blurred edges of objects represent the sources of motion information at the local level. At the global level, comparing the gradients of an entire image to a known general estimate can help deduce the PSF.

- **Non-blind deconvolution:** This involves recovering the initial estimate using a known PSF. Non-blind deconvolution methods address the problems of minimizing the huge impact that additive noise has in deblurring with a known PSF, the elimination of artifacts originating from approximate PSF estimations, and the truncation of data in the altered image.

Note Unblur is the incorrect technical term. *Deblur* is the correct technical term.

GAN Architecture

The input to the cov1 layer is a fixed-size 224x224 RGB image. The image is passed through a stack of convolutional (*conv*) layers, where the filters were used with a very small receptive field of 3×3 (which is the smallest size required to capture the notion of left/right, up/down, and center).

In one of the configurations, it also utilizes 1×1 convolution filters, which can be seen as linear transformations of the input channels (followed by nonlinearity). The convolution stride is fixed to one pixel; the spatial padding of the conv layer input is such that the spatial resolution is preserved after convolution (i.e., the padding is one pixel for 3×3 conv layers).

Spatial pooling is carried out by five max-pooling layers, which follow some of the conv layers (not all the conv layers are followed by max-pooling). Max-pooling is performed over a 2×2 pixel window, with stride 2.

Three fully-connected (FC) layers follow a stack of convolutional layers (which have a different depth in different architectures). The first two layers have 4,096 channels each, the third layer performs an 1,000-way ILSVRC classification and thus contains 1,000 channels (one for each class).

The final layer is the Softmax layer. The configuration of the fully connected layers is the same in all networks. All hidden layers are equipped with the rectification (ReLU) nonlinearity.

Required Libraries

For this project, we will use the basic libraries that you installed in the first chapter of this book. The following is a list of all the libraries required for this project:

- NumPy (see Chapter 1 for installation instructions)

- os (built-in Python 2 and up)

- Pandas (see Chapter 1 for installation instructions)

- Matplotlib (see Chapter 1 for installation instructions)

- Keras (see Chapter 1 for installation instructions)

- TensorFlow (see Chapter 1 for installation instructions)

- PIL (see Chapter 6 for installation instructions)

- random (built-in Python 2 and up)

- math (built-in Python 2 and up)

Looks like we have all the required libraries specific to this project. Let's focus on the types of layers and the number of each type of layer we want to use in this project.

GAN Architecture

Let's take a look at the "blueprints" for the GAN. Our model is going to consist of the following, as illustrated in Figure 7-5.

Generator

- Convolutional 2D layer: 4
- Dropout layer: 2
- Upsampling 2D : 1
- Dense layer: 1
- Activation layer: 2
- Activation function: Leaky ReLU
- Loss function: Binary cross-entropy

Discriminator

- Convolutional 2D layer: 4
- Convolutional 2D transpose: 1
- Max-pooling 2D: 1
- Dropout layer: 3
- Dense layer: 4
- Activation layer: 3
- Activation function: Leaky ReLU
- Loss function: Binary cross-entropy

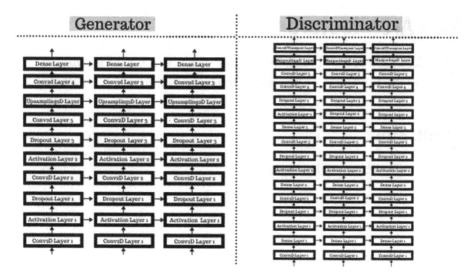

Figure 7-5. *GAN model*

Procedure

This section outlines the steps and code to use to build this project.

Step 1. Import the Libraries

Begin the project by importing the necessary libraries.

```
import numpy as np
import os
import pandas as pd
import matplotlib.pyplot as plt
import keras
import tensorflow as tf
from tensorflow.keras.layers import Dense, Dropout, Input,
InputLayer, Conv2D,UpSampling2D , Flatten,MaxPooling2D,Conv2DTr
anspose
from tensorflow.keras.models import Model,Sequential
```

```
from tensorflow.keras.optimizers import Adam
from tensorflow.keras import layers
from PIL import Image
import random
from math import ceil
```

Set the file path so that the Jupyter Notebook can access the dataset. Use the os.chdir command and enter the file path.

```
os.chdir('CERTH_ImageBlurDataset') #enter file path of dataset
os.curdir   #enter dataset directory
```

Now we are going to view the contents of the dataset:

```
os.listdir()    #list contents of current directory
```

Here is the output:

```
['Artificially-Blurred', 'Naturally-Blurred', 'Undistorted']
```

From the output, you can see that there are three folders in the dataset.

Note   For the sake of simplicity, we will refer to both the artificially-blurred and naturally-blurred images as "fake" and the undistorted images as "real."

Step 2. Dataset Preparation

Take 100 files at a time using init_size=100. Then begin going through the contents of the dataset using folders=os.listdir().

```
init_size=100
folders=os.listdir()
```

Then declare the variables that will be used to sort the dataset

```
filelist=[]#Keeps track of files.
fake_data=[]#stores the distorted images.
real_data=[]#stores the undistorted image.
```

Create the for loop to sort out the fake images. The im variable opens each image, one by one. Then the images are resized to 50x50 for convenience and uniformity. Keep in mind that a model cannot work with images directly. Therefore, you need to convert the images to arrays. Now, further simplify the arrays using a downsizing filter. Then add the array to fake_data, as follows.

```
for i in folders[0:3]:
    files=os.listdir(i)
    for j in files:
        im = Image.open(i+'\\'+j) # opening each image
        width = 50    #setting width of image
        height = 50 #setting height of image
        im5 = im.resize((width, height), Image.
        ANTIALIAS)    #resizing image
        x=np.asarray(im5)  #convert image to array
        x =(x-x.mean())/255.0# best down-sizing filter
        fake_data.append(x)
```

Create the for loop to sort out the real images. This procedure is similar to the previous code block, except this time, you are working with the "real" images.

```
for i in folders[2:]:
    files1=os.listdir(i)
    for j in files1:
        im = Image.open(i+'\\'+j)
        width = 50
```

```
height = 50
im5 = im.resize((width, height), Image.LANCZOS)
x=np.asarray(im5)
x =(x-x.mean()))/255.0# best down-sizing filter
real_data.append(x)
```

Step 3. Exploratory Data Analysis

Let's view the "fake" images first. By setting interpolation='nearest', it simply displays an image without trying to interpolate between pixels if the display resolution is not the same as the image resolution (which is most often the case). This will result in an image in which the pixels are displayed as a square of multiple pixels.

```
fake_data= np.asarray(fake_data)        #convert image to array
plt.imshow(fake_data[70], interpolation='nearest')
```

For the output, you'll get the image that's in the 70th position, as shown in Figure 7-6.

Note   Figures 7-6 and 7-7 may look different than the ones you see when running the project. Do not worry; this is just due to various factors such as the system you are working on.

Figure 7-6. *Fake image in the 70th position*

Now you can view the "real" images:

```
real_data= np.asarray(real_data)    #convert image to array
plt.imshow(real_data[50], interpolation='nearest')
```

For the output, you'll get the "real" image, which is in the 50th position, as shown in Figure 7-7.

Figure 7-7. *The real image, which is in the 50th position*

Step 4. Structure the Model

Next, you define a function with parameters for the Adam optimizer. The learning rate (lr), beta_1, and beta_2 are all set to their default values. Remember that beta_1 and beta_2 must be between 0 and 1.

Note   Since we have not set amsgrad to FALSE, we are using the AMSGrad variant of the Adam optimizer.

```
def adam_optimizer():
    return Adam(lr=0.001, beta_1=0.9, beta_2=0.999)
```

Structure the generator of the GAN using the create_generator() function.

```python
def create_generator():
    generator=tf.keras.models.Sequential()
    generator.add(InputLayer(input_shape=(50,100,100)))

    generator.add(Conv2D(32, (2, 2), activation='tanh',
    padding='same', strides=2))
    generator.add(layers.LeakyReLU(0.6))
    generator.add(layers.Dropout(0.4))

    generator.add(Conv2D(32, (2, 2), activation='tanh',
    padding='same'))
    generator.add(layers.LeakyReLU(0.3))
    generator.add(layers.Dropout(0.2))

    generator.add(Conv2D(32, (3, 3), activation='tanh',
    padding='same'))
    generator.add(UpSampling2D((2, 1)))
    generator.add(Conv2D(3, (5, 5), activation='tanh',
    padding='same'))

    generator.add(layers.Dense(units=3, activation='tanh'))
    generator.compile(loss='binary_crossentropy',
    optimizer=adam_optimizer())
    return generator
```

Create the generator and view the summary to ensure that all the layers are defined.

```python
g=create_generator()
g.summary()
```

Here's the output:

Layer (type)	Output Shape	Param #
conv2d_8 (Conv2D)	(None, 25, 50, 32)	12832
leaky_re_lu_5 (LeakyReLU)	(None, 25, 50, 32)	0
dropout_5 (Dropout)	(None, 25, 50, 32)	0
conv2d_9 (Conv2D)	(None, 25, 50, 32)	4128
leaky_re_lu_6 (LeakyReLU)	(None, 25, 50, 32)	0
dropout_6 (Dropout)	(None, 25, 50, 32)	0
conv2d_10 (Conv2D)	(None, 25, 50, 32)	9248
up_sampling2d_1 (UpSampling2	(None, 50, 50, 32)	0
conv2d_11 (Conv2D)	(None, 50, 50, 3)	2403
dense_4 (Dense)	(None, 50, 50, 3)	12

Total params: 28,623
Trainable params: 28,623
Non-trainable params: 0

This is how the summary of the generator should appear.

Next, structure the discriminator of the GAN using the create_ discriminator() function.

```python
def create_discriminator():
    discriminator=tf.keras.models.Sequential()
    discriminator.add(InputLayer(input_shape=(50,50,3)))

    discriminator.add(Conv2D(10, (2, 2), activation='tanh',
    padding='same', strides=2))
    discriminator.add(layers.Dense(units=100))
    discriminator.add(layers.LeakyReLU(0.2))
    discriminator.add(layers.Dropout(0.3))

    discriminator.add(Conv2D(10, (3, 3), activation='tanh',
    padding='same', strides=2))
    discriminator.add(layers.Dense(units=50))
    discriminator.add(layers.LeakyReLU(0.2))
    discriminator.add(layers.Dropout(0.3))

    discriminator.add(Conv2D(10, (3, 3), activation='tanh',
    padding='same', strides=2))
    discriminator.add(layers.Dense(units=25))
    discriminator.add(layers.LeakyReLU(0.2))
    discriminator.add(layers.Dropout(0.3))

    discriminator.add(Conv2D(1, (4, 4), activation='sigmoid',
    padding='same', strides=3))
    #discriminator.add(Conv2D(1, (4, 4), activation='tanh',
    padding='same'))
    discriminator.add(MaxPooling2D(pool_size = (2, 3)))
    #discriminator.add(Conv2DTranspose(1, (2,2), strides=(2,2)))
    discriminator.add(Flatten())
    discriminator.compile(loss='binary_crossentropy',
    optimizer=adam_optimizer())
    return discriminator
```

Create the discriminator and view the summary to ensure that all the layers have been defined.

```
d =create_discriminator()
d.summary()
```

Here's the output:

Layer (type)	Output Shape	Param #
conv2d_12 (Conv2D)	(None, 25, 25, 10)	130
dense_5 (Dense)	(None, 25, 25, 100)	1100
leaky_re_lu_7 (LeakyReLU)	(None, 25, 25, 100)	0
dropout_7 (Dropout)	(None, 25, 25, 100)	0
conv2d_13 (Conv2D)	(None, 13, 13, 10)	9010
dense_6 (Dense)	(None, 13, 13, 50)	550
leaky_re_lu_8 (LeakyReLU)	(None, 13, 13, 50)	0
dropout_8 (Dropout)	(None, 13, 13, 50)	0
conv2d_14 (Conv2D)	(None, 7, 7, 10)	4510
dense_7 (Dense)	(None, 7, 7, 25)	275
leaky_re_lu_9 (LeakyReLU)	(None, 7, 7, 25)	0

dropout_9 (Dropout)	(None, 7, 7, 25)	0
conv2d_15 (Conv2D)	(None, 3, 3, 1)	401
max_pooling2d_1 (MaxPooling2	(None, 1, 1, 1)	0
flatten_1 (Flatten)	(None, 1)	0

```
=================================================================
Total params: 15,976
Trainable params: 15,976
Non-trainable params: 0
```

This is how the summary of the discriminator should appear.

Now combine the VGG-16 using the create_gan(discriminator, generator) function.

```
def create_gan(discriminator, generator):
    d.trainable=False      #This enables us to treat the model as
    a combination of our custom GAN and the VGG16
    gan_input = Input(shape=(None,100,100))   #set the input shape.
    x = g(gan_input)
    gan_output= d(x)
    gan= Model(inputs=gan_input, outputs=gan_output)
    gan.compile(loss='binary_crossentropy', optimizer='adam')
    return gan
```

Create the GAN using create_gan(d,g) and view the summary to ensure that all the parameters are defined.

```
gan = create_gan(d,g)
gan.summary()  #view the structure to ensure it is correct.
```

Here is the output:

Layer (type)	Output Shape	Param #
input_7 (InputLayer)	(None, None, 100, 100)	0
sequential_2 (Sequential)	multiple	28623
sequential_3 (Sequential)	multiple	15976

Total params: 44,599
Trainable params: 28,623
Non-trainable params: 15,976

0
1

This is how the summary of the GAN should appear.

Step 5. Input Preparation

Here, you need to initialize the i counter to 0, the epoch number called epoch_num to 1, and the batch number called batches to 2.

Then, in the for loop, you take a random sample of the data and convert it to type float32 using tf.cast().

```
i=0      #set counter
epoch_num=1    #set number of epochs
batches=2      #set number of batches
for epoch in range(epoch_num):
    i=i+1
    for index in range(batches):
```

```
# [Batch Preparation]
print(index)
noise= np.random.normal(0,1, [batches,50,100,100])
noise = tf.cast(noise, tf.float32)
```

You now need to generate fake inputs for the model using the generator. For example, you can generate a fake output of arrays consisting only of ones using np.ones(gen_images.shape[0]):

```
# Generate fake inputs
gen_images = g.predict(x=noise,steps=10)
y_gen = np.ones(gen_images.shape[0])
```

Create a new set of randomly selected fake and real images using np.random.randint():

```
ran_real_image =real_data[np.random.randint(low=0,high=real_
data.shape[0],size=batches)] #get random set of real images
```

Select random real images using the following:

```
ran_fake_image =real_data[np.random.randint(low=0,high=real_
data.shape[0],size=batches)]#get random set of fake images
```

Construct different batches of real and fake data. Combine the randomly generated fake and real images into a new set using np.concatenate([ran_real_image, ran_fake_image]).

```
#Construct different batches of  real and fake data
X= np.concatenate([ran_real_image, ran_fake_image])
y_combined=np.zeros(2*batches)
y_combined[:batches]=0.9
```

```
d.trainable=True   #Train only the custom GAN.
d.train_on_batch(X, y_combined)
```

```
noise= np.random.randint(0,1, [batches,50,100,100])
noise = tf.cast(noise, tf.float32)
y_gen = np.ones(batches)
d.trainable=False
gan.train_on_batch(noise, y_gen)
noise= np.random.randint(0,1, [batches,50,100,100])
noise = tf.cast(noise, tf.float32)
gen_images = g.predict(x=noise,steps=10)
gen_images = gen_images
```

Step 6. View the Images

Once the model has been trained, you can view the images. We will
view them in the size 20x20 and set interpolation to nearest. Since we
do not need an axis to view the images, we will set it to off using plt.
axis('off').

```
dim=(20,20)
figsize=(20,20)
plt.figure(figsize=figsize)
for i in range(gen_images.shape[0]):
    plt.subplot(dim[0], dim[1], i+1)
    plt.imshow(gen_images[i]*256, interpolation='nearest')
    plt.axis('off')
    plt.tight_layout()
    os.chdir('output')
    plt.savefig('actual'+str(i)+'.png')
```

Step 7. Save Results

Now save the results directly to the system by first setting the file path
using os.chdir('output'). Then name the image file using result.
save('actual.png').

```
# Send Output to folder
result = Image.fromarray((gen_images[5]*256).astype(np.
uint8))   #obtain array form of image.
os.chdir('output')    #specify the file path to save the image.
result.save('actual.png')      #save the image
a=(gen_images[5]*255.0).astype(np.uint8)    #Unsigned Integers
of 8 bits. A uint8 data type contains all whole numbers from 0
to 255.
```

Troubleshooting

Here are some quick fixes to problems you may come across while working on this project.

- Ensure that to set the model to trainable at the correct time.

- If the results are not satisfactory, try shuffling the dataset before training.

- A large batch size can reduce the generalization ability of the model. Try using small batch sizes.

- Since we are working with VGG-16, which is a pertained model, make sure you use the same normalization and preprocessing as the model when training.

- Too much regularization can cause the network to underfit badly. Reduce regularization such as dropout, batch norm, weight/bias L2 regularization, etc.

- The network may need more time to train before it starts making meaningful predictions. If the loss is steadily decreasing, let it train some more.

Further Tests

Here are some ideas to experiment with and learn more from this project:

- Try removing the pretrained VGG-16 model and see what the result are with just the custom GAN. (Warning: GANs take a very long time to train, about 24+ hours. So test this only if your system is capable of handling the training time.)

- Add/remove layers to/from the generator and see how this affects the results.

- Add/remove layers to/from the discriminator and see how this affects the results.

- Vary the epochs.

- Try using just the VGG-16 and see how the results compare to the GAN.

Summary

Here's a quick recap of all that you learned in this chapter.

- Generative adversarial networks (GANs) are a powerful class of neural networks that are used for unsupervised learning.

- GANs consist of two components—a generator and a discriminator. The generator generates new data instances (usually images). The discriminator evaluates the images for authenticity.

- The mapping between the input and the output of mainstream neural networks are almost linear.

- The vanilla GAN is really simple; it tries to optimize the mathematical equation using stochastic gradient descent.

- Conditional GAN can be described as a deep learning method in which some conditional parameters, such as an additional parameter y and labels are put into place.

- Deep Convolutional GAN is one of the most successful implementations of GAN. It is composed of ConvNets in place of multi-layer perceptrons. It doesn't use max-pooling and the layers are not fully connected.

- The Laplacian Pyramid GAN is a linear image representation consisting of a set of band-pass images, spaced an octave apart, plus a low-frequency residual.

- Super resolution GAN is a deep neural network used along with an adversarial network in order to produce higher resolution images.

- GANs are used to generate examples for image datasets, generate photographs of human faces, generate realistic photographs, generate cartoon characters, image-to-image translation, text-to-image translation, semantic-image-to-photo translation, and face frontal view generation.

- The generative model describes how data is generated in terms of a probabilistic model. It captures the distribution of data and is trained in such a manner that it tries to maximize the probability of the discriminator making a mistake.

- The discriminator is a normal classification model. The discriminator model takes an example from the domain as input (real or generated) and predicts a binary class label of real or fake (a generated sample).

- When training the discriminator, hold the generator values constant; and when training the generator, hold the discriminator constant. Each should train against a static adversary. This gives the generator a better read on the gradient it must learn by.

References

Here are the references used in this chapter:

- https://machinelearningmastery.com/what-are-generative-adversarial-networks-gans/

- https://towardsdatascience.com/step-by-step-vgg16-implementation-in-keras-for-beginners-a833c686ae6c

- https://pathmind.com/wiki/generative-adversarial-network-gan

- https://neurohive.io/en/popular-networks/vgg16/

Further Reading

Interested in learning more about some of the topics covered in this chapter? Here are some great links to check out:

- Image deblurring: www.mathcs.emory.edu/~nagy/courses/fall06/ID_lecture1.pdf

- GANs: https://developers.google.com/machine-learning/gan

- VGG: www.robots.ox.ac.uk/~vgg/research/very_deep/

- VGG-16: www.researchgate.net/figure/A-schematic-of-the-VGG-16-Deep-Convolutional-Neural-Network-DCNN-architecture-trained_fig2_319952138

- AMSGrad version of Adam: https://openreview.net/forum?id=ryQu7f-RZ

CHAPTER 8

Image Manipulation

Think you have a keen eye for spotting tampered images? Now what if the image has been manipulated so well that the average person is easily fooled? Neural networks can aid in finding subtle features of images and identify which ones are authentic and which ones have been modified. This is called *image forensics*.

In this project we will use a CNN. Since we already discussed CNNs in Chapter 6, we will go straight to the project description and proceed from there.

Project Description

In this project we are going to use a CNN to look for image anomalies, such as identical patches of pixels, to detect which images have been doctored. In particular, this dataset consists of images that have been forged using the *copy-move technique*. The model trains on the ground truth images.

We use the "Unmodified/original images with JPEG compression" files from the dataset as our original images, which we call `real_data`. We use the "Copies that were pasted multiple times" files from the dataset as our manipulated data, which we will call `tampered_data`.

© Vinita Silaparasetty 2020
V. Silaparasetty, *Deep Learning Projects Using TensorFlow 2*,
https://doi.org/10.1007/978-1-4842-5802-6_8

Important Terminology and Concepts

Cameras create a digital watermark or a digital signature of the image the instant it is taken. Any modifications made later can be detected by checking the value of that digital watermark. The ease and prevalence of image-editing software tools make it simple for anyone to alter the content of images or to create new images without leaving any obvious traces of tampering. Existing software allows individuals to create photorealistic computer graphics and hybrid-generated visual content that viewers often find indistinguishable from photographic images.

Multimedia Forensics

Multimedia forensics comes from classical forensic science in that it uses scientific methods to gain probative facts from physical or digital evidence. The task of multimedia forensic tools is to expose the traces left in multimedia content during each step of its life, by exploiting existing knowledge on digital imaging and in multimedia security research.

It relies on the observation that each phase of the image history—from the acquisition process, to its storing in a compressed format, to any post-processing operation—leaves a distinctive trace on the data, as a sort of digital fingerprint. It is then possible to identify the source of the digital image and determine whether it is authentic or modified by detecting the presence, the absence, or the incongruence of such features intrinsically tied to the digital content.

Generally, the approaches used to detect manipulated images can be divided into the following:

- **Active approach:** For the assessment of trustworthiness, we exploit the data acquired from the source (i.e., in the camera). The active approach can be further classified into two segments: the data-hiding approach (e.g., watermarks) and the digital signature approach.

- **Passive/blind approach:** Through this approach, we try to make an assessment with only the digital content at our disposal. It works in the absence of any protecting techniques and without using any prior information about the image. Blind methods use the image function and the fact that forgeries can add specific detectable changes to images.

The history of a digital image is reconstructed in order to verify its originality and assess its quality. It is relatively easy to validate an image when the image source is known. In practical cases, though, almost no information is known about the image. Therefore, investigators need to authenticate the image history using the blind method.

Note   Digital cameras are equipped with a watermarking chip or a digital signature chip that can be easily exploited using a private key that is hard-wired in the camera itself. The chip authenticates every image that the camera takes before storing it on its memory card.

The history of a digital image can be represented as a composition of several steps, collected into four main phases: acquisition, coding, editing, and saving. These steps are shown in Figure 8-1.

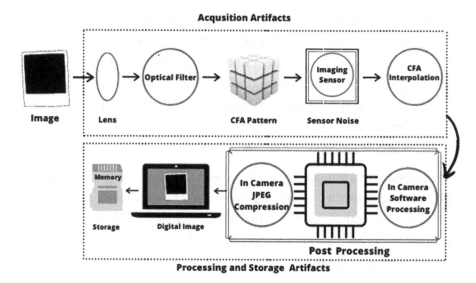

Figure 8-1. *History of a digital image*

Acquisition

During *acquisition*, the light coming from the real scene framed by the camera is focused by the lenses on the camera sensor (a CCD or a CMOS). This is where the digital image signal is generated. Before reaching the sensor, the light is filtered by the CFA (color filter array), a thin film on the sensor that selectively permits a certain component of light to pass through it to the sensor. Each pixel has only one particular main color (Red, Green, or Blue), which is gathered. The sensor output is successively interpolated to obtain all three main colors for each pixel, through the *demosaicing* process, in order to obtain the digital color image. The obtained signal undergoes additional in-camera processing that can include white balancing, color processing, image sharpening, contrast enhancement, and gamma correction.

Coding

The processed signal is stored in the camera memory; to save storage, in most cameras, the image is lossy compressed, and for commercial devices, the JPEG format is usually the preferred one. Lossy image compression is one of the most common operations performed on digital images. This is due to the convenience of handling smaller amounts of data to store and/or transmit. Indeed, most digital cameras compress each picture directly after taking a shot.

Editing

The generated image can be post-processed, for example, to enhance or to modify its content. Any image editing can be applied to an image during its life: the most commonly used editing methods are geometric transformation (rotation, scaling, etc.), blurring, sharpening, contrast adjustment, image splicing (the composition of an image using parts of one or more parts of images), and cloning (or copy-move, the replication of a portion of the same image).

Note   Splicing is probably more common than a copy-move forgery, because it is far more flexible and allows the creation of images with a very different content with respect to the original.

Saving

After editing, very often the image is saved in the JPEG format, so that a recompression will occur. Traces of manipulation are referred to as fingerprints or footprints and are categorized as the following:

- **Acquisition fingerprints:** Each component in a digital acquisition device modifies the input and leaves intrinsic fingerprints in the final image output, due to the specific optical system, image sensor, and camera software. The image acquisition pipeline is common for most of the commercially available devices; however, since each step is performed according to specific manufacturer choices, the traces can depend on the particular camera brand and/or model. This means that each stage of the camera introduces imperfections or intrinsic image regularities, which leave telltale footprints in the final image that represent a signature of the camera type or even of the individual device into the image. The presence of inconsistencies in these artifacts can be taken as evidence of tampering.

- **Coding fingerprints:** Lossy compression inevitably leaves itself characteristic footprints, which are related to the specific coding architecture. The presence of inconsistencies in an image's coding artifacts can be taken as evidence of tampering.

- **Editing fingerprints:** Each processing applied to the digital image, even if not visually detectable, modifies its properties, thereby leaving peculiar traces according to the processing used.

- **Sensor-based footprints:** Sensor pattern noise is mainly due to imperfections of the image sensor, resulting in slight differences between the sensed scene and the image acquired by the camera. The dominating component of sensor pattern noise is the photoresponse nonuniformity (PRNU) noise. It is a high-frequency multiplicative noise, generally stable throughout the camera's lifetime in normal operating conditions. These properties make it ideal not only for device identification, but also for single device linking and, if inconsistencies in the PRNU pattern within the image are found in certain regions, for forgery detection.

Along with PRNU, another important artifact left by cameras during acquisition is that due to the presence of the CFA (color filter array). Excluding professional triple-CCD/CMOS cameras, the incoming light is filtered by the CFA before reaching the sensor (CCD or CMOS), so that for each pixel, only one particular color is gathered.

The following are types of image-tampering analyses:

- **Detecting traces of resampling:** Two or more images can be spliced together to create high-quality and consistent image forgeries.

  In this case, geometric transformations such as scaling, rotation, or skewing are needed.

  Geometric transformations typically require a resampling and interpolation step. Thus, we need sophisticated resampling/interpolation detectors.

- **Noise inconsistencies analysis:** A commonly used tool to conceal traces of tampering is adding locally random noise to the altered image regions, which cause inconsistencies in the image's noise. Therefore, the presence of various noise levels in an image often signifies tampering.

- **Cyclostationary analysis:** Cyclostationary signals exhibit periodicity. Cyclostationary detectors find the traces of geometric transformation by detecting specific correlations between its spectral components. It has proven to give promising results.

- **Enhancement detection:** This includes enhancement operations like smoothing, contrast enhancement, histogram equalization, and median filtering. The pixels in adjacent rows and columns share the same value. These "streaking artifacts" can be analyzed by considering first-order differences for groups of two pixels and then studying their corresponding histograms. This simple approach yields extremely high detection rates, provided that images are not compressed.

- **Seam carving detection:** Automatically detects if there are any paths of pixels (seams) of the image along which no relevant content is present. If detected, these paths are eliminated, and the image size is reduced. We may think of this technique as a sort of content-dependent cropping.

- **Splicing detection based on lighting/shadows:** One of the most common hurdles when trying to create a believable forgery is to take into account how objects in the scene interact with the light source. Cutting an object from one photo and pasting it into another requires one to adapt object illumination and to introduce consistent shadows into the scene. When this is not done, inconsistencies in lighting direction and shadows can reveal that the image has been modified.

- **Splicing detection based on inconsistencies in geometry/perspective:** This involves identifying the presence of inconsistencies in the geometrical and perspective setting of the scene in an image, motion blur, and perspective.

230

Copy-Move Forgeries

This section discusses copy-move forgery in detail, as it is our primary focus in this project. *Copy-move forgery* is a specific type of image tampering where a part of the image is copied and pasted on another part, usually to conceal unwanted portions of the image. In Figure 8-2, the reflection of the tree is circled because it was not present in the original image. It has been digitally added.

Figure 8-2. *Example of a copy-move forgery*

Hence, the goal in detecting copy-move forgeries is to find image areas that are the same or extremely similar. If the copied parts are from the same image, some components (e.g., noise and color) will be compatible with the rest of the image. That means this kind of attack is not detectable using forensic methods that look for incompatibilities in statistical measures. Properly designed methods have thus been proposed to cope with this manipulation.

First of all, such techniques will have to cope with the problem of the computational complexity, since the direct application of an exhaustive search of cloned areas would be too expensive. In addition, it has to be considered that the cloned areas could be not equal, but just similar, since the tamperer in creating the forgery could exploit image-processing tools to hide the tampering. Therefore, the forgery-detection method should be designed in order to be robust with respect to this set of possible modifications.

Instead of looking for the whole duplicated region, the image is segmented into overlapping square blocks, and then we look for similar connected image blocks. By assuming that the cloned region is bigger than the block size, and thus that this region is composed of many overlapping cloned blocks, each cloned block will be moved with the same shift, and thus the distance between each duplicated block pair will be the same as well. Therefore, the forgery detection will look for a minimum number of similar image blocks within the same distance that are connected to each other to form two image areas exhibiting the same shape.

All the analyzed methods follow the same block matching-based procedure: an image is first segmented into overlapping square blocks of size, each block moves by one pixel from the upper-left corner to the lower-right corner. From each block, a set of features is extracted and properly quantized to remove possible slight differences between cloned blocks.

Assuming that similar blocks are represented by similar features, a matching process, based on the lexicographically sorting, is then applied to the block feature vectors to find the duplicated blocks. Finally, a forgery decision is made by checking if there are more than a certain number of block pairs connected to each other within the same shift. This takes into account the fact that most natural images will have many similar blocks.

Here are the types of features selected to represent each image block:

- Discrete cosine transform (DCT) coefficients

- Color-related features

- Principal component analysis (PCA) of pixels

- Fourier-Mellin transform (FMT) as block signature

- Log-Polar Fourier transform as a signature

- Scale-invariant feature transform (SIFT) local features, used to find matching regions within the same image

About the Dataset

Name: Image Manipulation Dataset

Contents:

- Unmodified/original images

- Unmodified/original images with JPEG compression

- One-to-one splices

- Splices with added Gaussian noise

- Splices with added JPEG artifacts

- Rotated copies

- Scaled copies

- Combined effects

- Copies that were pasted multiple times

Source: www5.cs.fau.de/research/data/image-manipulation/

Created by: V. Christlein, Ch. Riess, J. Jordan, Co. Riess, and E. Angelopoulou

Paper: "An Evaluation of Popular Copy-Move Forgery Detection Approaches," *IEEE Transactions on Information Forensics and Security,* vol. 7, no. 6, pp. 1841-1854, 2012.

Required Libraries

For this project, we will use the basic libraries that you installed in the first chapter of this book. The following is a list of all the libraries required for this project:

- NumPy (see Chapter 1 for installation instructions)

- os (built-in Python 2 and up)

- Pandas (see chapter 1 for installation instructions)

- Matplotlib (see Chapter 1 for installation instructions)

- Keras (see Chapter 1 for installation instructions)

- TensorFlow (see Chapter 1 for installation instructions)

- PIL (see Chapter 6 for installation instructions)

- random (built-in Python 2 and up)

- math (built-in Python 2 and up)

- Imageio (installation instructions are in this chapter)

- cv2 (see Chapter 6 for installation instructions)

- Skimage (see Chapter 6 for installation instructions)

You should have all the required libraries except Imageio. Let's install it now. Use this command to install Imageio using PIP:

```
Pip3 install imageio
```

To check the installation, use this command:

`Pip3 show imageio`

With this, you should have all the libraries you need for this project.

Troubleshooting

Ensure that Python and Pillow have been installed correctly, as they are prerequisites for Imageio.

CNN Architecture

To detect image forgery in a CNN, you need a model with the correct number of layers in the correct order. Figure 8-3 shows the model we will use in this project.

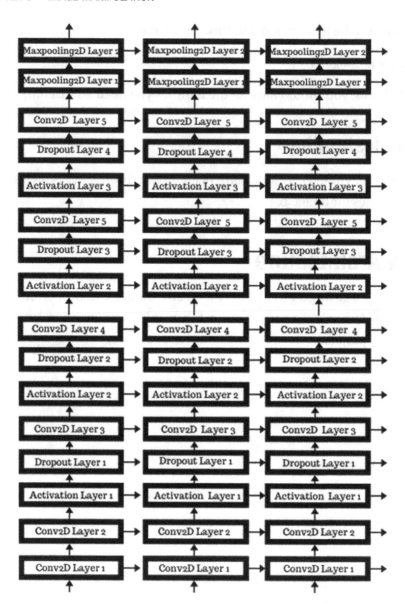

Figure 8-3. *Architecture of the CNN for this project*

Let's take a look at the "blueprint" for the CNN. This model is going to consist of the following layers:

- Convolutional 2D layer: 6

- Dropout layer: 4

- Max-pooling layer: 2

The convolutional 2D layer creates a convolution kernel that is convolved with the layer input to produce a tensor of outputs. The dropout layer helps to avoid overfitting by "dropping" some of the values obtained during training. The max-pooling layer operates on spatial data and thus is ideal for this project.

We use the Leaky ReLU activation function, as it avoids saturation (the loss of signal to either zero gradient or the dominance of chaotic noise arising from digital rounding). It also solves the dead ReLU problem. This ensures that we get the best results possible.

We will use the binary cross-entropy loss function, as it minimizes the distance between two probability distributions—predicted and actual.

Procedure

We are finally ready to implement the GRU. Let's open a new Jupyter Notebook and get to work.

Step 1. Import the Libraries

Begin by loading the necessary libraries.

```
from tensorflow.keras.applications.vgg16  import VGG16
import numpy as np
import os
import pandas as pd
```

```
import matplotlib.pyplot as plt
import keras
import tensorflow as tf
from tensorflow.keras.layers import Dense, Dropout, Input,
InputLayer, Conv2D,UpSampling2D , Flatten,MaxPooling2D,Conv2DTr
anspose
from tensorflow.keras.models import Model,Sequential
from keras.datasets import mnist
from tensorflow.keras.optimizers import Adam
from tensorflow.keras import layers
from PIL import Image
import random
from math import ceil
import imageio
import cv2
from skimage.data import astronaut
from skimage.filters import gaussian,sobel
from skimage import transform,io
```

Set the file path using os.chdir(''):

```
os.chdir('D:\\Proj\\vinita\\Project 3- Image Manipulation\\
manipulation_data\\Real_data\\')
```

Step 2. Preparing the Dataset

This step involves several sub-steps, described next.

Step 2a. Sort and Collect the Authentic Data

First, create the filelist=[] list to store all the image files. Then create the tampered_data=[] list to store the images that have been manipulated.

Finally, create the real_data=[] list, which stores the original images that have not been manipulated.

Now initialize the counter i=0. In the for loop, os.walk() will yield two lists for each directory it visits—splitting them into files and directories. os.sep() separates the file path.

Then search for the image files and display their file paths, so that you know the loop is working once you execute it.

Note   The gt file format is a simple binary format designed to store graph-tool Graph instances in a compact and fast manner, including all types of property maps supported by the library.

Now resize the image to 300x300 to maintain uniformity. Finally, add the image to the real_data list.

```
rootdir = os.getcwd()
filelist=[]
tampered_data=[]
real_data=[]
i=0
for subdir, dirs, files in os.walk(rootdir):
    for file in files:
        filepath = subdir + os.sep + file
        if (filepath.find('gt') >0):
            i=i+1
            print(filepath)
            width = 300
            height = 300
            image1 = cv2.imread(filepath,0)
            transformed_image = transform.resize(image1,
            (300,300), mode='symmetric', preserve_range=True)
```

```
transformed_image=(transformed_image-transformed_
image.mean())/255
real_data.append(transformed_image)
```

Step 2b. Sort and Collect the Manipulated Data

This process for collecting the manipulated data is similar to the previous code block.

```
for subdir, dirs, files in os.walk(rootdir):
    for file in files:
        filepath = subdir + os.sep + file

        if (filepath.find('gt') > 0):
            i=i+1
            print(filepath)
            im = Image.open(filepath)
            width = 300
            height = 300
            image1 = cv2.imread(filepath,0)
            transformed_image = transform.resize(image1,
            (300,300), mode='symmetric', preserve_range=True)
            transformed_image=(transformed_image-transformed_
            image.mean())/255
            tampered_data.append(transformed_image)
```

Step 2c. Transform and Convert the Data to an Array

You can view the mean using the .mean() function.

Now view the maximum using the .max() function, which returns the item with the highest value.

Then view the minimum using the .min() function, which returns the item with the lowest value.

240

After this, you can convert the data into arrays using np.asarray().

```
transformed_image=(transformed_image-transformed_image.
mean())/255
```

```
transformed_image.max()
transformed_image.min()
```

```
real_data=np.asarray(real_data)
tampered_data=np.asarray(tampered_data)
```

Step 2d. Create the Combined Dataset

We have preprocessed the data, so now you are ready to combine both arrays to create a single dataset by using np.concatenate().

Now reshape the data using combined_input.reshape(). Set the trainsize using the ceil() function, which returns the smallest integral value greater than 0.8.

We set the testsize using the ceil() function, which returns the smallest integral value greater than 0.2.

Now select a random section of the training data and testing data using np.random.randint():

```
combined_input=np.concatenate([real_data, tampered_data])
```

```
y_combined=np.zeros(real_data.shape[0]+tampered_data.shape[0])
y_combined[:real_data.shape[0]]=1
```

```
combined_input=combined_input.reshape(624,300,300,1)
```

```
trainsize= ceil(0.8 * combined_input.shape[0])
testsize= ceil(0.2 * combined_input.shape[0])+1
```

```
trainsel=np.random.randint(low=0,high=combined_input.
shape[0],size=trainsize)
```

```
testsel=np.random.randint(low=0,high=combined_input.
shape[0],size=testsize)
train_inp=combined_input[trainsel,]
test_inp=combined_input[testsel,]

train_out=y_combined[trainsel,]
test_out=y_combined[testsel,]
```

Step 2e. Define the Optimizer

Define the optimizer in which we set Adam to its default values.

```
def adam_optimizer():
    return Adam(lr=0.001,beta_1=0.9)
```

Step 3. Structure the Model

Let's create the CNN for this project using the following code:

```
model = Sequential()
model.add(InputLayer(input_shape=(300, 300, 1)))
model.add(Conv2D(32, (3, 3), activation='tanh', padding='same',
strides=2))

model.add(Conv2D(32, (3, 3), activation='tanh',
padding='same'))
model.add(layers.LeakyReLU(0.6))
model.add(layers.Dropout(0.4))

model.add(Conv2D(32, (3, 3), activation='tanh', padding='same',
strides=2))
model.add(layers.LeakyReLU(0.3))
model.add(layers.Dropout(0.2))
```

```
model.add(Conv2D(32, (3, 3), activation='tanh', padding='same',
strides=2))
model.add(layers.LeakyReLU(0.3))
model.add(layers.Dropout(0.2))

model.add(Conv2D(32, (3, 3), activation='tanh', padding='same',
strides=2))
model.add(layers.LeakyReLU(0.3))
model.add(layers.Dropout(0.2))

model.add(Conv2D(1, (3, 3), activation='tanh',
padding='same',strides=2))
model.add(MaxPooling2D(pool_size = (3, 3)))
model.add(MaxPooling2D(pool_size = (2, 2)))
model.add(Flatten())
print(model.summary())
```

Step 4. Train the Model

Compile the model by using Adam as the optimizer and binary_
crossentropy as the loss function.

Then train the model, setting the batch size to 100 and number of
epochs to 3.

```
model.compile(loss='binary_crossentropy', optimizer=adam_
optimizer())
model.fit(x=train_inp, y=train_out, batch_size=100,epochs=3)
```

Step 5. Test the Model

Obtain predictions for the training and test data using model.predict():

```
train_pred = model.predict(train_inp)
test_pred = model.predict(test_inp)
```

Step 6. Check the Results

Check the interpolation of the training and test data using np.interp().

For a better understanding of the results, you can generate a histogram of the interpolations using plt.hist().

Finally, combine the results of the training and test data to see the overall performance of this model using np.concatenate().

```
check=np.interp(train_pred, (train_pred.min(), train_pred.
max()), (0,1))
check1=np.interp(test_pred, (test_pred.min(), test_pred.max()),
(0,1))
```

```
plt.hist(check)
plt.hist(check1)
```

```
train_check = np.concatenate((train_out.reshape(-1,1),check.
reshape(-1,1)),axis=1)
test_check = np.concatenate((test_out.reshape(-1,1),check1.
reshape(-1,1)),axis=1)
```

You have successfully trained this model to detect manipulation in images.

Further Tests

Here are some ideas to experiment with to learn more from this project:

- Try increasing and decreasing the number of max-pooling layers in the CNN.

- Add an upsampling layer to see how the results differ.

- Try min-pooling instead of max-pooling.

- Try increasing the dropout layers.

- Try increasing and decreasing the number of epochs to see how that affects the results of the model.

Summary

Here is a quick recap of all that you learned in this chapter.

- Cameras create a digital watermark/digital signature from the image the instant it is taken.

- Existing software allows forgers to create photorealistic computer graphics or hybrid generated visual content that viewers can find indistinguishable from the original photographic images.

- Multimedia forensics comes from classical forensic science in that it uses scientific methods to gain probative facts from physical or digital evidence.

- The task of the multimedia forensic tools is to expose traces left in the multimedia content during each step of its life, by exploiting existing knowledge about digital imaging and about multimedia security research.

- The approaches to detecting manipulated images can be divided into active and passive.

  - **Active approach:** For the assessment of trustworthiness, this exploits data acquired from the source (i.e., in the camera). The active approach can be further classified into two segments: the data-hiding approach (e.g., watermarks) and the digital signature approach.

245

- **Passive/blind approach:** Using this approach we try to make an assessment using only the digital content. It works in the absence of any protecting techniques and without using any prior information about the image. Blind methods use the image function and the fact that forgeries can add specific detectable changes to images.

- Digital cameras are equipped with a watermarking chip or a digital signature chip that can be easily exploited using a private key hard-wired in the camera itself. That chip authenticates every image that the camera takes before storing it on its memory card.

- The history of a digital image can be represented as a composition of several steps, collected into four main phases: acquisition, coding, editing, and saving.

- The image acquisition pipeline is common for most commercially available devices; however, since each step is performed according to specific manufacturer choices, the traces can depend on the particular camera brand and/or model.

- Sensor pattern noise comes mainly from imperfections of the image sensor, resulting in slight differences between the sensed scene and the image acquired by the camera.

- Splicing is probably more common than copy-move forgery, because it is far more flexible and allows forgers to create images having very different content with respect to the original.

- Types of image tampering detection include: detecting traces of resampling, noise inconsistencies analysis, cyclostationary analysis, enhancement detection, seam carving detection, splicing detection based on lighting/shadows, and splicing detection based on inconsistencies in geometry/perspective.

- Copy-move forgery is a specific type of image tampering whereby a part of the image is copied and pasted on another part, usually to conceal unwanted portions of the image.

References

Here are the sources used in this chapter.

- `https://pdfs.semanticscholar.org/12cf/2682ed6a2 4dcb3a5ac7dcf2c08b71f6a18d1.pdf`

- `www.yundle.com/terms-definitions/i/image-manipulation`

Further Reading

Interested in learning more about some of the topics covered in this chapter? Here are some great links to check out:

- Image forensics: `https://link.springer.com/ article/10.1007/s11042-010-0620-1`

- Copy-move forgery: `www.imedpub.com/articles/ fusion-approaches-system-of-copymove-forgery-detection.php?aid=22116`

- GT files: `https://file.org/extension/gt`

- Dying ReLU problem: `https://machinelearning.wtf/terms/dying-relu/`

CHAPTER 9

Neural Network Collection

Chapter 3 mentioned that there are a lot of neural networks that are currently in use and more being developed regularly. This chapter will guide you as to which ones you can refer to for future projects on deep learning. This chapter is divided into three main parts: neural networks, optimization functions, and loss functions.

The first part provides examples of neural networks that you can easily use in your own projects. Each neural network is accompanied by an explanation to help you understand them so that you can make the right choice for your deep learning projects. The second part of the chapter features a collection of optimizers and the final part covers loss functions, with tips on how to select the right parameters for your model.

Neural Network Zoo Primer

The first artificial neural network was invented in 1958 by psychologist Frank Rosenblatt. He designed the *perceptron* (discussed in Chapter 2), which was intended to replicate how the human brain processes visual data and learns to recognize objects. Ever since the inception of neural network architectures, there has been an onslaught of new models.

© Vinita Silaparasetty 2020
V. Silaparasetty, *Deep Learning Projects Using TensorFlow 2*,
https://doi.org/10.1007/978-1-4842-5802-6_9

Since new models were introduced in quick succession, there was a need to organize and document these networks in some way, to make them easier to track and improve.

On September 14, 2016, Fjodor Van Veen and Stefan Leijnen, from the Asimov Institute, decided to create a chart of every model used in deep learning. They depicted the models as node maps. It is the most comprehensive chart of models in use today. This chart is titled the "Neural Network Zoo." This chapter references the chart and elaborates on it.

Neural Networks

This main section reviews a series of neural networks designed for use in future projects. Each neural network section is set up in the following manner:

- Description of a main neural network currently in existence

- List of the subcategories of each neural network and a list of associated layers

- List of applications of each neural network

- Example implementation of the model

Recurrent Neural Networks (RNNs)

RNNs are used in deep learning sand in the development of models that simulate the activity of neurons in the human brain (see Figure 9-1). They are especially powerful when it's critical to predict an outcome and are distinct from other types of artificial neural networks because they use feedback loops to process a sequence of data that informs the final output, which can also be a sequence of data. These feedback loops allow information to persist; the effect is often described as *memory*. The logic behind a RNN is to consider the sequence of the input.

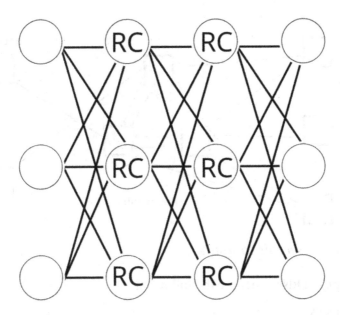

Figure 9-1. *Recurrent neural network. RC indicates the recurrent cell*

Like feedforward neural networks, RNNs can process data from initial input to final output. Unlike feedforward neural networks, RNNs use feedback loops such as Backpropagation Through Time (BPTT) throughout the computational process to loop information back into the network. This connects inputs together and is what enables RNNs to process sequential and temporal data. They are used for reservoir computing.

Reservoir Computing

Reservoir computing (see Figure 9-2) is an extension of neural networks in which the input signal is connected to a fixed (non-trainable) and random dynamic system (the reservoir), thus creating a higher dimension representation (embedding). This embedding is then connected to the desired output via trainable units.

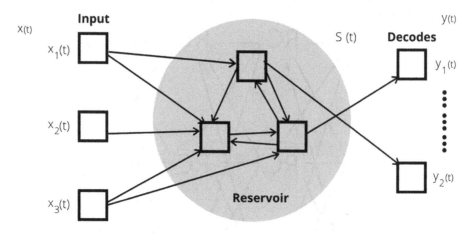

Figure 9-2. *Reservoir computing*

The types of RNNs include the following:

- LSTM

- Peephole connections

- Gated recurrent units

- Multiplicative LSTM

- LSTM with attention

- Hopfield network

- Markov chain

- Bidirectional associative memory

The layers used in an RNN are as follows:

- Embedding

- SimpleRNN

- SimpleRNNCell

- Dense

- Dropout

Applications of an RNN are as follows:

- Speech recognition

- Text classification

- Image recognition

Here's the implementation of RNN in TensorFlow 2.0:

```
rrn = tf.keras.Sequential()
rnn.add(layers.Embedding(input_dim=1000, output_dim=64))
rnn.add(layers.SimpleRNN(128))
rnn.add(layers.Dense(10, activation='softmax'))
rnn.add(layers.SimpleRNN(90))
rnn.compile(loss='binary_crossentropy', optimizer='rmsprop'
```

Multiplicative LSTM

Multiplicative LSTMs (mLSTMs) were introduced by Benjamin Krause in 2016 (see Figure 9-3). They are a type of recurrent neural network architecture for sequence modeling that combines the long short-term memory (LSTM) and multiplicative recurrent neural network architectures. mLSTM is characterized by its ability to have different recurrent transition functions for each possible input, which makes it more expressive for autoregressive density estimation. It's a hybrid architecture that combines the factorized hidden-to-hidden transition of mRNNs with the gating framework from LSTMs.

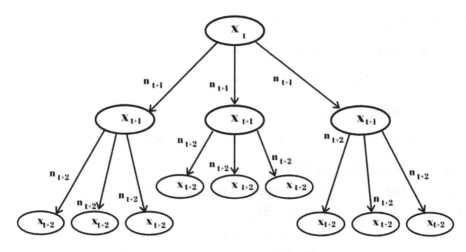

Figure 9-3. *Multiplicative LSTM (mLSTM)*

The layers in an mLSTM are as follows:

- Embedding

- Multiplicative LSTM

- Dense

- Dropout

- ConvLSTM2D

- ConvLSTM2DCell

- LSTMCell

- CuDNNLSTM

mLSTM is used with sequences of discrete mutually exclusive elements, Here's its implementation in TensorFlow 2.0:

```
mlstm = tf.keras.models.Sequential()
mlstm.add(Embedding(1000, 64, input_length=10))
mlstm.add(MultiplicativeLSTM(512, dropout_W=0.2, dropout_U=0.2)
```

```
mlstm.add(Dense(1024, activation='linear')
mlstm.add(MultiplicativeLSTM(50, dropout_W=0.1, dropout_U=0.1)
mlstm.add(Dropout(0.2)
mlstm.compile(loss='categorical_crossentropy',
optimizer='rmsprop'
```

ANNs with Attention

Attention in machine learning refers to a model's ability to focus on specific elements in the data (see Figure 9-4).

We build an architecture that consumes all the hidden states rather than using the last hidden state as a proxy. This is what "attention" mechanisms do. Each generated output is not just a function of the final hidden state but rather a function of *all* the hidden states. It's not an operation that merely combines all hidden states.

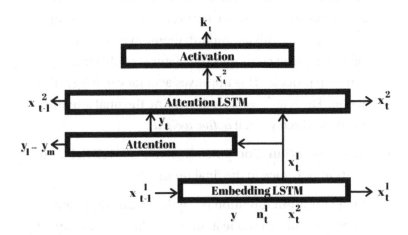

Figure 9-4. *LSTM with attention*

Types of attention include the following:

- **Global attention:** Uses all encoder hidden states to define the attention-based context vector for each decoder step.

- **Local attention:** Uses only a few hidden states that fall within a smaller window. This window is centered on the encoder's hidden state.

- **Hard attention:** Instead of a weighted average of all the hidden states, it uses attention scores to select a single hidden state.

- **Soft attention:** Calculates the context vector as a weighted sum of the encoder hidden states, as shown in the previous figures.

- **Latent attention:** A weight is learned on each feature to determine its importance for prediction of the trigger or the action. Unlike standard attention methods, latent attention computes the feature weights in a two-step process. This improves accuracy to trigger the action. The latent weights determine the final attention weights, which we call *active weights.*

- **Active attention:** Computes each token's weight based on its importance in the final prediction.

- **Area attention:** Attention is applied to an entire "area," without limiting a single item. It is defined as a group of structurally adjacent items in the memory. An "area" is formed by combining adjacent items in the memory.

The layers in an attention ANN are as follows:

- Scaled dot-product attention

- Multihead attention layer

An application of an attention ANN is with natural language processing.

Note   Other layers depend on the type of network being used, such as RNN, CNN and so on.

Here's its implementation in TensorFlow 2.0:

```
#RNN with Attention
rrn = tf.keras.Sequential()
rnn.add(layers.Embedding(input_dim=1000, output_dim=64))
rnn.add(layers.SimpleRNN(128))
rnn.add(layers.Attention( [query_seq_encoding, value_seq_
encoding]))
rnn.add(layers.Dense(10, activation='softmax'))
rnn.add(layers.SimpleRNN(90))
rnn.compile(loss='binary_crossentropy', optimizer='rmsprop'
```

Transformers

Transformers have a memory-hungry architectural style (see Figure 9-5). They are feedforward encoders/decoders with attention. They do not require cell-state memory. They pick and choose from an entire sequence fragment at once, using attention to focus on the most important parts.

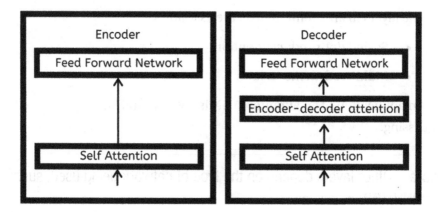

Figure 9-5. *Transformers*

The layers in a transformer are as follows:

- Input layer

- Hidden layer: Usually a dense layer

- Output layer

- GaussianNoise

- GaussianDropout

An application of transformers is with sequence transduction.
Here's the implementation in TensorFlow 2.0:

```
# Encoder

def create_encoder():

encoder = tf.keras.models.Sequential()
encoder.add(Dense(50, activation='relu', input_shape(1,1,None)))
encoder.add(Dropout(rate=dropout))
encoder.add(Dense(units=10, activation='relu'))
encoder.add(Dense(units=20))
encoder.add(Dropout(rate=dropout))
```

```
encoder.add(Dropout(rate=dropout))
return encoder

e = create_encoder( )

#Decoder

def create_decoder( ):

decoder = tf.keras.models.Sequential()
decoder.add(Dense(50, activation='relu', input_shape(1,1,None)))
decoder.add(Dropout(rate=dropout)
decoder.add(Dense(units=10, activation='relu'))
decoder.add(Dense(units=20)
decoder.add(Dropout(rate=dropout))
decoder.add(Dropout(rate=dropout))
return decoder

d = create_decoder()

# Definition of transformer

def create_transformer(encoder, decoder):
    d.trainable=False
    transformer_input = Input(shape=(None,100,100))
    x = g(transformer_input)
    transformer_output= d(x)
    transformer= Model(inputs=transformer_input,
    outputs=transformer_output)
    transfomer.compile(loss='binary-crossentropy',
    optimizer='adam')
    return transformer

transformer = create_transfomer(e,d)
```

Autoencoder

An *autoencoder* is an unsupervised artificial neural network that learns how to efficiently compress and encode data (see Figure 9-6). It then learns how to reconstruct the data from the latent-space representation, in order to create a representation that is as close to the original input as possible. It ignores the noise in the data to reduce data dimensions.

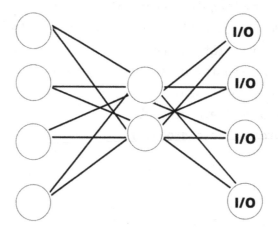

Figure 9-6. *Autoencoder. I/O indicates the matched input/output cells*

An autoencoder consists of the following components:

- **Encoder:** The model learns how to reduce the input dimensions and compress the input data into an encoded representation.

- **Bottleneck:** This layer contains the compressed representation of the input data.

- **Decoder:** The model learns how to reconstruct the data from the encoded representation to be as close to the original input as possible.

- **Reconstruction loss:** Measures the performance of the decoder using back propagation in order to minimize the network's reconstruction loss.

The encoder part of the network is used for encoding and sometimes even for data compression purposes. It has a decreasing number of hidden units in each layer. Thus, this part is forced to pick up only the most significant and representative features of the data.

The second half of the network performs the decoding function. This part has an increasing number of hidden units in each layer to enable it to reconstruct the original input from the encoded data.

Constraints are applied to obtain useful features from the autoencoder. Depending on the constraints applied or the lack of them, there are two types of autoencoders:

- **Undercomplete:** In this case, we force the autoencoder to learn the most salient features of the training data. If the dimension of the latent representation is the same as the input, the encoder can learn to perform the copying task without extracting any useful information about the distribution of the data.

- **Overcomplete:** In this case, the dimension of the latent representation is greater than the input. In this case, even a linear encoder and linear decoder can learn to copy the input to the output without learning anything useful about the data distribution.

Ideally, we need to avoid these two types of autoencoders mentioned. Carefully choose the code dimension as well as the capacity of the encoder and decoder based on the complexity of distribution to be modeled. The key is to achieve the right balance.

The layers in an autoencoder are as follows:

- Input layer

- Hidden layer: Usually a dense layer

- Output layer

- GaussianNoise

- GaussianDropout

Applications of an autoencoder include:

- Anomaly detection

- Image denoising

- Dimensionality reduction

Here's its implementation in TensorFlow 2.0:

```
lstm_autoencoder = Sequential()
# Encoder
lstm_autoencoder.add(LSTM(40, activation='relu', input_
shape=(timesteps, n_features), return_sequences=True))
lstm_autoencoder.add(LSTM(18, activation='relu', return_
sequences=False))
lstm_autoencoder.add(RepeatVector(timesteps))
# Decoder
lstm_autoencoder.add(LSTM(12, activation='relu', return_
sequences=True))
lstm_autoencoder.add(LSTM(30, activation='relu', return_
sequences=True))
lstm_autoencoder.add(TimeDistributed(Dense(n_features)))
lstm_autoencoder.compile(loss='rmse', optimizer=adam)
```

Variational Autoencoders

Variational autoencoders (VAEs) are powerful *generative* models (see Figure 9-7). They work with sequential or nonsequential data, continuous or discrete data, and labeled or completely unlabeled data.

Variational autoencoders can be CNN based. This means they will have layers similar to that of a CNN.

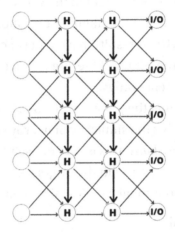

Figure 9-7. *Variational autoencoder. The H indicates the hidden cells*

Variational autoencoders are ideal for generative tasks due to their continuous latent spaces, which allow for easy random sampling and interpolation. They achieve this by generating two vector outputs:

- A vector of means

- A vector of standard deviations

This stochastic generation allows for slight variations in the encoding on each pass, even for the same mean and standard deviations.

They require encodings that are as close as possible to each other while still being distinct. This enables smooth interpolation and construction of *new* samples.

In order to force this, we introduce the Kullback–Leibler divergence (KL divergence) into the loss function. The KL divergence between two probability distributions simply measures how much they *diverge* from each other.

For VAEs, the KL loss is equivalent to the *sum* of all the KL divergences between the chosen point and the standard deviation.

Now, using purely KL loss results in a latent space in encodings placed randomly, near the center of the latent space, with little regard for similarity among nearby encodings.

Optimizing the two together, however, results in the generation of a latent space that maintains the similarity of nearby encodings on the *local scale* via clustering, yet *globally,* this is very densely packed near the latent space origin (compare the axes with the original).

The layers in a convolutional variational autoencoder are as follows:

- Convolutional

- Pooling

- Upsampling

- Dropout

- Dense

Applications of a variational autoencoder are as follows:

- Drawing

- Image generation

- Facial expression editing

- Forecasting from static images

- Synthetic music generation

Here's its implementation in TensorFlow 2.0:

```
#Encoder

def create_encoder():
input_img = Input(shape=(30, 30, 3))
vae_encoder = tf.keras.models.Sequential()
vae_encoder.add(Conv2D(32, (3, 3), activation='relu',
padding='same', input_shape=input_img)))
vae_encoder.addConv2D(32, (3, 3), activation='relu',
padding='same')
vae_encoder.addMaxPooling2D((2, 2), padding='same')
vae_encoder.addConv2D(64, (3, 3), activation='relu',
padding='same')
vae_encoder.addConv2D(64, (3, 3), activation='relu',
padding='same')
vae_encoder.addMaxPooling2D((2, 2), padding='same')
vae_encoder.addConv2D(128, (3, 3), activation='relu',
padding='same')
vae_encoder.addConv2D(128, (3, 3), activation='relu',
padding='same')
vae_encoder.addMaxPooling2D((2, 2), padding='same')
vae_encoder.compile(loss='categorical_crossentropy',
optimizer='rmsprop')
return encoder

e =create_encoder()

#Decoder

def create_decoder():
vae_decoder = tf.keras.models.Sequential()
vae_decoder = Conv2D(32, (3, 3), activation='relu',
padding='same')
```

```
vae_decoder = Conv2D(32, (3, 3), activation='relu',
padding='same')
vae_decoder = UpSampling2D((2, 2), interpolation='bilinear')
vae_decoder = Conv2D(64, (3, 3), activation='relu',
padding='same')
vae_decoder = Conv2D(64, (3, 3), activation='relu',
padding='same')
vae_decoder = UpSampling2D((2, 2), interpolation='bilinear')
vae_decoder = Conv2D(128, (3, 3), activation='relu',
padding='same')
vae_decoder = Conv2D(128, (3, 3), activation='relu',
padding='same')
vae_decoder = UpSampling2D((2, 2), interpolation='bilinear')
vae_decoder = Conv2D(3, (3, 3), activation='sigmoid',
padding='same')
vae_encoder.compile(loss='KL divergence', optimizer='rmsprop')
return decoder

d= create_decoder()

def create_vae(encoder, decoder):
    e.trainable=False
    vae_input = input_img
    vae= Model(inputs=vae_input, outputs=vae_output)
    vae.compile(loss='KL divergence', optimizer='rmsprop')
    return vae
vae = create_vae(e,d)
```

Denoising Autoencoders

A denoising autoencoder (DAE) is a stochastic version of the autoencoder
trained to reconstruct the input from a corrupted version of the same input
(see Figure 9-8).

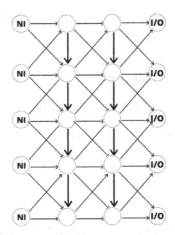

Figure 9-8. *Denoising autoencoder. I/O indicates the matched input/ output cells and NI indicates the noisy input cell*

When there are more nodes in the hidden layer than there are inputs, an autoencoder learns the "null function," meaning that the output equals the input. Denoising autoencoders solves this problem by randomly turning some of the input values to zero, essentially corrupting the data.

When calculating the loss function, it is important to compare the output values to the original input, not to the corrupted input. That way, the risk of learning the identity function instead of extracting features is eliminated.

The layers in a convolutional denoising autoencoder are as follows:

- Convolutional

- Pooling

- Upsampling

- Dropout

- Dense

Applications of a denoising autoencoder include:

- Watermark removal

- Image dimensionality reduction

- Image grayscale to color conversion

Here's its implementation in TensorFlow 2.0:

```
# Encoder

def create_encoder():

dae_encoder.add(Conv2D(32, (3, 3), activation='relu',
padding='same', input_shape=(28, 28, 1)))

dae_encoder.add(MaxPooling2D((2, 2), padding='same')
dae_encoder.add(Conv2D(32, (3, 3), activation='relu',
padding='same')
return encoder

e =create_encoder()

# Decoder

def decoder():

dae_decoder.add(Conv2D(32, (3, 3), activation='relu',
padding='same')
dae_decoder.add(UpSampling2D((2, 2))
dae_decoder.add(Conv2D(32, (3, 3), activation='relu',
padding='same')
dae_decoder.add(UpSampling2D((2, 2))

return decoder

d= create_decoder()
```

```
dae = Model(e, d)

dae.compile(optimizer='adadelta',loss='binary_crossentropy')
```

Recurrent Autoencoders

The recurrent autoencoder model summarizes sequential data through an encoder structure into a fixed-length vector and then reconstructs the original sequence through the decoder structure (see Figure 9-9). The summarized vector can be used to represent time-series features.

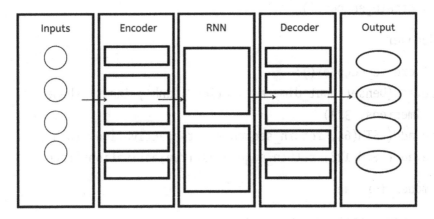

Figure 9-9. *Recurrent autoencoder*

The layers in a recurrent autoencoder are as follows:

- Embedding

- SimpleRNN

- SimpleRNNCell

- Dense

- Dropout

An application of a recurrent autoencoder is for sensor signal analysis.

Here's its implementation in TensorFlow 2.0:

```
#encoder

def create_encoder():

rae.add(Dense(128, activation='tanh', input_shape=(timesteps,
input_dim,))
rae.add(LSTM(64,return_sequences=True)
rae.add(LSTM(32,return_sequences=True)
return encoder

e = create_encoder()

#decoder

def create_decoder():
rae.add(Dense(input_dim, activation='tanh', inputs_shape
=(timesteps, 32))
rae.add(LSTM(64, return_sequences=True,activation='tanh')
rae.add(LSTM(128, return_sequences=True,activation='tanh')

# model for rae

def create_rae(encoder, decoder):
    e.trainable=False
    rae_input = input_val
    rae= Model(inputs=rae_input, outputs=rae_output)
    rae.compile(loss='binary_crossentropy', optimizer='rmsprop')
    return rae
rae = create_rae(e,d)
```

Sparse Autoencoders

Sparse autoencoders (SAE) provide an alternative method for introducing a bottleneck without reducing the number of nodes in the hidden layers (see Figure 9-10). Instead, the loss function penalizes activation within a layer.

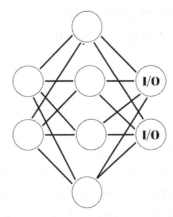

Figure 9-10. *Sparse autoencoder. I/O indicates the matched input/ output cells*

The layers in a sparse autoencoder are as follows:

- Input layer

- Hidden layer: Usually a dense layer

- Output layer

- GaussianNoise

- GaussianDropout

One application of a sparse autoencoder is with classification problems.

Here's its implementation in TensorFlow 2.0:

```
#encoder

def create_encoder():

sae.add(Dense(28, input_shape=(timesteps, input_dim,))
sae.add(LSTM(64,return_sequences=True)
sae.add(LSTM(32,return_sequences=True)
return encoder

e =create_encoder()

#decoder

def create_decoder():
sae.add(Dense(input_dim,inputs_shape =(timesteps, 32))
sae.add(LSTM(60, return_sequences=True,activation='tanh')
sae.add(LSTM(18, return_sequences=True,activation='tanh')
return decoder

d =create_decoder()

# model for sae

def create_sae(encoder, decoder):
    e.trainable=False
    sae_input = input_val
    sae= Model(inputs=sae_input, outputs=sae_output)
    sae.compile(loss='KL divergence', optimizer='rmsprop')
    return sae
sae = create_sae(e,d)
```

Note   The dimension of the latent space should be greater than the dimension of the input space.

Stacked Autoencoders

Stacked autoencoders are neural networks with multiple layers of sparse autoencoders (see Figure 9-11). When we add more hidden layers to an autoencoder, it helps reduce high-dimensional data to a smaller code representing important features. Each hidden layer is a more compact representation than the last hidden layer. For further layers we use uncorrupted input from the previous layers. After training a stack of encoders, we can use the output as an input to a standalone supervised machine learning model, as with support vector machines or multiclass logistic regression.

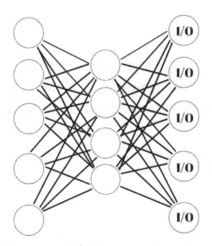

Figure 9-11. *Stacked autoencoder. I/O indicates the matched input/ output cells*

The layers in a stacked autoencoder are as follows:

- Input layer

- Hidden layer: Usually a dense layer

- Output layer

- GaussianNoise

- GaussianDropout

273

One application of a stacked autoencoder is for handwriting analysis. Here's its implementation in TensorFlow 2.0:

```
#encoder 1

def create_encoder1():
sae.add(Dense(28, input_shape=(timesteps, input_dim,))
sae.add(LSTM(64,return_sequences=True)
sae.add(LSTM(32,return_sequences=True)
return encoder

e1 = create_encoder1()

#decoder 1

def decoder1():
sae.add(Dense(input_dim,inputs_shape =(timesteps, 32))
sae.add(LSTM(60, return_sequences=True,activation='tanh')
sae.add(LSTM(18, return_sequences=True,activation='tanh')
return decoder

d1 =create_decoder1()

#encoder 2

def encoder2():
sae.add(Dense(28, input_shape=(timesteps, input_dim,))
sae.add(LSTM(64,return_sequences=True)
sae.add(LSTM(32,return_sequences=True)
return encoder

e2 =create_encoder1()

#decoder 2
```

```
def decoder2():
sae.add(Dense(input_dim,inputs_shape =(timesteps, 32))
sae.add(LSTM(60, return_sequences=True,activation='tanh')
sae.add(LSTM(18, return_sequences=True,activation='tanh')
return decoder

d2 =create_decoder2()

# model for sae

def create_sae(encoder, decoder):
    e.trainable=False
    sae_input = input_val
    sae= Model(inputs=sae_input, outputs=sae_output)
    sae.compile(loss='KL divergence', optimizer='rmsprop')
    return sae
sae = create_sae(e,d)
```

Convolutional Autoencoders

Normally there is a huge loss of information when slicing and stacking data. Instead of stacking the data, convolution autoencoders keep the spatial information of the input image data as it is (see Figure 9-12). It extracts information in what is called the *convolution layer*. For example, a flat 2D image is extracted to a thick square, then continues to become a long cubic, and another longer cubic. This process is designed to retain the spatial relationships in the data. This is the encoding process in an autoencoder. In the middle, there is a fully connected autoencoder. After that comes the decoding process that flattens the cubics to a 2D flat image.

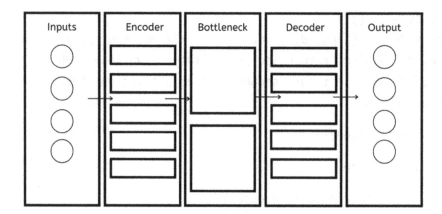

Figure 9-12. *Convolutional autoencoder*

The layers in a convolutional autoencoder are as follows:

- Convolutional

- Pooling

- Upsampling

- Dropout

- Dense

Applications of a convolutional autoencoder include:

- Handwriting analysis

- Image noise reduction

Here's its implementation in TensorFlow 2.0:

```
#Encoder

def create_encoder():
cae_encoder = tf.keras.Sequential()
cae_encoder.add(Conv2D(16, (3, 3), activation='relu',
padding='same', input_shape=(28, 28, 1)))
```

```
cae_encoder.add(MaxPooling2D((2, 2), padding='same')
cae_encoder.add(Conv2D(8, (3, 3), activation='relu',
padding='same')
cae_encoder.add(MaxPooling2D((2, 2), padding='same')
cae_encoder.add(Conv2D(8, (3, 3), activation='relu',
padding='same')
cae_encoder.add(MaxPooling2D((2, 2), padding='same')
return encoder

e =create_encoder()

#Decoder

def create_decoder():

cae_decoder.add(Conv2D(8, (3, 3), activation='relu',
padding='same')
cae_decoder.add(UpSampling2D((2, 2))(x)
cae_decoder.add(Conv2D(8, (3, 3), activation='relu',
padding='same')
cae_decoder.add(UpSampling2D((2, 2))
cae_decoder.add(Conv2D(16, (3, 3), activation='relu')
cae_decoder.add(UpSampling2D((2, 2))
cae_decoder.add(Conv2D(1, (3, 3), activation='sigmoid',
padding='same')

d =create_decoder()

autoencoder = Model(e, d)

autoencoder.compile(optimizer='adadelta', loss='binary_
crossentropy')
```

Stacked Denoising Autoencoders

In stacked denoising autoencoders, input corruption is used only for initial denoising (see Figure 9-13). This helps learn about important features present in the data. A stacked denoising autoencoder is simply many denoising autoencoders strung together.

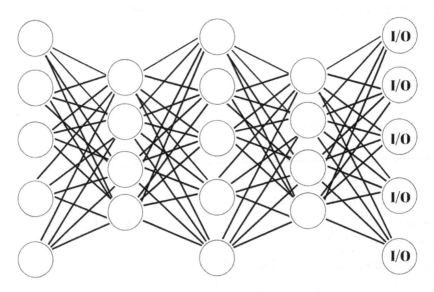

Figure 9-13. *Stacked denoising autoencoder. I/O indicates the matched input/output cells*

A key function of SDAs is unsupervised pretraining, layer by layer, as input is fed through. Once each layer is pretrained to conduct feature selection and extraction on the input from the preceding layer, a second stage of supervised fine-tuning can follow.

Stochastic Corruption in SDAs

Denoising autoencoders shuffle data around and learn about that data by attempting to reconstruct it. The act of shuffling is the noise, and the job of the network is to recognize the features within the noise that will allow it to classify the input. When a network is being trained, it generates a model and measures the distance between that model and the benchmark through a loss function. Its attempts to minimize the loss function involve resampling the shuffled inputs and reconstructing the data, until it finds those inputs that bring its model closest to the ground truth.

The layers in a stacked convolutional denoising autoencoder are as follows:

- Convolutional
- Pooling
- Upsampling
- Dropout
- Dense

Applications of a stacked denoising autoencoder include:

- Watermark removal
- Image dimensionality reduction
- Image grayscale to color conversion

Here's its implementation in TensorFlow 2.0:

```
# Encoder1

def create_encoder1():

dae_encoder.add(Conv2D(32, (3, 3), activation='relu',
padding='same', input_shape=(28, 28, 1)))

dae_encoder.add(MaxPooling2D((2, 2), padding='same')
dae_encoder.add(Conv2D(32, (3, 3), activation='relu',
padding='same')
return encoder1

E1 =create_encoder1()
```

```python
# Decoder1

def create_decoder1():

dae_decoder.add(Conv2D(32, (3, 3), activation='relu',
padding='same')
dae_decoder.add(UpSampling2D((2, 2)))
dae_decoder.add(Conv2D(32, (3, 3), activation='relu',
padding='same')
dae_decoder.add(UpSampling2D((2, 2)))

return decoder1

d1= create_decoder1()

# Encoder2

def create_encoder2():

dae_encoder.add(Conv2D(32, (3, 3), activation='relu',
padding='same', input_shape=(28, 28, 1)))

dae_encoder.add(MaxPooling2D((2, 2), padding='same')
dae_encoder.add(Conv2D(32, (3, 3), activation='relu',
padding='same')
return encoder2

e2 =create_encoder2()

# Decoder2

def create_decoder2():

dae_decoder.add(Conv2D(32, (3, 3), activation='relu',
padding='same')
dae_decoder.add(UpSampling2D((2, 2)))
```

```
dae_decoder.add(Conv2D(32, (3, 3), activation='relu',
padding='same')
dae_decoder.add(UpSampling2D((2, 2))

return decoder2

d2= create_decoder2()

# model for scae

def create_scae(e2, d2):
    e.trainable=False
    scae_input = input_val
    scae= Model(inputs=scae_input, outputs=scae_output)
    scae.compile(loss='KL divergence', optimizer='rmsprop')
    return scae
scae = create_scae(e2,d2)
```

Contractive Autoencoders

A contractive autoencoder is an unsupervised deep learning technique
that helps a neural network encode unlabeled training data (see
Figure 9-14). This is accomplished by constructing a loss term that
penalizes large derivatives of the hidden layer activations with respect
to the input training examples, essentially penalizing instances where a
small change in the input leads to a large change in the encoding space.

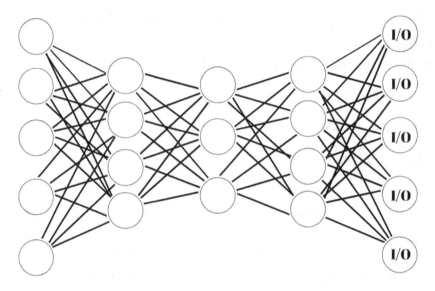

Figure 9-14. *Contractive autoencoder. I/O indicates the matched input/output cells*

The layers in a stacked contractive autoencoder are as follows:

- Convolutional

- Pooling

- Upsampling

- Dropout

- Dense

Applications of a contractive autoencoder include:

- Watermark removal

- Image dimensionality reduction

- Image grayscale to color conversion

- Information retrieval

- Anomaly detection

Here's its implementation in TensorFlow 2.0:

```
#Encoder

def create_encoder():
input_img = Input(shape=(30, 30, 3))
vae_encoder = tf.keras.models.Sequential()
vae_encoder.add(Conv2D(32, (3, 3), activation='relu',
padding='same', input_shape=input_img)))
vae_encoder.addConv2D(32, (3, 3), activation='relu',
padding='same')
vae_encoder.addMaxPooling2D((2, 2), padding='same')
vae_encoder.addConv2D(64, (3, 3), activation='relu',
padding='same')
vae_encoder.addConv2D(64, (3, 3), activation='relu',
padding='same')
vae_encoder.addMaxPooling2D((2, 2), padding='same')
vae_encoder.addConv2D(128, (3, 3), activation='relu',
padding='same')
vae_encoder.addConv2D(128, (3, 3), activation='relu',
padding='same')
vae_encoder.addMaxPooling2D((2, 2), padding='same')
vae_encoder.compile(loss='categorical_crossentropy',
optimizer='rmsprop')
return encoder

e =create_encoder()

#Decoder

def create_decoder():

vae_decoder = tf.keras.models.Sequential()
vae_decoder = Conv2D(32, (3, 3), activation='relu',
padding='same')
```

```python
vae_decoder = Conv2D(32, (3, 3), activation='relu',
padding='same')
vae_decoder = UpSampling2D((2, 2), interpolation='bilinear')
vae_decoder = Conv2D(64, (3, 3), activation='relu',
padding='same')
vae_decoder = Conv2D(64, (3, 3), activation='relu',
padding='same')
vae_decoder = UpSampling2D((2, 2), interpolation='bilinear')
vae_decoder = Conv2D(128, (3, 3), activation='relu',
padding='same')
vae_decoder = Conv2D(128, (3, 3), activation='relu',
padding='same')
vae_decoder = UpSampling2D((2, 2), interpolation='bilinear')
vae_decoder = Conv2D(3, (3, 3), activation='sigmoid',
padding='same')
vae_encoder.compile(loss='binary_crossentropy',
optimizer='rmsprop')
return decoder

d= create_decoder()

def create_vae(encoder, decoder):
    e.trainable=False
    vae_input = input_img
    vae= Model(inputs=vae_input, outputs=vae_output)
    vae.compile(loss='binary_crossentropy', optimizer='rmsprop')
    return vae
vae = create_vae(e,d)
```

Markov Chains

Markov chains are a way to statistically model random processes (see Figure 9-15). A Markov chain is a probabilistic automaton based on a principle of "memorylessness." In other words, the next state of the process depends only on the previous state and not the sequence of states. The probability distribution of state transitions is typically represented as the Markov chain's *transition matrix*. If the Markov chain has j possible states, the matrix will be a jxj matrix, such that entry (n, m) is the probability of transitioning from state n to state m. Additionally, the transition matrix must be a *stochastic matrix,* which is a matrix whose entries in each row must add up to exactly 1. Markov chains essentially consist of a set of transitions, which are determined by some probability distribution, that satisfy the Markov property. It is a set of mathematical systems that hop from one "state" (a situation or set of values) to another.

In probability theory and statistics, the term "Markov property" refers to the memoryless property of a stochastic process.

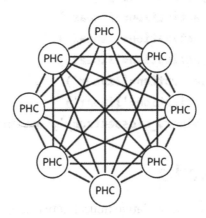

Figure 9-15. *Markov chain. PHC indicates the probabilistic hidden cell*

The layers in Markov chains are as follows:

- HamiltonianMonteCarlo

- Dense

Applications of Markov chains include:

- Text generation

- Financial modeling

- Video modeling

- DNA modeling

Here's its implementation in TensorFlow 2.0:

```
mc = tf.keras.models.Sequential()
mc.add(HamiltonianMonteCarlo(target_log_prob_fn=get_
unnormalized_log_probability(data),num_leapfrog_steps=3,step_
size=step_size,step_size_update_fn=tfp.mcmc.make_simple_step_
size_update_policy(),seed=1398)
mc.add(Dense(102, activation='linear')
mc.add(Dense(104, activation='linear')
mc.add(Dense(124, activation='linear')
mc.add(Dense(14, activation='linear')
mc.add(Dense(12, activation='linear')
mcr.compile(loss='binary_crossentropy', optimizer='rmsprop')
```

Hopfield Networks

A Hopfield network is an associative neural network model (see Figure 9-16). Hopfield networks are associated with the concept of simulating human memory through pattern recognition and storage. It is a type of recurrent neural network. However, Hopfield networks return patterns of the same size.

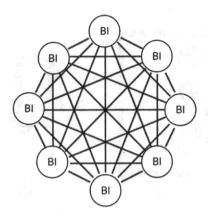

Figure 9-16. *Hopfield network. BI indicates the backfeed input cell*

How Human Memory Works

Human memory is not located in one singular place in the brain, rather it is a brain-wide process in which several different areas of the brain act in conjunction with one another (sometimes referred to a *distributed processing*). A simple task is actively and seamlessly reconstructed by the brain from many different areas: Each element of a memory (sights, sounds, words, and emotions) is encoded in the same part of the brain that originally created that fragment (visual cortex, motor cortex, language area, etc.), and recall of a memory effectively reactivates the neural patterns generated during the original encoding. Consider it to be a complex web, in which the threads symbolize the various elements of a memory, that join at intersections called nodes to form a whole rounded memory (see Figure 9-17).

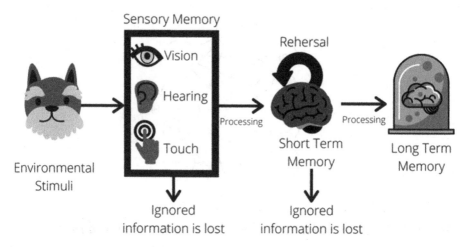

Figure 9-17. *How human memory works*

The layers in a Hopfield network are as follows:

- Embedding

- Dense

- Dropout

Applications of a Hopfield network include:

- Pattern recognition

- Image detection and recognition

- Enhancement of X-ray images

- Medical image restoration

Here's its implementation in TensorFlow 2.0:

```
hn = tf.keras.models.Sequential()
hn.add(HamiltonianMonteCarlo(target_log_prob_fn=get_
unnormalized_log_probability(data),num_leapfrog_steps=3)
hn.add(Dense(12, activation='linear'))
hn.add(Dense(14, activation='linear'))
```

```
hn.add(Dense(24, activation='linear')
hn.add(Dense(14, activation='linear')
hn.add(Dense(12, activation='linear')
hn.compile(loss='binary_crossentropy', optimizer='rmsprop')
```

Bidirectional Associative Memory

Bidirectional associative memory (BAM) was introduced by Bart Kosko in 1988. It is a type of recurrent neural network (see Figure 9-18).

Types of associative memory include:

- Auto-associative

- Hetero-associative

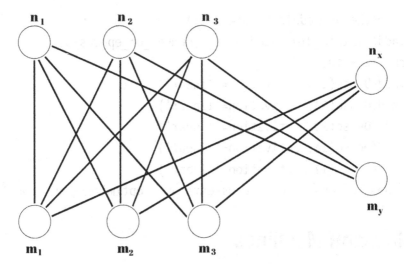

Figure 9-18. *Bidirectional associative memory*

BAM is hetero-associative, so given a pattern, it can return another pattern that's potentially a different size. It is similar to the Hopfield network in that they are both forms of associative memory.

The layers in bidirectional associative memory are as follows:

- Embedding

- Dense

- Dropout

Applications of bidirectional associative memory include:

- Pattern recognition

- Image detection and recognition

- Enhancement of X-Ray images

- Medical image restoration

Here's its implementation in TensorFlow 2.0:

```
bam = tf.keras.models.Sequential()
bam.add(visible_dim, hidden_dim, number_of_epochs=5,
batch_size= 10)
bam.add(Dense(21, activation='linear'))
bam.add(Dense(34, activation='linear'))
bam.add(Dense(20, activation='linear'))
bam.add(Dense(14, activation='linear'))
bam.add(Dense(12, activation='linear'))
bam.compile(loss='binary_crossentropy', optimizer='rmsprop')
```

Boltzmann Machines

The restricted Boltzmann machine (RBM) is an undirected graphical model (see Figure 9-19). It was initially introduced as "Harmonium" by Paul Smolensky in 1986. Restricted Boltzmann machines achieve state-of-the-art performance in collaborative filtering. A Boltzmann machine is a stochastic (non-deterministic) or generative deep learning model that only has visible (input) and hidden nodes. Energy-based models (EBMs) are a type of RBM that capture dependencies between variables by associating a scalar energy to each configuration of the variables. Inferences consist of clamping the value of observed variables and finding configurations of the remaining variables that minimize the energy. Learning consists of finding an energy function in which observed configurations of the variables are given lower energies than unobserved ones. EBMs can be seen as an alternative to probabilistic estimation for prediction, classification, or decision-making tasks because there is no requirement for proper normalization.

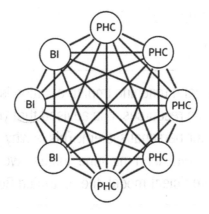

Figure 9-19. *Boltzmann machine. BI indicates the backfeed input cell and PHC indicates the probabilistic hidden cell*

Types of Boltzmann machines include the following:

- Restricted Boltzmann machines (RBMs)

- Deep belief networks (DBNs)

- Deep Boltzmann machines (DBMs)

The layers in a Boltzmann machine are as follows:

- Embedding

- Pooling

- Dense

- Dropout

Applications of the Boltzmann machine include:

- Dimensionality reduction

- Classification

- Regression

- Collaborative filtering

- Feature learning

- Topic modeling

Note   A full Boltzmann machine implementation is extremely difficult and exhausts resources. It is advised that you not implement this structure on your personal system. This is why we will not look at an example of a Boltzmann machine. Instead we will look at an example of a more efficient model, the restricted Boltzmann machine.

Restricted Boltzmann Machines

Restricted Boltzmann machines (RBMs) were invented by Geoffrey Hinton and are a two-layered artificial neural network (one layer being the visible layer and the other one being the hidden layer). These two layers are connected by a fully bipartite graph with generative capabilities (see Figure 9-20). They have the ability to learn a probability distribution over a set of inputs. RBMs are a special class of Boltzmann machine and they are restricted in terms of the connections between the visible and the hidden units. This makes it easy to implement them when compared to other Boltzmann machines. This means that every node in the visible layer is connected to every node in the hidden layer but no two nodes in the same group are connected to each other. This restriction allows for more efficient training algorithms than what is available for the general class of Boltzmann machines, in particular, the gradient-based contrastive divergence algorithm.

Types of RBMs include:

- Relational restricted Boltzmann machines

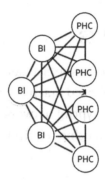

Figure 9-20. *Restricted Boltzmann machine. BI indicates the backfeed input cell and PHC indicates the probabilistic hidden cell*

The layers in a restricted Boltzmann machine are as follows:

- Embedding
- Pooling
- Dense
- Dropout

Applications of a restricted Boltzmann machine include the following:

- Dimensionality reduction
- Classification
- Regression

- Collaborative filtering

- Feature learning

- Topic modeling

Here's its implementation in TensorFlow 2.0:

```
rbm_2 = BernoulliRBM(learning_rate=0.05, n_iter=50,
n_components=150, random_state=0, verbose=True)
```

Deep Belief Networks

A deep belief network (DBN) is a sophisticated type of generative neural network that uses an unsupervised machine learning model to produce results (see Figure 9-21). This type of network illustrates some of the work that has been done recently in using relatively unlabeled data to build unsupervised models.

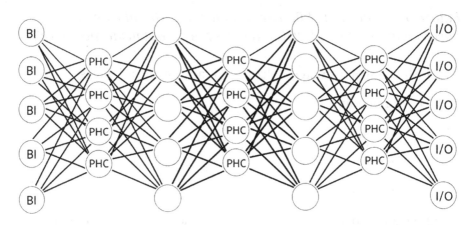

Figure 9-21. *Deep belief network. BI indicates the feedback input cell; PHC indicates the probabilistic hidden cell; and I/O indicates the matched input/output cells*

A deep belief network can be defined as a stack of restricted Boltzmann machines, in which each RBM layer communicates with both the previous and subsequent layers. The nodes of any single layer don't communicate with each other laterally.

This stack of RBMs might end with a Softmax layer to create a classifier, or it may simply help cluster unlabeled data in an unsupervised learning scenario.

With the exception of the first and final layers, each layer in a deep belief network has a double role—it serves as the hidden layer to the nodes that come before it and as the input (or "visible") layer to the nodes that come after it.

Types of deep belief networks (DBNs):

- Greedy layerwise training

- Wake-sleep algorithms

Deep belief networks (DBNs) are networks consisting of several middle layers of the restricted Boltzmann machine (RBM) and the last layer as a classifier.

Applications of deep belief networks include the following:

- Natural language processing

- Image generation

- Image recognition

- Video recognition

Here's its implementation in TensorFlow 2.0:

```
rbm_2 = BernoulliRBM(learning_rate=0.05, n_iter=50,
n_components=150, random_state=0, verbose=True)
rbm_2 = BernoulliRBM(learning_rate=0.05, n_iter=50,
n_components=150, random_state=0, verbose=True)
```

```
rbm_2 = BernoulliRBM(learning_rate=0.05, n_iter=50,
n_components=150, random_state=0, verbose=True)
rbm_2 = BernoulliRBM(learning_rate=0.05, n_iter=50,
n_components=150, random_state=0, verbose=True)
rbm.compile(loss='binary_crossentropy', optimizer='rmsprop')
```

Deconvolutional Networks

Deconvolutional networks, also known as deconvolutional neural networks, are very similar in nature to CNNs, but executed in reverse (see Figure 9-22). A signal may be lost due to having been convoluted with other signals. A convolutional neural network emulates the workings of a biological brain's frontal lobe function in image processing. The frontal lobe helps categorize and classify objects, in addition to distinguishing one item from another.

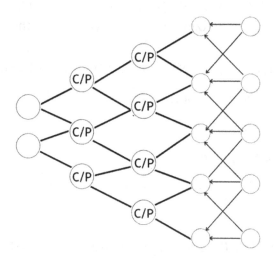

Figure 9-22. Deconvolutional network. C/P indicates convolutional or pool cells

The backward function can be seen as a reverse engineering of convoluted neural networks. It constructs layers captured as part of the entire image from the machine vision field of view and separates what has been convoluted.

Note   The deconvolution layer is more accurately described as a *transposed convolutional layer.* It performs a cross-correlation.

The layers in deconvolutional networks are as follows:

- Convolutional
- Conv2DTranspose
- Pooling
- Upsampling2D
- Dropout
- Dense

Applications of deconvolutional networks include the following:

- Image synthesis
- Image analysis

Here's its implementation in TensorFlow 2.0:

```
model = Sequential()

    model.add(Dense(25*15*20, input_shape=(56,)))
    model.add(Activation('relu'))

    model.add(Dense(25*15*20))
    model.add(Activation('relu'))

    model.add(Reshape((25,15,20)))
```

```
model.add(Conv2DTranspose(20, kernel_size=(3,3),
strides=(2,2), padding='same'))
model.add(Activation('relu'))

model.add(Conv2DTranspose(20, kernel_size=(3,3),
strides=(2,2), padding='same'))
model.add(Activation('relu'))

model.add(Conv2DTranspose(20, kernel_size=(3,3),
strides=(2,2), padding='same'))
model.add(Activation('relu'))

model.add(Conv2D(1, kernel_size=(3,3), strides=(1,1),
padding='same'))
model.add(Activation('relu'))

model.add(Lambda(lambda t: t[:,2:-2,2:-3,0]))

model.summary()
```

Deep Convolutional Inverse Graphics Networks

The deep convolutional inverse graphics network (DCIGN) is a combination of a CNN encoder and a deep neural network (DNN) decoder (see Figure 9-23). It has a long name, fitting for its long structure. However, the name is misleading, as it is not a network but rather a *variational autoencoder* (VAE).

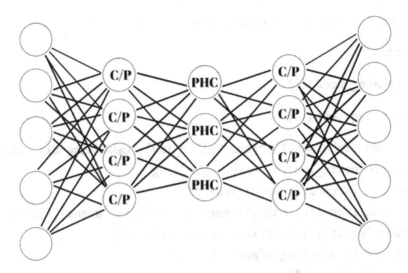

Figure 9-23. *Deep convolutional inverse graphics networks. C/P indicates convolutional or pool cells and I/O indicates the matched input/output cells*

The layers in a deconvolutional network include the following:

- Convolutional

- Conv2DTranspose

- Pooling

- Upsampling2D

- Dropout

- Dense

Applications of a deconvolutional network include the following:

- Automatic semantic image segmentation

- Upscaling images

- Image manipulation

Here's its implementation in TensorFlow 2.0:

```
#Encoder

def create_encoder():

model = Sequential()

model.add (Embedding(len(vocabulary_inv), embedding_dim, input_
length=sequence_length, name="embedding")
model.add (Dropout(dropout_prob[0])
model.add (Convolution1D(filters=num_filters, kernel_size=sz,
padding="valid", activation="relu",strides=1)
model.add (MaxPooling1D(pool_size=2)
model.add (Flatten()
model.add (Dropout(dropout_prob[1])
model.add (Dense(hidden_dims, activation="relu")
model.add (Dense(1, activation="sigmoid")

model.compile(loss="binary_crossentropy", optimizer="adam",
metrics=["accuracy"])

return encoder

e =create_encoder()

#Decoder

def decoder():

model = Sequential()

model.add ( Dense(n_hidden_1, activation='relu')
model.add ( Dense(n_hidden_2, activation='relu')
model.add ( Dense(n_hidden_3, activation='relu')
model.add ( Dense(n_output, activation='sigmoid')
model = Model(input_bits, out_put)
```

```
model.compile(optimizer='adam', loss='mse', metrics=[bit_err])
model.summary()

return decoder

d =create_decoder()

def create_dcign(encoder, decoder):
    e.trainable=False
    vaedcign_input = input_img
    dcign= Model(inputs=dcign_input, outputs=dcign_output)
    dcign.compile(loss='binary_crossentropy',
optimizer='rmsprop')
    return dcign
Dcign = create_dcign(e,d)
```

Liquid State Machines

A liquid state machine (LSM) is a type of spiking neural network (see Figure 9-24). Nodes are connected to each other at random and receive a time-varying input from external sources as well as other nodes. The connections are recurrent, which turns the inputs into a spatial temporal pattern of activations in the network node, which are read out by linear discriminant units. It is inspired by spiking in the human brain. Liquid state machines consist of leaky integrate and fire (LIF) neurons. They are not explicitly trained.

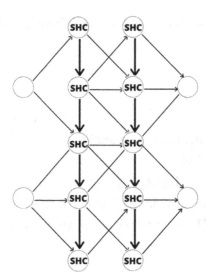

Figure 9-24. *Liquid state machines. SHC indicates a spiking hidden cell*

Human Brain Spiking

Spikes are very fast brain waves that earned their name due to their shape on the electroencephalogram (EEG). Each may be followed by slow delta waves. Spikes are distinct from other brain activity on an EEG (see Figure 9-25). Polyspikes are a series of spikes that happen quickly.

Figure 9-25. *Spikes in the human brain*

The layers in an LSM are as follows:

- Convolutional

- Conv2DTranspose

- Pooling

- Upsampling2D

- Dropout

- Dense

Applications of LSM include video activity recognition.

Here's its implementation in TensorFlow 2.0:

```
model = Sequential()

model.add (Embedding(len(vocabulary_inv), embedding_dim, input_
length=sequence_length, name="embedding")
model.add (Dropout(dropout_prob[0])
model.add (Convolution1D(filters=num_filters, kernel_size=sz,
padding="valid", activation="relu",strides=1)
model.add (MaxPooling1D(pool_size=2)
model.add (Flatten()
model.add (Dropout(dropout_prob[1])
model.add (Dense(hidden_dims, activation="relu")
model.add (Dense(1, activation="sigmoid")

model.compile(loss="binary_crossentropy", optimizer="adam",
metrics=["accuracy"])
```

Echo State Networks (ESNs)

An echo state network is a type of recurrent neural network (see Figure 9-26). The weights between the input, the hidden layer (the reservoir) *Win,* and the weights of the reservoir *Wr* are randomly assigned and not trainable.

The weights of the output neurons (the readout layer) are trainable and can be learned so that the network can reproduce specific temporal patterns. The hidden layer (or the reservoir) is very sparsely connected (typically <10% connectivity). The reservoir architecture creates a recurrent nonlinear embedding of the input, which can be then connected to the desired output. These final weights will be trainable. It is possible to connect the embedding to a different predictive model (such as a trainable NN or a ridge regression/ SVM for classification problems).

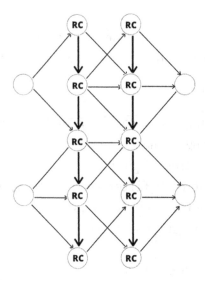

Figure 9-26. *Echo state network. RC indicates a recurrent cell*

The layers in an ESN include the following:

- Embedding

- SimpleRNN

- SimpleRNNCell

- Dense

- Dropout

Applications of ESNs include stock price predictions.

Here's its implementation in TensorFlow 2.0:

```
#Use ESN library with tensor flow and Keras

from ESN import EchoStateRNNCell
Import tensorflow
Import Keras

rrn = tf.keras.Sequential()
rnn.add(layers.Embedding(input_dim=1000, output_dim=64))
rnn.add(layers. EchoStateRNNCell(128))
rnn.add(layers.Dense(10, activation='softmax'))
rnn.add(layers. EchoStateRNNCell(90))
rnn.compile(loss='binary_crossentropy', optimizer='rmsprop'
```

Deep Residual Network (ResNet)

The core idea of ResNet was to introduce an "identity shortcut connection" that skips one or more layers (see Figure 9-27). Kaiming He, Xiangyu Zhang, Shaoqing Ren, and Jian Sun argue that stacking layers shouldn't degrade the network performance, because we could simply stack identity mappings (layer that doesn't do anything) upon the current network, and the resulting architecture would perform the same.

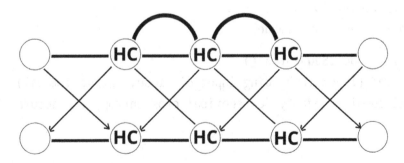

Figure 9-27. *Deep residual network. HC indicates the hidden cell*

This indicates that the deeper model should not produce a training error higher than its shallower counterparts. They hypothesize that letting the stacked layers fit a residual mapping is easier than letting them directly fit the desired underlying mapping. And the residual block explicitly allows it to do precisely that.

Due to its similar architecture, ResNet can be thought of as a special case of a highway network. However, highway networks themselves do not perform as well as ResNets. This tells us that it is more important to keep these "gradient highways" clear than to go for a larger solution space.

Following this intuition, the authors refined the residual block and proposed a preactivation variant of residual block, in which the gradients can flow through the shortcut connections to any other earlier layer, unimpeded.

ResNet is one of the early adopters of batch normalization (the batch norm paper authored by Ioffe and Szegedy was submitted to ICML in 2015). The basic building blocks for ResNets are the conv and identity blocks.

The only layer in a DRN is the embedding layer. One application of DRN is for image recognition.

Here's its implementation in TensorFlow 2.0:

```
#Use DRN library with tensorflow and Keras

import keras
Import tensorflow
import keras_resnet.models

Model = model.Sequential()
model.add(layers.Embedding(input_dim=1000, output_dim=64))
model.compile("adam", "categorical_crossentropy", ["accuracy"])
```

ResNeXt

ResNeXt follows the same split-transform-merge paradigm as ResNet, except in this variant, the outputs of different paths are merged by adding them together (see Figure 9-28). The authors, UC San Diego and Facebook AI Research (FAIR), introduced a hyper-parameter called cardinality—the number of independent paths—to provide a new way of adjusting the model capacity. Experiments show that accuracy can be gained more efficiently by increasing the cardinality than by going deeper or wider.

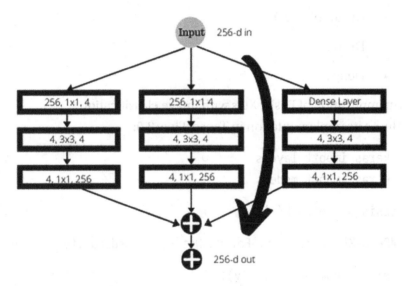

Figure 9-28. *ResNeXt*

The authors state that compared to Inception, this novel architecture is easier to adapt to new datasets/tasks, as it has a simple paradigm and only one hyper-parameter to be adjusted, while Inception has many hyper-parameters (like the kernel size of the convolutional layer of each path) to tune.

In practice, the "split-transform-merge" is usually done by a pointwise grouped convolutional layer, which divides its input into groups of feature maps and performs normal convolution respectively. Their outputs are depth-concatenated and then fed to a 1x1 convolutional layer.

The layers in a ResNeXt are as follows:

- Convolutional

- Conv2DTranspose

- Pooling

- Upsampling2D

- Dropout

- Dense

An application of ResNeXt is with image classification.

Here's its implementation in TensorFlow 2.0:

```
from keras import layers
from keras import models

def residual_network(x):

    #ResNeXt by default. For ResNet set `cardinality` = 1 above.

    def add_common_layers(y):
        y = layers.BatchNormalization()(y)
        y = layers.LeakyReLU()(y)

        return y

    def grouped_convolution(y, nb_channels, _strides):
        # when `cardinality` == 1 this is just a standard
        convolution
        if cardinality == 1:
            return layers.Conv2D(nb_channels, kernel_size=(3, 3),
            strides=_strides, padding='same')(y)
```

```
    assert not nb_channels % cardinality
    _d = nb_channels // cardinality

    # in a grouped convolution layer, input and output
    channels are divided into `cardinality` groups,
    # and convolutions are separately performed within each
    group
    groups = [ ]
    for j in range(cardinality):
        group = layers.Lambda(lambda z: z[:, :, :, j * _d:j
        * _d + _d])(y)
        groups.append(layers.Conv2D(_d, kernel_size=(3, 3),
        strides=_strides, padding='same')(group))

    # the grouped convolutional layer concatenates them as
    the outputs of the layer
    y = layers.concatenate(groups)

    return y

def residual_block(y, nb_channels_in, nb_channels_out, _
strides=(1, 1), _project_shortcut=False):

    #Our network consists of a stack of residual blocks.
    These blocks have the same topology,
    and are subject to two simple rules:

    #If producing spatial maps of the same size, the blocks
    share the same hyper-parameters (width and     filter
    sizes).
    #Each time the spatial map is down-sampled by a factor
    of 2, the width of the blocks is multiplied by a factor
    of 2.

    shortcut = y
```

```
# we modify the residual building block as a bottleneck
design to make the network more economical
y = layers.Conv2D(nb_channels_in, kernel_size=(1, 1),
strides=(1, 1), padding='same')(y)
y = add_common_layers(y)

# ResNeXt (identical to ResNet when `cardinality` == 1)
y = grouped_convolution(y, nb_channels_in,
_strides=_strides)
y = add_common_layers(y)

y = layers.Conv2D(nb_channels_out, kernel_size=(1, 1),
strides=(1, 1), padding='same')(y)
# batch normalization is employed after aggregating the
transformations and before adding to the shortcut
y = layers.BatchNormalization()(y)

# identity shortcuts used directly when the input and
output are of the same dimensions
if _project_shortcut or _strides != (1, 1):
    # when the dimensions increase projection
    shortcut is used to match dimensions (done by 1×1
    convolutions)
    # when the shortcuts go across feature maps of two
    sizes, they are performed with a stride of 2
    shortcut = layers.Conv2D(nb_channels_out, kernel_
    size=(1, 1), strides=_strides, padding='same')
    (shortcut)
    shortcut = layers.BatchNormalization()(shortcut)

y = layers.add([shortcut, y])
```

```
    # relu is performed right after each batch
    normalization,
    # expect for the output of the block where relu is
    performed after the adding to the shortcut
    y = layers.LeakyReLU()(y)

    return y

# conv1
x = layers.Conv2D(64, kernel_size=(7, 7), strides=(2, 2),
padding='same')(x)
x = add_common_layers(x)

# conv2
x = layers.MaxPool2D(pool_size=(3, 3), strides=(2, 2),
padding='same')(x)
for i in range(3):
    project_shortcut = True if i == 0 else False
    x = residual_block(x, 128, 256, _project_
    shortcut=project_shortcut)

# conv3
for i in range(4):
    # down-sampling is performed by conv3_1, conv4_1, and
    conv5_1 with a stride of 2
    strides = (2, 2) if i == 0 else (1, 1)
    x = residual_block(x, 256, 512, _strides=strides)

# conv4
for i in range(6):
    strides = (2, 2) if i == 0 else (1, 1)
    x = residual_block(x, 512, 1024, _strides=strides)
```

```
# conv5
for i in range(3):
    strides = (2, 2) if i == 0 else (1, 1)
    x = residual_block(x, 1024, 2048, _strides=strides)

x = layers.GlobalAveragePooling2D()(x)
x = layers.Dense(1)(x)

return x

image_tensor = layers.Input(shape=(img_height, img_width,
img_channels))
network_output = residual_network(image_tensor)

model = models.Model(inputs=[image_tensor], outputs=[network_
output])
print(model.summary())
```

Source:
https://gist.github.com/mjdietzx/0cb95922aac14d446a6530f87b3a04
ce

Neural Turing Machines

The authors Alex Graves, Greg Wayne, and Ivo Danihelka designed the
neural Turing machine, which interacts with external memory resources
using attentional processes (see Figure 9-29). We create a memory
structure in the form of an array, then read and write from it. It is important
to note that we do not have an unlimited memory capacity to hold all the
information, and we access information by similarity or relevancy.

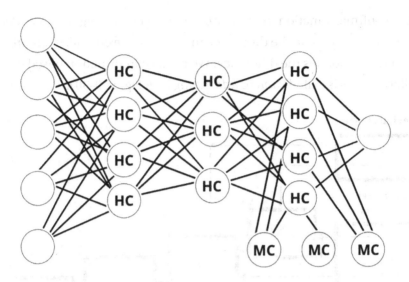

Figure 9-29. *Neural Turing machine. HC indicates hidden cells and MC indicates memory cells*

For example, imagine a memory structure m_t, which contains x rows, each with y elements. Each row represents a piece of information (memory). We retrieve information from our memory using the weight *we,* including factors like our current input, previous focus, and possible shifting and blurring.

Reading

In conventional programming, memory is accessed by the index of $m_t[i]$. We then derive a reading mechanism where our result is a weighted sum of our memory, where the sum of all weights equals one. In word embedding, we use linear algebra to manipulate relationships. Sometimes we merge information based on accumulated knowledge. A controller extracts features (c_t) from the input and we use it to compute the weights.

To compute the weight, *we,* measure the similarity between c_t and each of our memory entries. Calculate a score, s, using cosine similarity. Here, n is our extracted feature c_t, and m is each individual row in our memory.

Apply a Softmax function to the score to compute the weight. β_t is added to amplify or attenuate the difference in scores. For example, if it is greater than one, it amplifies the difference. We retrieve information based on similarity. This is called *content addressing* (see Figure 9-30).

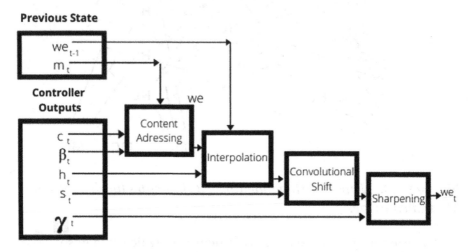

Figure 9-30. *The process of memory writing*

The memory writing process is made up of the previous state and new input. We erase part of the previous state where *pt* is an erase vector. Then, we write our new information, where *adt* is what we want to add. Here, through a controller that generates *we*, we read and write from our memory.

Applications of neural Turing machines are as follows:

- Natural language processing

- Meta learning

Here's its implementation in TensorFlow 2.0:

```
import tensorflow as tf
from ntm_cell import NTMCell
from ntm import NTM
```

```
Model = model.Sequential()
model.add(NTMCell(input_dim=1000, output_dim=64))
model.compile("adam", "categorical_crossentropy", ["accuracy"])
```

Capsule Networks

CAPSNet was proposed by Geoffrey Hinton in 2017 (see Figure 9-31). It aims to solve the problem of convolutional neural networks (CNN). CNNs are good at classifying images, but they fail when images are rotated or tilted, or when an image has the features of the desired object, but not in the correct order or position. The reason a CNN has trouble classifying these types of images is that it performs multiple phases of convolution and pooling. The pooling step sums and reduces the information in each feature discovered in the image. In this process, it loses important information such as the position of the feature and its relation to other features.

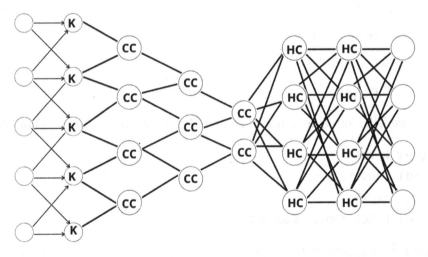

Figure 9-31. *Capsule network. HC indicates hidden cells; K indicates kernels; and CC indicates capsule cells*

CAPSNet Architecture

CAPSNet is based on the concept of neural "capsules." It starts with the convolution step, just like a regular CNN. But instead of the pooling step, when the network discovers features in the image, it reshapes them into vectors, "squashes" them using a special activation function, and feeds each feature into a *capsule*. This is a specialized neural structure that deals only with this feature. Each capsule in the first layer begins processing and then feeds its result to one or more levels of secondary capsules, nested within the first capsule. This is called *routing by agreement*. The primary capsule detects the learned features, while preserving contextual information like position and relation to other elements.

Applications of CAPSNet include the classification of images.

The layers of CAPSNet are as follows:

- Convolutional

- Conv2DTranspose

- Pooling

- Upsampling2D

- Dropout

- Dense

Here's the implementation of a neural Turing machine in TensorFlow 2.0:

```
import keras
Import tensorflow
Import capsNet
from capsNet import CapsNet

Model = model.Sequential()
model.add(layers.Embedding(input_dim=1000, output_dim=64))
model.compile("adam", "categorical_crossentropy", ["accuracy"])
```

LeNet-5

LeNet is one of the simplest architectures proposed by Yann LeCun (see Figure 9-32). It has two convolutional and three fully-connected layers. The average-pooling layer as we know it now was called a *sub-sampling layer* and it had trainable weights (which isn't the current practice of designing CNNs nowadays).

This architecture has become the standard template—stacking convolutions and pooling layers, and ending the network with one or more fully-connected layers.

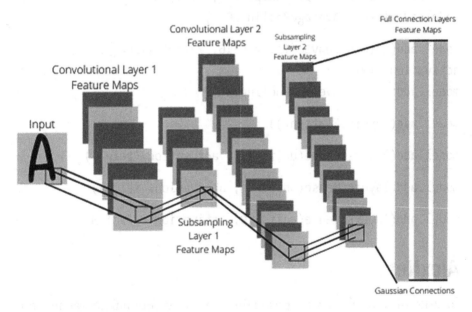

Figure 9-32. *LeNet-5*

One application of LeNet-5 is with handwriting recognition. The layers of LeNet-5 are as follows:

- Convolutional

- Conv2DTranspose

- Pooling

- Upsampling2D

- Dropout

- Dense

Here's its implementation in TensorFlow 2.0:

```
model = keras.Sequential()

model.add(layers.Conv2D(filters=6, kernel_size=(3, 3),
activation='relu', input_shape=(32,32,1)))
model.add(layers.AveragePooling2D())

model.add(layers.Conv2D(filters=16, kernel_size=(3, 3),
activation='relu'))
model.add(layers.AveragePooling2D())

model.add(layers.Flatten())

model.add(layers.Dense(units=120, activation='relu'))

model.add(layers.Dense(units=84, activation='relu'))

model.add(layers.Dense(units=10, activation = 'softmax'))
```

AlexNet

In 2012, Alex Krizhevsky proposed the deep convolutional neural network. The AlexNet contains eight neural network layers, five convolutional and three fully-connected (see Figure 9-33). This laid the foundation for the traditional CNN, a convolutional layer followed by an activation function followed by a max-pooling operation (sometimes the pooling operation is omitted to preserve the spatial resolution of the image). AlexNet just stacked a few more layers onto LeNet-5. He was the first to implement rectified linear units (ReLUs) as activation functions.

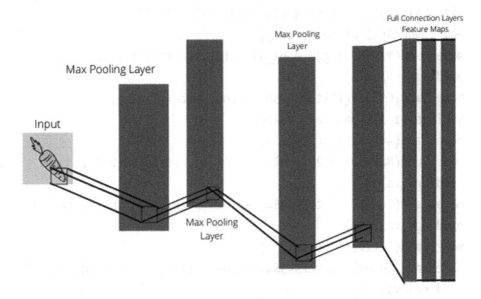

Figure 9-33. *AlexNet*

The layers of an AlexNet are as follows:

- Convolutional
- Conv2DTranspose
- Pooling
- Upsampling2D
- Dropout
- Dense

One application of AlexNet is with machine vision.

Here's its implementation in TensorFlow 2.0:

```
model = Sequential()
model.add(Conv2D(filters=96, input_shape=(224,224,3), kernel_
size=(11,11), strides=(4,4), padding='valid'))
model.add(Activation('relu'))
model.add(MaxPooling2D(pool_size=(2,2), strides=(2,2),
padding='valid'))
model.add(Conv2D(filters=256, kernel_size=(11,11),
strides=(1,1), padding='valid'))
model.add(Activation('relu'))
model.add(MaxPooling2D(pool_size=(2,2), strides=(2,2),
padding='valid'))
model.add(Conv2D(filters=384, kernel_size=(3,3), strides=(1,1),
padding='valid'))
model.add(Activation('relu'))
model.add(Conv2D(filters=384, kernel_size=(3,3), strides=(1,1),
padding='valid'))
model.add(Activation('relu'))
model.add(Conv2D(filters=256, kernel_size=(3,3), strides=(1,1),
padding='valid'))
model.add(Activation('relu'))
model.add(MaxPooling2D(pool_size=(2,2), strides=(2,2),
padding='valid'))
model.add(Flatten())
model.add(Dense(4096, input_shape=(224*224*3,)))
model.add(Activation('relu'))
model.add(Dropout(0.4))
model.add(Dense(4096))
model.add(Activation('relu'))
```

```
model.add(Dropout(0.4))
model.add(Dense(1000))
model.add(Activation('relu'))
model.add(Dropout(0.4))
model.add(Dense(17))
model.add(Activation('softmax'))
model.compile(loss=keras.losses.categorical_crossentropy,
optimizer='adam', metrics=["accuracy"])
```

GoogLeNet

GoogLeNet (see Figure 9-34) is a 22 layer deep network designed by the
Google team in 2014 for classification and detection in the "ImageNet
Large-Scale Visual Recognition Challenge" 2014 (ILSVRC2014). To
optimize quality, the architectural decisions were based on the Hebbian
principle and the intuition of multiscale processing.

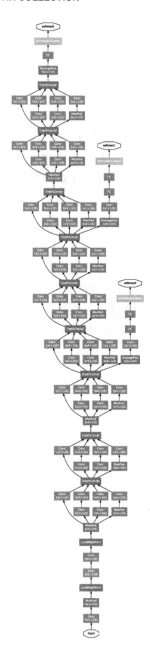

Figure 9-34. *GoogLeNet*
Image Source: *https://arxiv.org/pdf/1409.4842v1.pdf*

The Hebbian theory is a neuro-scientific theory that attempts to explain synaptic plasticity, the adaptation of brain neurons during the learning process. It states that an increase in synaptic efficacy arises from a presynaptic cell's repeated and persistent stimulation of a postsynaptic cell.

The layers of GoogLeNet are as follows:

- Convolutional

- Conv2DTranspose

- Pooling

- Upsampling2D

- Dropout

- Dense

Applications of GoogLeNet include the following:

- Object detection

- Object classification

Here's its implementation in TensorFlow 2.0:

```
model = Sequential()
model.add(Conv2D(10, (1,1), padding='same', activation='relu')
(input_img)
model.add(Conv2D(10, (3,3), padding='same', activation='relu')
(layer_1)
model.add(Conv2D(10, (1,1), padding='same', activation='relu')
(input_img)
model.add(Conv2D(10, (5,5), padding='same', activation='relu')
(layer_2)
model.add(MaxPooling2D((3,3), strides=(1,1), padding='same')
(input_img)
model.add(Conv2D(10, (1,1), padding='same', activation='relu')
(layer_3)
```

```
model.add(dense_1 = Dense(1200, activation='relu')(flat_1)
model.add(dense_2 = Dense(600, activation='relu')(dense_1)
model.add(dense_3 = Dense(150, activation='relu')(dense_2)
model.add(Dense(nClasses, activation='softmax')(dense_3)
model.compile(optimizer='adam', loss='categorical_
crossentropy', metrics=['accuracy'])
```

Xception

The Xception network was designed by François Chollet and is an adaptation of Inception, where the Inception modules have been replaced with depthwise separable convolutions (see Figure 9-35). Xception takes the Inception hypothesis to the *eXtreme* (hence the name).

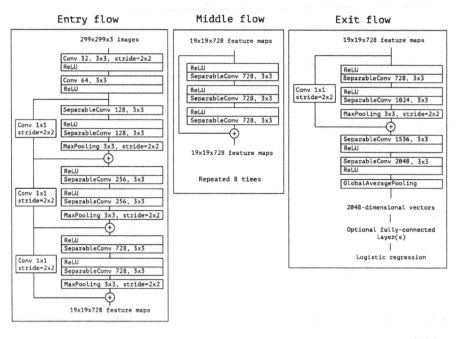

Figure 9-35. *Xception*
Source: *https://miro.medium.com/max/1128/1*hOcAEj9QzqgBXcwU zmEvSg.png*

The layers in an Xception network are as follows:

- Convolutional

- Conv2DTranspose

- Pooling

- Upsampling2D

- Dropout

- Dense

Applications of Xception include the following:

- Object detection

- Object classification

Here's its implementation in TensorFlow 2.0:

```
model = Sequential()
model.add(Conv2D(32, (3, 3), strides=(2, 2), use_bias=False,
name='block1_conv1')
model.add(Conv2D(64, (3, 3), use_bias=False, name='block1_
conv2')
model.add(Conv2D(128, (1, 1), strides=(2, 2), padding='same',
use_bias=False)
model.add(SeparableConv2D(128, (3, 3), padding='same', use_
bias=False, name='block2_sepconv1')
model.add(SeparableConv2D(128, (3, 3), padding='same', use_
bias=False, name='block2_sepconv2')
model.add(MaxPooling2D((3, 3), strides=(2, 2), padding='same',
name='block2_pool')
model.add(Conv2D(256, (1, 1), strides=(2, 2), padding='same',
use_bias=False)
```

```
model.add(SeparableConv2D(256, (3, 3), padding='same', use_
bias=False, name='block3_sepconv1')
model.add(SeparableConv2D(256, (3, 3), padding='same', use_
bias=False, name='block3_sepconv2')
model.add(MaxPooling2D((3, 3), strides=(2, 2), padding='same',
name='block3_pool')
model.add(Conv2D(728, (1, 1), strides=(2, 2), padding='same',
use_bias=False)
model.add(SeparableConv2D(728, (3, 3), padding='same', use_
bias=False, name='block4_sepconv1')
model.add(SeparableConv2D(728, (3, 3), padding='same', use_
bias=False, name='block4_sepconv2')
model.add(MaxPooling2D((3, 3), strides=(2, 2), padding='same',
name='block4_pool')
model.add(SeparableConv2D(728, (3, 3), padding='same', use_
bias=False, name=prefix + '_sepconv1')
 model.add(SeparableConv2D(728, (3, 3), padding='same', use_
 bias=False, name=prefix + '_sepconv2')
model.add(SeparableConv2D(728, (3, 3), padding='same', use_
bias=False, name=prefix + '_sepconv3')
 model.add(Conv2D(1024, (1, 1), strides=(2, 2),padding='same',
 use_bias=False)
 model.add(SeparableConv2D(728, (3, 3), padding='same', use_
 bias=False, name='block13_sepconv1')
model.add(SeparableConv2D(1024, (3, 3), padding='same', use_
bias=False, name='block13_sepconv2')
model.add(MaxPooling2D((3, 3), strides=(2, 2), padding='same',
name='block13_pool')
model.add(SeparableConv2D(1536, (3, 3), padding='same', use_
bias=False, name='block14_sepconv1')
```

```
model.add(SeparableConv2D(2048, (3, 3),padding='same', use_
bias=False, name='block14_sepconv2')
model.add(layers.GlobalMaxPooling2D())
model.compile(optimizer='adam', loss='categorical_
crossentropy', metrics=['accuracy'])
```

Optimizers

This section covers the optimizers that you should be aware of for your deep learning projects.

Stochastic Gradient Descent

A gradient is the slope of a function. The degree of change of a parameter given the amount of change in another parameter. Mathematically, it can be described as the partial derivatives of a set of parameters with respect to its inputs. The larger the gradient, the steeper the slope (see Figure 9-36).

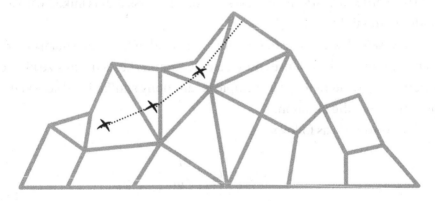

Figure 9-36. *Stochastic gradient descent*

Gradient descent is a convex function. It is an iterative method used to find the values of the parameters of a function. It minimizes the cost function as much as possible. The parameters are initially defined as a particular value and from that, gradient descent is executed in an iterative process to find the optimal values of the parameters, using calculus, to find the minimum possible value of the given cost function.

In gradient descent, the "batch" denotes the total number of samples from a dataset that is used for calculating the gradient for each iteration. In typical gradient descent optimization, such as batch gradient descent, the batch is taken to be the whole dataset. Although using the whole dataset is useful for getting to the minima in a less noisy or less random manner, a problem arises when our datasets get huge.

Suppose you have a million samples in your dataset. If you use a typical gradient descent optimization technique, you will have to use all of the one million samples to complete one iteration while performing the gradient descent, and this has to be done for every iteration until the minima is reached. Hence, it becomes computationally very expensive to perform.

The word *stochastic* means a system or a process that is linked with a random probability.

A few samples are selected randomly instead of the whole dataset for each iteration. In SGD, it uses only a single sample, i.e., a batch size of one, to perform each iteration. The sample is randomly shuffled and selected for performing the iteration.

The formula is as follows:

$$w_{new} = w - \alpha \frac{\partial L}{\partial w}$$

Where:

- $\partial L / \partial w$ is the gradient component
- α is the learning rate

- w_{new} is the new weight

- w is the weight

The advantages of SGD include the following:

- Stochastic gradient descent with momentum renders some speed to the optimization and also helps escape local minima better.

- Uses SGD and Nesterov for shallow networks.

The disadvantages of SGD include the following:

- It doesn't work well when the parameters are in different scales, as a low learning rate will make the learning slow, while a large learning rate might lead to oscillations.

- It can't handle saddle points efficiently.

- There's a common learning rate for all parameters.

Here's its implementation in Keras:

```
keras.optimizers.SGD(learning_rate=0.01, momentum=0.0,
nesterov=False)
```

RMSProp

The RMSProp optimizer is similar to the gradient descent algorithm with momentum. Momentum takes past gradients into account to smooth out the steps of gradient descent. It can be applied with batch gradient descent, mini-batch gradient descent, or stochastic gradient descent.

RMSProp is an adaptive learning rate that tries to improve on AdaGrad. Instead of taking the cumulative sum of squared gradients, it takes the exponential moving average (again!) of these gradients.

The RMSProp optimizer restricts the oscillations in the vertical direction. Therefore, we can increase our learning rate and our algorithm could take larger steps in the horizontal direction, thus converging faster.

Gradients of very complex functions like neural networks have a tendency to either vanish or explode as the energy is propagated through the function. The more complex the function is, the worse this problem becomes.

RMSProp uses a moving average of squared gradients to normalize the gradient itself. That has an effect of balancing the step size. Decreasing the step for large gradients avoids exploding, and increasing the step for small gradients avoids vanishing.

The formula is as follows:

$$w_{t+1} = w_t - \frac{\alpha}{\sqrt{v_t + \epsilon}} \cdot \frac{\partial L}{\partial w_t}$$

When:

$$v_t = \beta v_{t-1} + (1 - \beta) \left[\frac{\partial L}{\partial w_t} \right]^2$$

Where:

- $\alpha = 0.001$
- $\beta = 0.9$ (recommended by the authors of the paper)
- $\varepsilon = 10^{-6}$

The advantages of RMSProp are as follows:

- Handles saddle points well
- Good for deep nets
- Pseudo curvature information
- Ideal for mini-batch learning

The disadvantages of RMSProp are as follows:

- If the learning rate is big, the weights slosh to and fro across the ravine.

- If the learning rate is too big, this oscillation diverges.

Here's its implementation in Keras:

```
keras.optimizers.RMSprop(learning_rate=0.001, rho=0.9)
```

AdaGrad

AdaGrad penalizes the learning rate too harshly for parameters that are frequently updated and gives more learning rate to sparse parameters that are not updated as frequently. It is ideal for datasets with sparse data, such as tf-idf, etc. This is because it makes big updates to infrequent parameters and small updates to frequent parameters. The AdaGrad algorithm is just a variant of preconditioned stochastic gradient descent.

The main benefit of AdaGrad is that we don't need to tune the learning rate manually. Most implementations use a default value of 0.01.

The formula is as follows:

$$w_{t+1} = w_t - \frac{\alpha}{\sqrt{v_t + \in}} \cdot \frac{\partial L}{\partial w_t}$$

When:

$$v_t = v_{t-1} + \left[\frac{\partial L}{\partial w_t} \right]^2$$

Where:

- $\alpha = 0.01$

- $\varepsilon = 10^{-7}$

One advantage of AdaGrad is that it handles saddle points well. One disadvantage of AdaGrad is that its learning rate is always decreasing and decaying.

Here's its implementation in Keras:

```
keras.optimizers.Adagrad(learning_rate=0.01)
```

AdaDelta

AdaDelta is similar to RMSProp. The only difference is that AdaDelta doesn't require an initial learning rate constant to start with. AdaDelta is an extension of AdaGrad and it monotonically reduces the learning rate. It does this by restricting the window of the past accumulated gradient to the fixed size of w. Running average at time, t, then depends on the previous average and the current gradient. In AdaDelta we do not need to set the default learning rate, as we take the ratio of the running average of the previous time steps to the current gradient.

The formula is as follows:

$$w_{t+1} = w_t - \frac{\sqrt{D_{t-1} + \epsilon}}{\sqrt{v_t + \epsilon}} \cdot \frac{\partial L}{\partial w_t}$$

When:

$$D_t = \beta D_{t-1} + (1 - \beta)[\Delta w_t]^2$$

$$v_t = \beta v_{t-1} + (1 - \beta)\left[\frac{\partial L}{\partial w_t}\right]^2$$

$$\Delta w_t = w_t - w_{t-1}$$

Where:

- $\beta = 0.95$

- $\varepsilon = 10^{-6}$

The advantages of AdaDelta are as follows:

- It handles saddle points well.

- It is an extension of AdaGrad, which tends to remove the decaying learning rate problem.

- We don't need to set a default learning rate.

Here's its implementation in Keras:

```
keras.optimizers.Adadelta(learning_rate=1.0, rho=0.95)
```

Adam

Adam combines the good properties of AdaDelta and RMSProp and hence tends to do better with most problems.

The formula is as follows:

$$w_{t+1} = w_t - \frac{\alpha}{\sqrt{\hat{v}_t + T}} \cdot \hat{m}_t$$

When:

$$\hat{m}_t = \frac{m_t}{1 - \beta_1^t}$$

$$\hat{v}_t = \frac{v_t}{1 - \beta_2^t}$$

$$m_t = \beta_1 m_{t-1} + (1 - \beta_1) \frac{\partial L}{\partial w_t}$$

$$v_t = \beta_2 v_{t-1} + (1 - \beta_2) \left[\frac{\partial L}{\partial w_t} \right]^2$$

Where:

- $\alpha = 0.001$
- $\beta_1 = 0.9$
- $\beta_2 = 0.999$
- $\varepsilon = 10^{-8}$

The advantages of Adam are as follows:

- Handles saddle points well.
- Suitable for deep nets.
- Relatively low memory requirements (though higher than gradient descent and gradient descent with momentum).
- Usually works well even with little tuning of hyper-parameters.

Here's its implementation in Keras:

```
keras.optimizers.Adam(learning_rate=0.001, beta_1=0.9,
beta_2=0.999, amsgrad=False)
```

Note   When in doubt, Adam is the best choice.

Adamax

Adamax is helpful when there are sparse parameter updates. It is an adaptation of the Adam optimizer.

The formula is as follows:

$$w_{t+1} = w_t - \frac{\alpha}{v_t} \cdot \hat{m}_t$$

When:

$$\hat{m}_t = \frac{m_t}{1 - \beta_1^t}$$

$$m_t = \beta_1 m_{t-1} + (1 - \beta_1) \frac{\partial L}{\partial w_t}$$

$$v_t = \max\left(\beta_2 v_{t-1}, \left| \frac{\partial L}{\partial w_t} \right| \right)$$

Where:

- $\alpha = 0.002$
- $\beta_1 = 0.9$
- $\beta_2 = 0.999$

The advantages of Adamax are as follows:

- Infinite-order norm makes the algorithm stable
- Suitable for sparsely updated parameters

Here's its implementation in Keras:

```
keras.optimizers.Adamax(learning_rate=0.002, beta_1=0.9,
beta_2=0.999)
```

Nesterov Accelerated Gradient (NAG)

Nesterov accelerated gradient is a slight variation of normal gradient descent that can speed up training and improve convergence significantly. Nesterov momentum is a simple change to normal momentum. Here, the gradient term is not computed from the current position. This helps because, while the gradient term always points in the right direction, the momentum term may not. If the momentum term points in the wrong direction or overshoots, the gradient can still "go back" and correct it in the same update step.

The formula is as follows:

$$w_{t+1} = w_t - \alpha m_t$$

When:

$$m_t = \beta m_{t-1} + (1 - \beta)\frac{\partial L}{\partial w *}$$

Where:

- m is initialized to 0
- $\beta = 0.9$

Nadam

Nadam is Adam RMSProp with the Nesterov momentum. Nadam combines NAG and Adam. Nadam is employed for noisy gradients or for gradients with high curvatures. The learning process is accelerated by summing up the exponential decay of the moving averages for the previous and current gradient.

The formula is as follows:

$$w_{t+1} = w_t - \frac{\alpha}{\sqrt{\hat{v}_t} + \epsilon}\left(\beta_1 \hat{m}_t + \frac{1 - \beta_1}{1 - \beta_1^t} \cdot \frac{\partial L}{\partial w_t}\right)$$

When:

$$\hat{m}_t = \frac{m_t}{1 - \beta_1^t}$$

$$\hat{v}_t = \frac{v_t}{1 - \beta_2^t}$$

$$m_t = \beta_1 m_{t-1} + (1 - \beta_1)\frac{\partial L}{\partial w_t}$$

$$v_t = \beta_2 v_{t-1} + (1 - \beta_2)\left[\frac{\partial L}{\partial w_t}\right]^2$$

Where:

- $\alpha = 0.002$

- $\beta_1 = 0.9$

- $\beta_2 = 0.999$

- $\varepsilon = 10^{-7}$

Here's its implementation in Keras:

```
keras.optimizers.Nadam(learning_rate=0.002, beta_1=0.9,
beta_2=0.999)
```

Loss Functions

Recall that when a network is being trained, it generates a model and measures the distance between that model and the benchmark through a loss function. Its attempts to minimize the loss function involve resampling the shuffled inputs and reconstructing the data, until it finds those inputs that bring its model closest to the ground truth. The following sections discuss the various loss functions you will come across.

Mean Squared Error (MSE)

Mean squared error (MSE) is one of the most common loss functions. The MSE loss function is widely used in linear regression to measure the performance of the model. To calculate MSE, square the difference between the predictions and the ground truth. Then calculate the average across the whole dataset.

Here's its implementation in Keras:

```
keras.losses.mean_squared_error(y_true, y_pred)
```

Mean Absolute Error (MAE)

Here we find the mean of the absolute error, which is the difference between the inferred value of a quantity and its actual value. The *absolute error* of the sum or difference of a number of quantities is less than or equal to the sum of their absolute errors. The formula is as follows:

$$\mathbf{MAE} = \frac{1}{n}\sum_{i=1}^{n}|x_i - x|$$

Where:

- n = The number of errors
- Σ = The summation symbol (which means "add them all up")
- |xi – x| = The absolute errors

Here's its implementation in Keras:

```
keras.losses.mean_absolute_error(y_true, y_pred)
```

Mean Absolute Percentage Error (MAPE)

The MAPE is often used when the quantity you want to predict is known to remain above zero. It is ideal for forecasting applications, especially in situations where enough data is available.

Here's its implementation in Keras:

```
keras.losses.mean_absolute_percentage_error(y_true, y_pred)
```

Mean Squared Logarithmic Error (MSLE)

The mean squared logarithmic error (MSLE) is a measure of the ratio between the true and predicted values. The mean squared logarithmic error is, as the name suggests, a variation of the mean squared error.

Here's its implementation in Keras:

```
keras.losses.mean_squared_logarithmic_error(y_true, y_pred)
```

Squared Hinge

The squared hinge loss is used for "maximum margin" binary classification. The hinge loss guarantees that, during training, the classifier will find the classification boundary that's the furthest apart from each of the different classes of data points as possible. In other words, it finds the classification boundary that guarantees the maximum margin between the data points of the different classes.

Here's its implementation in Keras:

```
keras.losses.squared_hinge(y_true, y_pred)
```

Hinge

It is used in SVMs and so is also called *SVM loss*. Hinge loss simplifies the mathematics needed for SVM, thus leading to effective results while maximizing the error. It is ideal when you need real-time decisions with a less accuracy. Hinge loss not only penalizes the wrong predictions but also the right predictions that are not confident.

Here's its implementation in Keras:

```
keras.losses.hinge(y_true, y_pred)
```

Categorical Hinge

Categorical hinge loss can be optimized as well and hence used for generating decision boundaries in multiclass machine learning problems.

Here's its implementation in Keras:

```
keras.losses.categorical_hinge(y_true, y_pred)
```

Log Cosh

Log cosh is the logarithm of the hyperbolic cosine of the prediction error. This means that it works mostly like the mean squared error, but will not be so strongly affected by the occasional wildly incorrect prediction.

Here's its implementation in Keras:

```
keras.losses.logcosh(y_true, y_pred)
```

Huber Loss

The Huber loss combines the best properties of MSE and MAE. It is quadratic for smaller errors and is linear otherwise. The same applies to its gradient.

Here's its implementation in Keras:

```
keras.losses.huber_loss(y_true, y_pred, delta=1.0)
```

Categorical Cross-Entropy

Categorical cross-entropy is a loss function that is used for single label categorization. This is when only one category is applicable for each data point.

Here's its implementation in Keras:

```
keras.losses.categorical_crossentropy(y_true, y_pred, from_
logits=False, label_smoothing=0)
```

Sparse Categorical Cross-Entropy

Sparse categorical cross-entropy is a loss function used to measure the dissimilarity between the distribution of observed class labels and the predicted probabilities of class membership. Categorical refers to the possibility of having more than two classes (instead of binary, which refers to two classes). Sparse refers to using a single integer from zero to the number of classes minus one (such as { 0; 1; or 2 } for a class label for a three-class problem), instead of a dense one-hot encoding of the class label (such as { 1,0,0; 0,1,0; or 0,0,1 } for a class label for the same three-class problem). Use sparse categorical cross-entropy when your classes are mutually exclusive.

Here's its implementation in Keras:

```
keras.losses.sparse_categorical_crossentropy(y_true, y_pred,
from_logits=False, axis=-1)
```

Binary Cross-Entropy

Binary cross-entropy is a loss function used on problems involving yes/no (*binary*) decisions. For instance, in multi-label problems, where an example can belong to multiple classes at the same time, the model tries to decide for each class whether the example belongs to that class or not.

Here's its implementation in Keras:

```
keras.losses.binary_crossentropy(y_true, y_pred, from_
logits=False, label_smoothing=0)
```

Kullback-Leibler Divergence

Kullback-Leibler divergence is an asymmetric measure of difference between two probability vectors.

Here's its implementation in Keras:

```
keras.losses.kullback_leibler_divergence(y_true, y_pred)
```

Poisson

The Poisson loss is a loss function used for regression when modeling count data. Minimizing the Poisson loss is equivalent to maximizing the likelihood of the data under the assumption that the target comes from a Poisson distribution, conditioned on the input. The loss takes the form of:

$$L(y,\hat{y}) = \frac{1}{N}\sum_{i=0}^{N}(\hat{y}_i - y_i log \hat{y}_i)$$

where $\hat{y}$ is the predicted expected value.

Here's its implementation in Keras:

```
keras.losses.poisson(y_true, y_pred)
```

References

Here are the references used in this chapter:

- www.asimovinstitute.org/neural-network-zoo/
- www.computerworld.com/article/2591759/
  artificial-neural-networks.html
- www.countbayesie.com/blog/2017/5/9/kullback-
  leibler-divergence-explained
- https://openreview.net/pdf?id=Hk4kQHceg
- https://searchenterpriseai.techtarget.com/
  definition/recurrent-neural-networks
- https://towardsdatascience.com/attention-in-
  neural-networks-e66920838742
- https://arxiv.org/pdf/1508.04025.pdf
- proceedings.mlr.press/v37/xuc15.pdf
- https://papers.nips.cc/paper/6284-latent-
  attention-for-if-then-program-synthesis.pdf
- www.sciencedirect.com/topics/engineering/deep-
  belief-network
- https://searchenterpriseai.techtarget.
  com/definition/deconvolutional-networks-
  deconvolutional-neural-networks

- https://maelfabien.github.io/deeplearning/
  inception/#

- https://peltarion.com/knowledge-center/
  documentation/modeling-view/build-an-ai-model/
  loss-functions/mean-squared-logarithmic-error

- https://peltarion.com/knowledge-center/
  documentation/modeling-view/build-an-ai-model/
  loss-functions/categorical-crossentropy

- https://towardsdatascience.com/10-gradient-
  descent-optimisation-algorithms-86989510b5e9

Further Reading

Interested in learning more about some of the topics covered in this chapter? Here are some great links to check out:

- Autoencoders:

  http://ufldl.stanford.edu/tutorial/
  unsupervised/Autoencoders/

- VAEs: www.jeremyjordan.me/variational-
  autoencoders/

- RAEs: https://arxiv.org/abs/1807.03710

- ELMs:

  www.ntu.edu.sg/home/egbhuang/pdf/ELM-
  Tutorial.pdf

- RNNs:

  www.geeksforgeeks.org/introduction-to-
  recurrent-neural-network/

- Multiplicative LSTMs:

  https://arxiv.org/abs/1609.07959

- ANNs with attention:

  https://pathmind.com/wiki/attention-
  mechanism-memory-network

- Transformers:

  https://towardsdatascience.com/transformers-
  141e32e69591

- Denoising autoencoders:

  https://pathmind.com/wiki/denoising-
  autoencoder

- Sparse autoencoders:

  https://web.stanford.edu/class/cs294a/
  sparseAutoencoder.pdf

- Stacked autoencoders:

  https://medium.com/@venkatakrishna.
  jonnalagadda/sparse-stacked-and-variational-
  autoencoder-efe5bfe73b64

- Convolutional autoencoders:

  https://towardsdatascience.com/
  convolutional-autoencoders-for-image-noise-
  reduction-32fce9fc1763

- Stacked denoising autoencoders:

  http://deeplearning.net/tutorial/SdA.html

- Contractive autoencoders:

  https://deepai.org/machine-learning-glossary-and-terms/contractive-autoencoder

- Markov chains: http://setosa.io/ev/markov-chains/

- Hopfield networks:

  www.sciencedirect.com/topics/computer-science/hopfield-network

- Bidirectional associative memory:

  https://uomustansiriyah.edu.iq/media/lectures/5/5_2017_02_28!06_30_52_PM.pdf

- Boltzmann machines: http://artificialintelligence-notes.blogspot.com/2012/09/what-is-boltzmann-machine.html

- Restricted Boltzmann machines:

  https://medium.com/datadriveninvestor/deep-learning-restricted-boltzmann-machine-b76241af7a92

- Deep belief networks:

  http://deeplearning.net/tutorial/DBN.html

- Deconvolutional networks:

  https://searchenterpriseai.techtarget.com/definition/deconvolutional-networks-deconvolutional-neural-networks

- DCGIN: https://medium.com/@Medmain/two-sides-of-the-same-network-efd3a0f3b425?source=rss-------1

- Liquid state machines:

  www.frontiersin.org/articles/10.3389/
  fnins.2019.00686/full

- Echo state networks:

  https://towardsdatascience.com/gentle-
  introduction-to-echo-state-networks-
  af99e5373c68

- Deep residual networks:

  https://towardsdatascience.com/introduction-
  to-resnets-c0a830a288a4

- Neural Turing machines:

  https://arxiv.org/abs/1410.5401

- Capsule neural networks:

  https://towardsdatascience.com/capsule-
  networks-the-new-deep-learning-network-
  bd917e6818e8

- LeNet-5:

  http://yann.lecun.com/exdb/lenet/

- AlexNet: https://medium.com/analytics-vidhya/
  cnns-architectures-lenet-alexnet-vgg-googlenet-
  resnet-and-more-666091488df5

- GoogLeNet:

  https://leonardoaraujosantos.gitbooks.io/
  artificial-inteligence/content/googlenet.html

- Xception:

  www.iitk.ac.in/esc101/05Aug/tutorial/
  essential/exceptions/definition.html

APPENDIX

Portfolio Tips

This appendix is a bonus reference for entry-level individuals who are looking for their first job. Here, I introduce you to a framework for solving real-world problems. This framework is especially helpful in the work environment. Although each problem will be unique to its industry and will require specific methods, the framework presented is the basic procedure that is used by data analysts.

Data Analyst Portfolios

A portfolio is important, as it can help get you employment. It acts as public evidence of your skills. If you are looking for a serious paid job in data science, do some projects with real-world data. As you learn more and improve yourself, your portfolio should also be updated.

After publishing your projects online, keep updating and improving on them.

Portfolios are places for you to showcase:

- Independent projects
- Open source development
- Written communication
- Presentation skills

© Vinita Silaparasetty 2020
V. Silaparasetty, *Deep Learning Projects Using TensorFlow 2*,
https://doi.org/10.1007/978-1-4842-5802-6

What employers look for:

- Extracting insights from raw data and presenting those insights to others.

- Building systems that offer direct value to the customer.

- Building systems that offer direct value to others in the organization.

- Sharing your expertise with others in the organization.

- Ability to estimate the value of a project.

- Ability to use developed thought processes.

- Lessons learned from your projects.

The following sections describe the components of a good portfolio.

LinkedIn Profile

LinkedIn should be your online curriculum vitae. An important part of LinkedIn is the search tool; you need to show up appropriately when employers search for people with your qualifications. Recruiters also often search for people on LinkedIn. LinkedIn allows you to see which companies have searched for you and who has viewed your profile. It is imperative to create a profile that best showcases your strengths and helps you make contact with recruiters.

Best practices:

- Add your capstone projects or thesis work to your profile. Add relevant links to the GitHub repository and slides that you used to present these projects.

- Get endorsements on LinkedIn for your skills. It is not a major deciding factor to employers, but it does give you a little more credibility in the eyes of the employer.

- Ask for recommendations. This is given the same amount of importance as skill endorsements. Every small advantage you can get goes a long way in helping you secure your dream job.

- Do a keyword search and add keywords that apply to you to your profile.

- Use the About section to your advantage. Ensure that your enthusiasm for data science is evident in this section.

- Follow data science influencers and companies to stay up to date on data science related events.

- Upload a professional profile picture. Wear formal attire in the photo.

- Ensure that your experience is linked with the official company page. A logo of the company will appear alongside the experience field.

Mistakes to avoid:

- Never lie on your LinkedIn profile. You won't believe the number of people who think they can get away with it.

- Do not stuff keywords. Pick only the most relevant ones that truly apply to you.

- Do not post selfies or group photos as your profile picture.

GitHub Profile

A GitHub profile is a powerful signal that you are a competent data scientist. In the projects section of a resume, people often leave links to their GitHub where the code is stored for their projects. You can also have writeups and markdowns there. GitHub lets people see what you have built and how you have built it. At some companies, hiring managers look at an applicant's GitHub.

Kaggle

Participating in Kaggle competitions, creating a kernel, and contributing to discussions are ways to show some competency as a data scientist. Kaggle gives you experience in analyzing data and building models.

However, it does not give you practice with end-to-end projects that are done in the industry.

You do not have the chance to practice:

- Defining the problem statement

- Data collection

- Data cleaning

Blogging Platforms

Writing about a project or a data science topic allows you to share with the community and encourages you to write out your work processes and thoughts. This is a useful skill when interviewing. You gain experience writing and get practice structuring a data-driven argument. This is probably the most relevant skill that blogging develops since it's hard to practice elsewhere, and it's an essential part of any data science career

Convert your projects into tutorial style posts so that others can benefit from and follow along with your work. By writing a blog, you can practice communicating findings to others.

It is another way to advertise yourself. One of the major benefits I have found is that the process of people critiquing my projects and suggesting improvements (through the comments section of the blog) means I am ready to address these same issues with interviewers, because they aren't the first ones to point out these same flaws.

Sharing Your Portfolio

People often forget that software engineers and data scientists also Google their issues. If these same people have their problems solved by reading your public work, they will think better of you and reach out to you.

Since data scientists do use online resources in the course of their work, when they find you in their frequented communities, they begin to accept you as one of them. That's true even if you have not worked as a data scientist before.

A major component of data science is about communication and presenting data, so it is good to have these online profiles. Besides the fact that these platforms help provide valuable experience, they can also help you get noticed and lead people to your resume.

Twitter

Twitter is where you will find the data science community. This is the perfect place to share your projects, get feedback, and make valuable connections in a slightly less formal environment as compared to LinkedIn.

Facebook

Join relevant Facebook groups to expand your network. Share your posts and portfolio projects there and get helpful feedback from other data scientists.

LinkedIn Groups

Join relevant LinkedIn groups to connect with like-minded individuals. This will help you stay informed, get an idea of what your peers are doing, and is a great place to get an audience for your portfolio, blog articles, etc.

Tableau Public (Optional)

If you are good at visualization, Tableau Public is the place for you. Share your amazing visuals with others, get inspiration for your next project, and get valuable feedback on your work. Tableau is the first choice for many employers when it comes to visualization tools.

Types of Projects

The basic categories of projects that every data science portfolio must have are described in this section.

Data Cleaning Project

This is most of the work a data scientist does, and it's a critical skill to demonstrate. This project involves taking messy data, cleaning it, and doing analyses on it. A data cleaning project demonstrates that you can reason about data, and can take data from many sources and consolidate it into a single dataset.

You'll want to go from raw data to a version that's easy to analyze. In order to do this, you'll need to follow these steps:

1. Find a messy dataset. Some sources are given later in this chapter. Find any supplemental datasets if you can. For example, if you downloaded a dataset on flights, are there any datasets you can find via Google that you can combine with it?

2. Pick a question to answer using the data. This question acts as a starting point, but will change as you explore and understand the data.

3. Conduct an exploratory data analysis to help identify an interesting angle to explore. Ensure that exploring the angle you want is possible with the data.

4. Clean up the data. Unify multiple data files if you have them.

5. Present your results. Make sure that your code and logic can be followed, and add as many comments and markdown cells explaining your process as you can.

Data Storytelling Project

A data storytelling project demonstrates your ability to extract insights from data and persuade others. This has a large impact on the business value you can deliver, and it is an important piece of your portfolio. This project involves taking a set of data and telling a compelling narrative with it. A good storytelling project will make heavy use of visualizations.

Here is how you go about data storytelling:

1. Find an interesting dataset. Picking something that is related to current events can be more exciting to readers.

2. Pick a question to answer using the data. This question acts as a starting point, but will change as you explore and understand the data.

3. Conduct an exploratory data analysis to help identify an interesting angle to explore. Ensure that exploring the angle you want to is possible with the data. Identify interesting correlations in the data

4. Create charts and display your findings step-by-step.

5. Write a compelling narrative:

   - Pick the most interesting angle from your explorations.

   - Write a story around getting from the raw data to the findings you made.

   - Create compelling charts that enhance the story.

   - Write extensive explanations about what you were thinking during each step, and about what the code is doing.

   - Write extensive analysis of the results of each step and what they tell a reader.

   - Teach the reader something as you go through the analysis.

Explanatory Post

It's important to be able to understand and explain complex data science concepts. This helps a hiring manager understand how good you'd be at communicating complex concepts to other team members and customers. This is a critical piece of a data science portfolio, as it covers a good portion of real-world data science work.

It also proves that you understand concepts and how things work at a deep level, not just at a syntax level. This deep understanding is important in being able to justify your choices and walk others through your work.

In order to build an explanatory post, you'll need to pick a data science topic to explain, then write a blog post, taking someone from the very ground level all the way up to having a working example of the concept.

Here are the steps you'll need to follow:

1. Select a concept you know well or can learn.

    -   You could select an algorithm.

    -   Statistical concepts are a great topic too.

    -   Make sure that the concept has enough nuance to spend some time explaining.

    -   Make sure you fully understand the concept, and it's not too complex to explain well.

2. Pick a dataset to help you explain the concept.

3. Create an outline of your post.

    -   Assume that the reader has no knowledge of the topic you're explaining.

    -   Break the concept into small steps.

4. Write up your post.

    - Explain everything in clear and straightforward language.

    - Try having someone non-technical read it and gauge their reaction.

5. Share your post.

    - Share it on your blog.

    - Share it on social media.

Projects to Avoid

- Survival classification on the Titanic dataset (www.kaggle.com/c/titanic).

- Handwritten digit classification on the MNIST dataset (www.tensorflow.org/versions/r1.2/get_started/mnist/pros).

- Flower species classification using the Iris dataset (https://archive.ics.uci.edu/ml/datasets/iris).

- Twitter datasets are very commonly used for sentiment analysis. Try doing a different type of project with Twitter data.

- Predicting Boston housing prices. This is a model that predicts the value of a given house in the Boston real estate market using various statistical analysis tools. It identified the best price that a client can sell their house utilizing machine learning.

Note   Try creating spin-offs of your projects. Can you approach the same problem in a different way? This helps to showcase your ability to apply theoretical knowledge to a project.

Selecting a Topic

Consider these points when selecting your topic:

- In order to create a portfolio that will have employers clamoring to hire you, do your research to determine the hottest projects in machine learning and deep learning.

- Where do you want to work? What kind of project would showcase your skills to that potential employer?

- Now, select the ones that you are passionate about. Employers are quick to detect a fake and they prefer potential employees who are as passionate about the projects they are. You could even incorporate your interests into the project. For example, if you love movies, you could do a sentiment analysis on movie reviews or create a recommendation system based on movie reviews.

- Gauge the level of difficulty of the project. Research other projects that are similar to the one that you have chosen.

- Are you familiar with the tools required for the project you have chosen? Are there alternate tools you could use that you are more comfortable with?

  - Ensure that the skills you will learn by doing the project align with your personal learning goals.

  - What kind of tools would you like to learn/practice?

  - Does the project enable you to use these tools?

- Gauge the time it will take to complete the project.

- Ensure that you can easily obtain the necessary data.

  - Source: From where specifically are you going to obtain the data?

  - Format: In which format will it be? Can you handle that kind of format?

  - Necessary actions to take it: Will you scrape it? Ask someone for the dataset?

  Projects dedicated to web scraping, data collection, and dataset preparation are impressive additions to your portfolio.

  - Identify limitations:

  - Do you need to first learn about the tools before you start on the project? This will increase the time taken to complete the project.

  - Is the data not enough?

Note   Your portfolio should have a minimum of five very impressive projects. Then you can add more from there as you gain more experience.

Now that you have selected your topic, it is time to solve the problem the way a data scientist would. I have outlined a simple framework that you can use for your projects. It consists of the four components shown in Figure A-1.

Analytics Framework

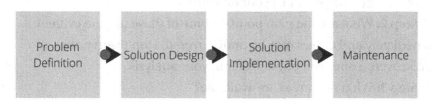

Figure A-1. *Analytics framework*

Note   You will notice that each component spills into the other and it is meant to do so.

Defining Problem Statements

The problem statement stage is the first and most important step of solving an analytics problem. It can make or break the entire project. When you start your project, the problem will not be clear enough, from an analytics point of view, to begin solving it right away. The problem needs to be well framed.

As a data scientist, you need to think of the problem statement in mathematical terms.

Remember: A good data science problem should be relevant, specific, and unambiguous.

Phase 1: Understanding the Goals and Expectations

This phase is crucial, as the information provided to you will be the basis for your analysis. So take your time and make sure to get all the information you need.

Step 1: Begin by determining your vision. What do you hope to achieve by solving the problem? List your objectives.

Step 2: What are the pain points? Some of these may be evident immediately and others may be undiscovered. Don't worry, the undiscovered ones will pop up later in your analysis.

Step 3: What resources are available?

- Data

- Reference material to use when you get stuck

- Do you require the cloud?

Step 4: What are the potential benefits?

- What new skills will you learn?

- What new concepts will you learn?

- Can your findings benefit others?

- Is it worth pursuing?

Step 5: Determine the duration of the project. Machine learning problems perform best with short term goals.

Step 6: Look for perspective. See the problem from a potential business's point of view and from their client's point of view. This will help you produce better results that will benefit both sides.

Step 7: Ensure that you have the domain knowledge required for the particular problem. Research as much as you need to. For example, if you are solving a problem regarding healthcare, learn more about the healthcare industry as a whole.

Pro Tips:

- Focus on a writing statement of the problem you want to solve. You will convert it into an analytics question in the next phase.

- Recall the five "Ws"—who, what, where, when, and why. Ensure that you answer them completely.

Phase 2: Translating the Goals to Data Analysis Goals

After the goals are clear, you need to translate them into data analysis goals to understand the scope of the project. For example:

Cafe A wants to increase their profits as compared to Cafe B.

So here you have the problem and the goal. Now you can translate this statement into the following analytical questions:

- What product is most popular?

- What product is least popular?

- How does the price of items at Cafe A compare to that of their competitors at Cafe B?

- How many customers does Cafe A have as compared to Cafe B?

- What are the peak hours at Cafe A and cafe B, and is there any convergence?

- What is the footfall to each cafe?

- What is the average age of the customers at each cafe?

- What is the number of repeat customers to each cafe?

Soon you notice that Cafe A sells less coffee than their competitor Cafe B.

This changes the problem statement from "How do we increase our profits?" to " How do we sell more coffee?"

Phase 3: Framing the Problem Statement

Write a statement that describes the problem, explains why solving the problem is important, and defines a starting point to begin solving it.

A problem statement generally follows this format :"The problem P, has the impact I, which affects B, so a good starting point would be S."

Let's break that statement down:

- **"The problem P. . .":** Here, you insert the problem as defined by the company.

- **". . . has the impact I ."** Insert the negative impacts/pain points of the problem.

- **". . . which affects B. . ."** Insert the parties that are affected. IT could be the business, the customers, or a third party.

- **"..., so a good starting point would be S."** Insert the benefits of solving the problem.

For the cafe scenario, the problem statement would be something like this:

> "The problem of low coffee sales has the impact of decreased profits, which affects Cafe A's bottom line, so a good starting point would be to compare their coffee prices with that of their competitors."

Phase 4: Choosing a Success Metric

To know if your problem statement is truly successful or not, you need to evaluate it at the end. The achievement should be measurable. Take cues from similar projects online to see which metrics they use.

Common metrics include:

- Model assessment: accuracy, performance, etc.

- Benchmarks: Increase coffee sales by at least 10% in the first month of implementing the solution.

Using Design Thinking

Use elements from the design thinking approach to help design an effective solution.

The solution-generation process helps produce ideas that reflect the genuine constraints and facets of that particular problem (see Figure A-2). Design thinking helps you prototype and test products and services so as to uncover new ways of improving the product, service, or design itself. Design thinking provides a solution-based approach to solving problems. It is an iterative process.

Solution Design

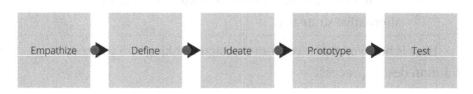

Design Thinking

Figure A-2. *Solution design*

Benefits of Design Thinking

- Acts as a one-stop reference and guidance throughout the project.

- Maps the problem statement to various aspects of the solution that will be built out.

- Provides the functional outline and technical architecture for the solution.

- Provides clarity about what to build, what tests to run, and what to expect from the end product.

- Helps you come up with estimates for the cost, timelines, and resource requirements for the project.

- Acts as a baseline for change control.

- Enjoys rapid iteration.

- Includes targeted feedback from relevant stakeholders, allowing a larger range of 13 possible solutions to be considered in the selection process.

- Avoids personal biases.

- Prevents selection of the first idea when a better idea may have come along.

- Includes ambiguous elements of the problem to reveal previously unknown parameters and uncover alternative strategies.

Here is how you can incorporate design thinking into your own solution design process.

Phase 1: Planning

Step 1: Empathize. Define the relevant beneficiaries at the beginning and keep them in mind along the way. Read through the content from subject-matter experts.

Step 2: Identify the type of analytics to be conducted. The common types of analyses that must be included in your project are as follows:

- **Predictive analytics:** A method of studying historical data to make a short term prediction.

- **Descriptive analytics:** Involves exploratory data analysis and helps to summarize data to get a better understanding of it.

- **Diagnostic analytics:** Helps to get to the root of the problem that you are trying to solve.

- **Prescriptive analytics:** In the industry, a data scientist must conduct prescriptive analyses to come up with actionable solutions for a business. In order to impress employers, you can suggest solutions to the problem you have chosen to work on. It is an entirely optional step in the case of portfolio projects.

Step 3: Identify the type of machine learning to be done.

- **Supervised :** Training a model using labeled data and target variables.

- **Unsupervised:** Training a model with unlabeled data and no target variables.

- **Semi-supervised learning:** The process is similar to supervised learning. The only difference is that the model is trained with data that is partially labeled. So it needs to be able to detect some of the input values on its own.

- **Reinforcement learning:** When a model is trained using a method of reward and punishment to encourage it to provide the desired output, it is called reinforcement learning.

- **Inductive learning:** From the perspective of inductive learning, we are given an input dataset and a set of the desired output samples. The problem is to estimate the function (i.e., to estimate the output for new samples in the future).

Step 4: Ideate. Think of all the possible solutions to the problem. You should ignore feasibility for now.

Step 5: Identify any limitations. The best solution in theory may not be the best solution in practice. This is due to the constraints that real-world problems pose. Always take into account the following:

- Resources: Data availability, system specs, etc.

- How the solution will be implemented within the time constraints

Step 6: Create a road map (a roadmap template is provided at the end of this chapter). By creating a roadmap, you can finish your project and organize it well.

- Identify milestones

- Set expectations for each

- Set deadlines for each

Phase 2: Model Design

The software design process can be perceived as a series of well-defined steps. Although it varies according to the design approach (function oriented or object oriented), you'll still have to decide whether you will be using an existing model and tweaking it or whether you need to build your model from scratch. Consider these types of designs:

- **Top-down design:** Top-down designs are suitable when the software solution needs to be designed from scratch and specific details are unknown.

  A system is composed of more than one sub-system and it contains a number of components, which are further divided into subsystems. Top-down design takes the whole software system as one entity and breaks it into parts to achieve more than one sub-system or component based on some characteristics. Each sub-system or component is then treated as a system and broken down further. This process continues until the lowest level of the system in the top-down hierarchy is achieved.

  Top-down design starts with a generalized model of the system and keeps defining the more specific parts of it. When all the components are composed, the whole system comes into existence.

- **Bottom-up design:** The bottom-up strategy is more suitable when a system needs to be created from some existing system, where the existing primitives can be used in the newer system.

The bottom-up design model starts with most specific and basic components. It proceeds with composing higher level components by using basic or lower level components. It keeps creating higher level components until the desired system is not evolved as one single component. With each higher level, the amount of abstraction is increased.

Phase 3: Prototyping

Rapid prototyping is proven to give similar results in less time compared to non-constrained prototyping.

Step 1: Formulate a hypothesis (or many of them).

Step 2: Create simple prototype models to test your hypotheses.

Phase 4: Black-Box Testing

We are going to use a method called black-box testing (see Figure A-3). It involves testing the functionality of an application without knowing the details of its implementation, including internal program structure, data structures, etc. It is also called specification-based testing. When applied to machine learning models, black-box testing means testing machine learning models without knowing the internal details, such as features of the machine learning model, the algorithm used to create the model, etc.

Black Box Testing

Figure A-3. *Sample black-box testing process*

Step 1: Identify the type of test to perform.

Black-Box Testing Techniques for Machine Learning Models

The following list explains some of the techniques that you could use to perform black-box testing on machine learning models:

- **Model performance:** The most basic method of testing, model performance uses test data/new datasets. It compares the model performance in terms of parameters such as accuracy/recall, loss, etc., to that of predetermined accuracy with the model already built and moved into production.

- **Metamorphic testing:** One or more properties are identified that represent the metamorphic relationship between input/output pairs. The test cases that result in success lead to another set of test cases, which could be used for further testing of machine learning models. Test cases are executed until one of the test cases fails. The defect is then logged and dealt with.

- **Dual coding:** Different models are built based on different algorithms and the prediction from each of these models is compared against the same dataset.

Solution Implementation

Solution implementation is an iterative process (see Figure A-4) that involves the following:

- Data collection

- Data exploration

- Data handling

- Data Mining

- Prototyping

- Storytelling

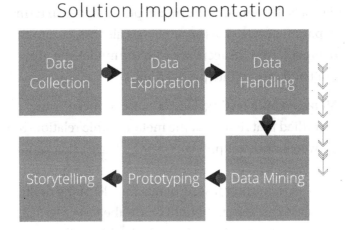

Figure A-4. Sample solution implementation process

Phase 1: Data Collection

If you need hot water, don't boil the ocean. In the data problem statement stage, you should already determine what sort of data you will need. Do not try to work with the entire database from the start.

On the other hand, sometimes you may need additional sources of data.

Phase 2: Data Exploration

Exploratory Data Analysis (EDA) refers to the critical process of performing initial investigations on data so as to discover patterns, spot anomalies, test hypotheses, and to check assumptions with the help of summary statistics and graphical representations.

It is the process of uncovering valuable insights from large datasets, often with the assistance of advanced statistical analysis and visualization. It involves running descriptive statistics of variables and checking for correlations.

Why EDA?

- Detection of mistakes
- Checking of assumptions
- Preliminary selection of appropriate models
- Determining relationships among the explanatory variables
- Assessing the direction and rough size of relationships between explanatory and outcome variables
- Identifying data types
- Checking for missing values
- Grouping data

Univariate EDA

Univariate analysis is the simplest form of data analysis where the data being analyzed contains only one variable. Since it's a single variable it doesn't deal with causes or relationships. The main purpose of univariate analysis is to describe the data and find patterns that exist within it. It is of two types:

> **Non-graphical methods:** They involve just the calculation of summary statistics.

> **Graphical methods:** They summarize the data in a diagrammatic/pictorial way.

Multivariate EDA

Multivariate data analysis refers to any statistical technique used to analyze data that arises from more than one variable. This essentially models reality where each situation, product, or decision involves more than a single variable. Usually the multivariate EDA will be bivariate (looking at exactly two variables), but occasionally, it will involve three or more variables. It is of two types:

> **Non-graphical methods:** They involve just the calculation of summary statistics.

> **Graphical methods:** They summarize the data in a diagrammatic/pictorial way.

Note   It is almost always a good idea to perform univariate EDA on each of the components of a multivariate EDA before performing the actual multivariate EDA.

Phase 3: Data Handling

As you conduct the EDA, you will notice the parts of the data that need to be "cleaned" to ensure your analysis goes smoothly. So the data handling phase goes hand in hand with the EDA phase.

Step 1: Clean the Data

1. Check and convert data types. Data types may come in the wrong format, which makes analysis difficult. For example, a column that is meant for numeric data may be stored as a string.

2. Drop irrelevant columns, which are columns that do not contribute to the analysis.

3. Use the .duplicated() function to detect duplicate values and drop them.

4. Check for inconsistent data entries. They are the representation of the same value in different ways. This may be due to whitespace, different use of case, punctuation marks, etc.

5. Incorporate string manipulation. This is an essential way of obtaining numeric data from strings.

Step 2: Handle Missing Data

1. Drop rows or columns with missing values or Nan values.

2. Fill in missing values or Nan values manually.

3. Imputation is a method that fills in the missing values with estimated ones. The objective is to employ known relationships that can be identified in the valid values of the dataset to assist in estimating the missing values.

The types of imputation are:

- **Mean/mode/median imputation:** It is one of the most frequently used methods. It consists of replacing the missing data of a given attribute by the mean or median (quantitative attribute) or mode (qualitative attribute) of all known values of that variable.

- **Substitution:** Imputation is done by replacing the original value with a different value.

- **Hot deck:** A randomly chosen value from an individual in the sample who has similar values in other variables.

- **Cold deck:** A systematically chosen value from an individual who has similar values in other variables.

- **Regression imputation:** The predicted value is obtained by regressing the missing variable on other variables.

- **Stochastic regression imputation:** The predicted value from a regression, plus a random residual value.

- **Interpolation and extrapolation:** An estimated value from other observations from the same individual. It usually only works with longitudinal data.

Step 3: Partition the Data

Split the data, ideally in the ratio of 60:20:20, as follows:

- Train (60%)

- Test (20%)

- Validate (20%)

Step 4: Handle Any Outliers

An outlier is a data point that differs significantly from other observations due to variability in the measurement. It may indicate experimental error.

1. Delete outlier values.

2. Transform variables to eliminate outliers. The natural log of a value reduces the variation caused by extreme values.

3. Use imputation only on artificial outliers. Mean/mode/median imputation is one of the most frequently used methods.

Phase 4: Data Mining

Data mining, as shown in Figure A-5, is the process of turning raw data into useful information. By looking for patterns in large batches of data, you can learn a lot of valuable information. To conduct data mining, use the popular technique known as CRISP-DM.

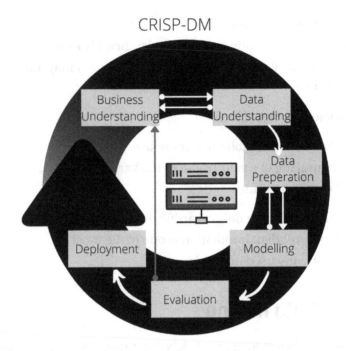

Figure A-5. *Data mining process*

Step 1: Business understanding. Involves understanding the project objectives and requirements, then converting this knowledge into a data mining problem definition and a preliminary plan. This has been covered in the "Problem Statement Definition" section.

Step 2: Data understanding. Starts with an initial data collection and proceeds with activities in order to get familiar with the data. This is covered in the "Data Handling" section.

Step 3: Data preparation. The data preparation phase covers the preparation of data to construct the final dataset from the initial raw data. This is covered in the section called "Data Handling."

Step 4: Modeling. This is where we select the sort of deep learning or machine learning model that would best suit our needs.

Step 5: Evaluation. Once the models have been built, they need to be tested to ensure that they generalize against unseen data and are not underfitted or overfitted.

Underfitting

Underfitting is a modeling error that occurs when a function does not fit the data points well enough. It is the result of a simple model with an insufficient number of training points. A model that is underfitted is inaccurate because the trend does not reflect the reality of the data.

Overcoming Underfitting

- Get more training data.

- Increase the size or number of parameters in the model.

- Increase the complexity or type of the model.

- Increase the training time until the cost function in the model is minimized.

Overfitting

Overfitting is a modeling error that occurs when a function too closely fits a limited set of data points. It is the result of an overly complex model with an excessive number of training points. A model that is overfitted is inaccurate because the model has effectively memorized the existing data points.

Overcoming Overfitting

- **Cross-validation.** This is done by splitting your dataset into test and training data. Build the model using the training set. The test set is used for in-time validation. This way you know what the expected output is and you will easily be able to judge the accuracy of your model.

- **Regularization.** This is a form of regression that regularizes, or shrinks, the coefficient estimates toward zero. This technique discourages learning a more complex model.

- **Early stopping.** When training a learner with an iterative method, you stop the training process before the final iteration. This prevents the model from memorizing the dataset.

- **Pruning.** This technique applies to decision trees.

  - **Pre-pruning:** Stop "growing" the tree earlier before it perfectly classifies the training set.

  - **Post-pruning:** Allows the tree to "grow" and perfectly classify the training set, and then post prune the tree.

- **Dropout.** This is a technique where randomly selected neurons are ignored during training.

Step 6: Deployment. This involves deploying a code representation of the model into an operating system to score or categorize new unseen data as it arises. You can then create a mechanism to use that new information in the solution of the original problem.

Phase 5: Prototyping

Step 1: This is where you begin creating a basic version of the selected models and then compare the performance of each.

Step 2: Now that you have narrowed it down to a few top-performing models, fine tune and compare them again.

Step 3: Continue with Step 2 until you have created the desired model.

Phase 6. Storytelling

The final step in a data science research project is to communicate the findings to the relevant stakeholders. This point is where the data scientist or research team needs to communicate the actions that should be taken based on their findings by consolidating them in a report or presentation. Ideally, all research projects end in a deeper understanding, in order to justify the investment of time spent researching.

Step 1: Focus on explanatory analysis over exploratory analysis. Explanatory analysis presents an important finding or recommendation, then explains the process that was taken to get there. Findings that are merely interesting and not useful are saved for in-depth descriptions of the project, or not included at all.

Step 2: Select the graph that best represents your findings. Start a visualization by writing out what needs to be communicated, then create exactly that. Often it is easier to create a set of charts and graphs, then pull insights and craft a story around what has been created.

There are several types of graphs that you can choose from (see Figures A-6 through A-17):

- **Line graph:** Line charts, or line graphs, are powerful visual tools that illustrate trends in data over a period of time or a particular correlation.

- Each value is plotted on the chart, then the points are connected to display a trend over the compared time span. Multiple trends can be compared by plotting lines of various colors.

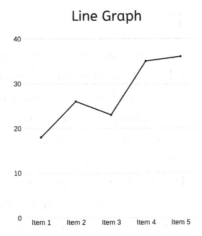

Figure A-6. *Sample line graph*

- **Bar graph:** A classic. The universally-recognized graph features a series of bars of varying lengths. One axis of a bar graph features the categories being compared, while the other axis represents the value of each.

  The length of each bar is proportionate to the numerical value or percentage that it represents. Bar graphs work great for visually presenting nearly any type of data. The graphs are ideal for comparing any sort of numeric value.

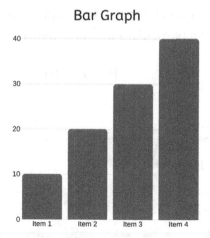

Figure A-7. *Sample bar graph*

- **Histogram:** A a specific type of bar chart, where the categories are ranges of numbers. Histograms therefore show combined continuous data.

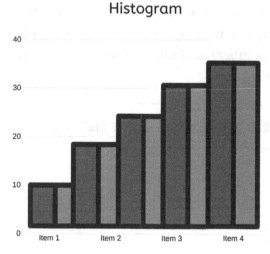

Figure A-8. *Sample histogram*

- **Pictogram:** A special type of bar graph. It uses pictures to represent a particular number of items.

Pictogram

Figure A-9. *Sample pictogram*

- **Cartesian graph:** Compares two sets of numbers, one of which is plotted on the x-axis and the other on the y-axis. The numbers can be written as Cartesian coordinates, which are represented as (x,y), where x is the number read from the x-axis, and y the number from the y-axis.

Note   Cartesian graphs do not always start at 0.

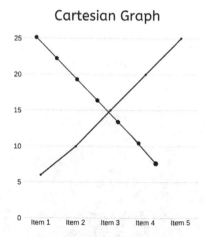

Figure A-10. *Sample Cartesian graph*

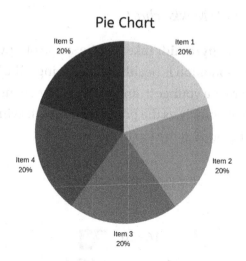

Figure A-11. *Sample pie chart*

- **Pie chart:** Great for comparing parts of a whole. The whole chart is 100% and the slices are percentages, which together equal 100%.

- **Mosaic or Mekko chart:** Used to compare multiple variables or multiple categories at the same time. They can be used for numeric as well as non-numeric variables.

Mekko Chart

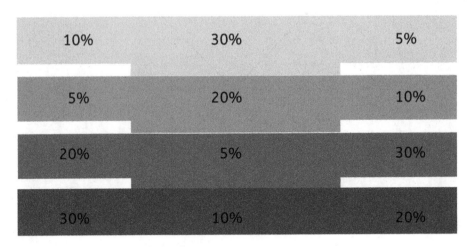

Figure A-12. *Sample Mekko chart*

- **Population pyramid:** Takes on the shape of a pyramid when a population is healthy and growing—the largest groups are the youngest, and each gender dwindles somewhat equally as the population ages, leaving the smallest groups at the top of the graph.

Population Pyramid

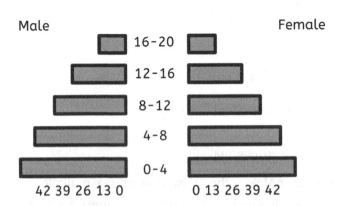

Figure A-13. *Sample population pyramid*

Note   A population pyramid that veers away from its shape might indicate an irregularity in a population during a particular period.

- **Spider chart:** Used to visually compare three or more quantitative variables. It is also called a radar chart. The chart usually consists of a series of radii, each representing a different category, that splay out from a center point like spokes.

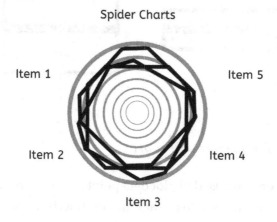

Figure A-14.   *Sample spider chart*

The length of each "spoke" is proportionate to the value being compared. For each category, the spokes are then connected to a line of a designated pattern or color, forming a star-like shape with points equal to the number of categories.

The result is a graphic representation that can reveal trends and compare categories all at the same time.

- **Box plot:** A box-and-whisker plot (sometimes called a box plot) is a graph that presents information from a five-number summary. This type of graph is used to show the shape of the distribution, its central value, and its variability.

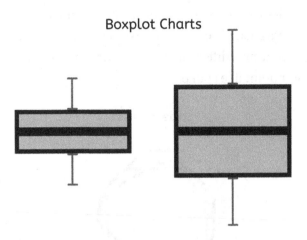

Boxplot Charts

Figure A-15. *Sample box plot chart*

- **Scatter plot:** Used to plot data points on a horizontal and a vertical axis in the attempt to show how much one variable is affected by another. Each row in the data table is represented by a marker whose position depends on its values in the columns set on the x and y axes.

Scatter Plot

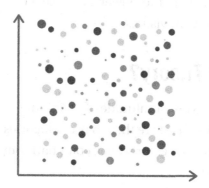

Figure A-16. *Sample scatter plot*

- **Choropleth map:** These are maps where areas are shaded according to a prearranged key, and each shade or color type represents a range of values.

Choropleth Map

Figure A-17. *Sample choropleth map*

Selecting colors is an important aspect to creating your visuals. You want them to be pleasant to the viewer. Let's use "color theory" to help select color pallets for your visuals.

What Is Color Theory?

Color theory encompasses a multitude of definitions, concepts, and design applications. However, there are three basic categories of color theory that are logical and useful—the color wheel, color harmony, and the context in which colors are used.

Color theories create a logical structure for color.

Follow these color theory guidelines when using color in your graphs:

- Use branded colors for marketing materials or presentations. Using the company's color scheme helps you align with your brand and keeps your messaging consistent. It also helps with brand recognition.

- Gradient colors can be great to show a pattern. Consider showing your most important values with bars and use colors to only show categories.

- If you need more than seven colors in a chart, consider using another chart type or group categories together.

- Consider using the same color for the same variables. If you are making a series of charts that involve the same variable, keep the color for each variable consistent in all the charts.

- Make sure to explain to readers what your colors mean. Every element of your graph should be explained: What does the height of the bar mean? What does the size of the markers on a map represent?

- Using gray for less important elements in your chart makes your highlight colors (which should be reserved for your most important data points) stick out even more. Gray is also helpful for general context data and less important annotations.

- Make sure your contrasts are high enough. In addition to having a high contrast ratio, avoid complementary hues (e.g., red and green, orange and blue) and bright colors for backgrounds.

- Consider semantic color association. When choosing a color palette, consider their meaning in the culture of your target audience. If possible, use colors that readers will associate with your data (e.g., red signifies danger in some cultures and luck in others).

- Use light colors for low values and dark colors for high values. When using color gradients, make sure that the bright colors represent low values, while the dark colors represent high values.

- Don't use a gradient color palette for categories and the other way around. Viewers will associate dark colors with "more/high" and bright colors with "less/low," such a color palette will imply a ranking of your categories. If the chart is too colorful, consider another chart type for your data.

- Consider using two hues for a gradient, not just one.

- Consider using diverging color gradients. If you want to emphasize how a variable diverts from a baseline, you may want to consider using a diverging palette.

- Using different shades in your gradients and color palettes has the big advantage that readers with a color vision deficiency will still be able to distinguish your colors.

Note   Avoid using too much color in your visuals.

Maintenance

Data is the most crucial component of a successful system. You may have found a dataset that provides you with accurate predictions at present, but data changes and will not continue to provide accurate predictions for eternity.

Other causes of system degradation include:

- Introduction of new technologies

- Changes in the industry

- Changes in data

- Degradation of tools

When designing a system, it is important to understand how your data is going to change over time. A well-architected system should take this into account, and a plan should be put in place for keeping your models updated. You need to constantly monitor the models in your projects too, so that employers know that you truly care about your work and that you keep up with the last changes.

The maintenance process can be automated to continuously evaluate and retrain your models. This type of system is often referred to as continuous learning, and it may look something like this:

- Save new training data as you receive it.

- When you have enough new data, test its accuracy against your model.

- If you see the accuracy of your model degrading over time, use the new data, or a combination of the new data and old training data, to build and deploy a new model.

Without maintenance, the model is likely to succumb to decay. This deterioration in predictive power sets in when environmental conditions under which a model was first put into production change sufficiently. Under any scenario, tending to a model demands the close scrutiny, critical thinking, and manual effort that only a highly trained data scientist can provide.

Uploading Your Project to GitHub

Step 1: Create a new repository.

Step 2: Select a repository name that's rich in relevant keywords.

Step 3: Give it a short description so that when readers see your project in search results, they will immediately understand what your project is about.

Step 4: Ensure that you set the repository to Public.

Step 5: Initialize the read.me for your repository. This is where you describe your project in more detail. You can use the template provided at the end of this chapter to create a good read.me file.

Step 6: Add a license. This ensures that readers give you credit when they use parts of your code. IT also shows that you take pride in your work but also enjoy sharing it with the community.

Step 7: Add badges with the tools you have used along with the version of each tool at the time of completion of the project.

Step 8: Add links to additional material that document and aid in the explanation of your project.

Step 9: Add visuals and screenshots of graphs to your read.me file.

Step 10: Save your read.me file.

Step 11: Upload the dataset folder. If you're including the data you used in your project's repository, you should ensure you have the legal right to redistribute it. If you do not have the rights to upload the data to your repository, just place a link and adequate credits to the original owner/creator of the dataset.

Step 12: Upload your coding files. If it is a Jupyter Notebook, you will have just one code file to upload. However, if you are creating .py files, make sure you create one for the model. Then create a .json file for the model itself and one .h5 file for the weights and other parameters of the trained model. This way, others can run your model on their own systems.

Tips for Documenting Projects

- Badges make your project look professional, but use them sparingly.

- Store data in the same folder as your notebook (or a subfolder) so that you can include a relative path that will work for anyone downloading your repository and running your code.

- Include information on any packages and version details for external packages and libraries you've used, to make it easier for others to download and run your code.

- If you're pulling data from somewhere using an API key or other access credentials, you do not want to share those credentials publicly! Thankfully, GitHub screens your code and warns you if any such private information is present in your code.

- You can connect Tableau with your repository using the Git app.

Appendix Checklist

- A portfolio is important, as it can help get you employment. It acts as public evidence of your skills.

- After publishing your projects online, keep updating and improving on them.

- Portfolios are a place for you to showcase independent projects, open source development, written communication, and presentation skills.

- Add your capstone projects or thesis work to your profile. Add relevant links to the GitHub repository and slides that you used to present the projects.

- Get endorsements on LinkedIn for your skills. It gives you a little more credibility in the eyes of the employer.

- Ask for recommendations on LinkedIn. This is given the same amount of importance as skill endorsements. Every small advantage you can get goes a long way in helping you secure your dream job.

- Do a keyword search and add keywords that apply to your LinkedIn profile.

- Use the About section to your advantage, and ensure that your enthusiasm for data science is evident in this section.

- Follow data science influencers and companies to stay up-to-date on data science related events.

- Upload a professional profile picture. Wear formal attire in the photo.

- Ensure that your experience is linked to the official company page, then a logo of the company will appear alongside the experience field.

- People often forget that software engineers and data scientists also Google their issues. If these same people have their problems solved by reading your public work, they will think better of you and reach out to you.

- Since data scientists do use online resources in the course of their work, when they find you in their frequented communities, they begin to accept you as one of them. This is true even if you have not worked as a data scientist before.

- Avoid adding these projects to your portfolio: Survival classification on the Titanic dataset, handwritten digit classification on the MNIST dataset, and flower species classification using the iris dataset.

- Your portfolio should have a minimum of five very impressive projects. You can add on more from there as you get more experience.

- The analytics methodology framework consists of problem definition, solution design, solution implementation, and maintenance.

- A good data science problem should be relevant, specific, and unambiguous.

- A problem statement generally follows the format: "The problem P, has the impact I, which affects B, so a good starting point would be S."

- Design thinking involves the following stages: empathize, define, ideate, prototype, and test

- Predictive analytics is a method of studying historical data to make a short-term prediction. It involves descriptive analytics, prescriptive analytics, and diagnostic analytics.

- Supervised learning involves using a model with labeled data and target variables, whereas unsupervised learning is when you use a model with unlabeled data and no target variables.

- Semi-supervised learning is similar to supervised learning. The only difference is that the model is trained with data that is partially labeled.

- Reinforcement learning is when a model is trained using a method of reward and punishment to encourage it to provide the desired output.

- Inductive learning is when we are given an input dataset and a set of the desired output samples. The problem is to estimate the function (i.e., to estimate the output for new samples in the future).

- Top-down design is more suitable when the software solution needs to be designed from scratch and the specific details are unknown.

- Bottom-up design is more suitable when a system needs to be created from some existing system, where the basic primitives can be used in the newer system.

- Black-box testing involves testing the functionality of an application without knowing the details of its implementation, including internal program structure, data structures, etc. It is also called specification-based testing.

- Model performance is the most basic method of testing. It uses test data/new datasets and compares the model performance in terms of parameters such as accuracy/recall, loss, etc., to that of predetermined accuracy with the model already built and moved into production.

- **Metamorphic testing** is when one or more properties are identified that represent the metamorphic relationship between input/output pairs. The test cases that result in success lead to another set of test cases, which could be used for further testing of machine learning models. Test cases are executed until one of the test cases fails. The defect is then logged and dealt with.

- Dual coding is when different models are built based on different algorithms and the prediction from each of these models is compared for the same dataset.

- Exploratory Data Analysis (EDA) refers to the critical process of performing initial investigations on data so as to discover patterns, spot anomalies, test hypotheses, and check assumptions with the help of summary statistics and graphical representations.

- Univariate analysis is the simplest form of data analysis where the data being analyzed contains only one variable. It doesn't deal with causes or relationships. It describes the data and finds patterns that exist within it.

- Multivariate data analysis refers to any statistical technique used to analyze data that arises from more than one variable. This essentially models reality where each situation, product, or decision involves more than a single variable. Usually the multivariate EDA will be bivariate (looking at exactly two variables), but occasionally it will involve three or more variables.

- Imputation is a method that fills in the missing values with estimated ones. The objective is to employ known relationships that can be identified in the valid values of the dataset to assist in estimating missing values.

- Mean/mode/median imputation is one of the most frequently used methods. It consists of replacing the missing data for a given attribute by the mean or median (quantitative attribute) or mode (qualitative attribute) of all known values of that variable. Use imputation only on artificial outliers.

- An outlier is a data point that differs significantly from other observations due to variability in the measurement. It could also indicate experimental error.

- Transform variables to eliminate outliers. The natural log of a value reduces the variation caused by extreme values.

- Split the data, ideally in the ratio of 60:20:20, into Train, Test, and Validate parts.

- Underfitting is a modeling error that occurs when a function does not fit the data points well enough. It is the result of a simple model with an insufficient number of training points. A model that is underfitted is inaccurate because the trend does not reflect the reality of the data.

- Overfitting is a modeling error that occurs when a function is too closely fit to a limited set of data points. It is the result of an overly complex model with an excessive number of training points. A model that is overfitted is inaccurate because the model has effectively memorized existing data points.

- Cross-validation is done by splitting your dataset into test data and training data. Build the model using the train dataset. The test set is used for in-time validation. This way you know what the expected output is and you will easily be able to judge the accuracy of your model.

- Regularization is a form of regression that regularizes, or shrinks, the coefficient estimates toward zero. This technique discourages learning a more complex model.

- Early stopping is, when training a learner with an iterative method, you stop the training process before the final iteration. This prevents the model from memorizing the dataset.

- Pruning applies to decision trees. Pre-pruning is when you stop "growing" the tree earlier, before it perfectly classifies the training set. Post-pruning allows the tree to "grow" perfectly to classify the training set, and then post prunes the tree.

- Dropout is a technique where randomly selected neurons are ignored during training.

- Degradation of a system occurs due to introduction of new technologies, changes in the industry, changes in data, and degradation of tools used.

- Imputation that is done by replacing the original value with a different value is called substitution.

- A hot deck is a randomly chosen value from an individual in the sample who has similar values on other variables.

- A cold deck is a systematically chosen value from an individual who has similar values on other variables.

- With regression imputation, the predicted value is obtained by regressing the missing variable on other variables.

- Stochastic regression imputation involves the predicted value from a regression plus a random residual value.

- Avoid using red, green, or blue for your visuals, so that color-blind individuals do not have trouble.

- Color theory encompasses a multitude of definitions, concepts, and design applications.

References

Here are the references used in this chapter:

- www.theanalysisfactor.com/seven-ways-to-make-up-data-common-methods-to-imputing-missing-data/

- www.datasciencecentral.com/profiles/blogs/crisp-dm-a-standard-methodology-to-ensure-a-good-outcome

- www.proglobalbusinesssolutions.com/six-steps-in-crisp-dm-the-standard-data-mining-process/

- www.interaction-design.org/literature/article/what-is-design-thinking-and-why-is-it-so-populars

- https://dzone.com/articles/qa-blackbox-testing-for-machine-learning-models

- www.dataquest.io/blog/what-to-consider-when-choosing-colors-for-data-visualization/

Further Reading

Interested in learning more about some of the topics covered in this appendix? Here are some great links to check out:

- Get exposure for your portfolio:

- www.dataquest.io/blog/how-to-share-data-science-portfolio/

- Optimize LinkedIn:

- `www.themuse.com/advice/the-31-best-linkedin-profile-tips-for-job-seekers`

- GitHub tutorial:

  `https://product.hubspot.com/blog/git-and-github-tutorial-for-beginners`

- Color blindness:

  `www.colourblindawareness.org/colour-blindness/`

- Color theory:

  `https://99designs.com/blog/tips/the-7-step-guide-to-understanding-color-theory/`

Resources for Building Your Portfolio

Here are some links to additional materials that will help you create a fantastic portfolio.

Sources for free datasets:

- Data Portals (`http://dataportals.org/`): A massive list of 551 (as of this writing) open data portals from all over the world, each of which has its own library of datasets to offer. You can browse geographically (or alphabetically) and you can also search by keyword. Most portals are government-run, open data portals.

- Data.gov (`http://data.gov/`): The home of virtually all U.S. government data, with nearly a quarter-million datasets on topics that range from industry to public health to finance.

- AWS Open Data (https://registry.opendata.aws/): Amazon's portal has all sorts of interesting and unexpected things, from web-crawling data to satellite monitoring data from space.

- Data.world (https://data.world/): Kind of like GitHub for data. You'll find all kinds of datasets here, although some of them will include common and popular datasets like the Titanic passenger data, and since they're user-uploaded, they may not always be accurate or reliable.

- /r/datasets (www.reddit.com/r/datasets/): A subreddit for sharing datasets. Years of history to browse through, new stuff every day, and you can even make requests!

- AcademicTorrents (http://academictorrents.com/): A site where scientists can upload datasets from their research and publications.

Data visualization resources:

- Data Viz project's big gallery of chart types (https://datavizproject.com/): This is perfect for reminding yourself about the wide variety of chart types out there and helping you find the best one to fit your data.

- Hubspot's Data Viz design (https://cdn2.hubspot.net/hub/53/file-863940581-pdf/Data_Visualization_101_How_to_Design_Charts_and_Graphs.pdf): Has some really helpful tips for designing specific types of charts.

- Our own guide to color on Data Viz (`www.dataquest.io/blog/what-to-consider-when-choosing-colors-for-data-visualization/`): Goes into a bit of depth about what you should think about when picking colors.

- Geckoboard (`www.geckoboard.com/learn/data-literacy/data-visualization-tips/`): Offers a printable poster that you can hang in your office if you want some wall-based inspiration and design help.

- UC Berkeley (`https://multimedia.journalism.berkeley.edu/tutorials/graphic-design-for-data-visualization/`): UCB has a 30-minute video on graphic design in the context of data that's quite helpful if you've got the time to sink into it.

- Google dataset search tool (`https://toolbox.google.com/datasetsearch`)

- Reddit datasets thread (`www.reddit.com/r/datasets/`)

- Awesome GitHub Repository with a list of datasets (`https://github.com/awesomedata/awesome-public-datasets`)

The next section shows a template you can follow when making your own `Read.me` file. To make the best use of it, just fill in your details in the spaces provided.

Read.me Template
Project Title

Badges for tools used with version:
    Duration:

Problem Statement

Objectives:

Hypothesis:

Explanation of concepts used:

Data analysis methods and techniques used techniques:

Resources:

References:

Acknowledgements:

Road Map Template

Milestone 1:

Tasks:

Requirements:

Deadline:

Milestone 2:

Tasks:

Requirements:

Deadline:

Milestone 3:

Tasks:

Requirements:

Deadline:

Milestone 4:

Tasks:

Requirements:

Deadline:

Milestone 5:

Tasks:

Requirements:

Deadline:

Milestone 6:

Tasks:

Requirements:

Deadline:

Milestone 7:

Tasks:

Requirements:

Deadline:

When preparing data for your projects, cleaning it is the most crucial step to getting the best results from your project.

Data Cleaning Checklist

Here is a handy checklist to make sure that you clean your data thoroughly:

- Identify missing values
- Identify outliers
- Check for overall plausibility and errors (e.g., typos)
- Identify highly correlated variables
- Identify variables with (nearly) no variance
- Identify variables with strange names or values
- Check variable classes (e.g., characters vs. factors)
- Remove/transform some variables (maybe your model does not like categorical variables)
- Rename some variables or values (especially interesting if it's a large number)
- Check for an overall pattern (statistical/ numerical summaries)
- Center/scale variables
- Remove HTML characters
- Decode encoded data
- Remove or substitute NULL values
- Handle zero values
- Handle negative values
- Handle date values
- Remove unnecessary values

- Remove stop-words

- Remove punctuation

- Remove expressions

- Split words that are attached

- Check the min and max of each column to ensure that they make sense

- Remove URLs

- Check grammar

- Check spelling

- Fix incorrect entries

- Ensure that geographic coordinates are within -180 to 180 degrees latitude or longitude

Index

A

Acquisition fingerprints, 227
Active attention, 256
AdaDelta, 332, 333
AdaGrad, 331, 332
Adam, 333, 334
Adamax, 335
Adam optimizer, 106, 179
AlexNet, 318, 319, 321
Anaconda
    activation, 22
    advanced options window, 17
    brew, updating, 25
    create button, 20
    destination window, 16
    environments button, 19
    GUI, 12
    introduction window, 13, 18
    license window, 15
    official website, 12
    opening terminal, 25
    Python 3.7 selection, 21
    Read Me window, 14
    running, 23, 24
Area attention, 256
Artificial neural network (ANN),
    68, 71, 84

activation signal, 50
attention, 255–257
components, 50
perceptron, 51
Autoencoders
    application, 262
    components, 260
    constraints, 261
    DAE, 266–269
    implementation, 262
    input/output cells, 260
    latent-space representation, 260
    layers, 262
    types, 261
    VAEs, 263–266
AveragePooling2D layer, 178
Axon, 49

B

Backpropagation Through
    Time (BPTT), 251
Backward propagation, 85, 89
Bidirectional associative
    memory (BAM), 289, 290
Binary cross-entropy, 106, 342
Biological neurons, 49, 50

Printed in the United States
By Bookmasters